# INSIDE TIME

Also by Ken Smith

THE PITY
WORK, DISTANCES/POEMS
TRISTAN CRAZY
FOX RUNNING
BURNED BOOKS
ABEL BAKER CHARLIE DELTA: EPIC SONNETS
THE POET RECLINING: SELECTED POEMS
TERRA
A BOOK OF CHINESE WHISPERS
WORMWOOD

# INSIDE TIME

**KEN SMITH**
**WITH DAVE WAIT**

**HARRAP**
London

First published in Great Britain 1989
by Harrap Books Ltd
19–23 Ludgate Hill, London EC4M 7PD
Reprinted 1989



ISBN 0 245–54720–7

Designed by Roger King Graphic Studios, Poole

Printed and bound in Great Britain
by Mackays of Chatham, Kent.

## ACKNOWLEDGEMENTS

To date, some pieces have been published in the following magazines:
AMBIT: *Bob Kirk* and *The Escape* (Dave Wait) and *The Protagonist.*
ANTIOCH REVIEW: *The Birdman, Angus in Exile* and *Alexander.*
STAND: *Lenny's Painting* and *Horns and Blue Lights.*

The painting used for the endpapers is by Jim Curran, a prisoner serving a life sentence in Wormwood Scrubs.

## AUTHOR'S NOTE

The characters portrayed in this book are real and the events described all took place, but fictional names and descriptive detail have been used in places where I have felt that this would protect privacy.

# CONTENTS

# FOREWORD

Prison. The word is a frightener to keep the rest of us on the straight and narrow. We think of prisons and we confront dark mysteries we'd be safer not to explore. Prisons are the dungeons in our fairy-tales and legends, and part of our defence from them is to mythologize them and their inhabitants. We are curious, incredulous, prepared to be horror-struck, but curiosity doesn't take us far. The realities of prison numb, the tales of these who have been there are suspect precisely because they have been there; the word *prison* unstitches reason. Here live monstrous clichés of the archetypal villain — the hood, the lag, the nonce, the brutal screw — but most of them in reality are ordinary enough, beyond the distinction of being prisoners or their keepers. Prison is the musty, ill-lit place of cobwebs and creepies under the stairs where we keep the furniture of nightmares. The system itself promotes silence and mystery — officers are bound to silence by their employers, the Government, as are governors and civil servants, by reason of their careers and their pensions. The military-style hierarchy of prison government excludes information from the lower ranks, and the rules are only partially and sparingly revealed. Inside, everyone operates on scant information, and where there is a vacuum there is always speculation.

There are brave accounts of survival – Jimmy Boyle's, Rod Caird's, Jack Abbot's, Zeno's *Life* about his nine years in Wormwood Scrubs' D Wing. Twenty years after his release, his successors, reading his book, commented how little anything had changed, surprised and not surprised, identifying with his feelings. At times the prisoner as protagonist tellingly describes his condition, but it is hard to write in prison, to hold the imagination and the attention long, and most would sooner forget it all. And it is even more difficult to write in retrospect; released, most prisoners want to get as far away as possible. In any case the first rule is that a prisoner is always in the wrong, not to be trusted, to be disbelieved.

In the absence of hard information there is no shortage of interest, however. The media constantly reflects our anxieties — about crime and criminals and about prisons. There is a developing prison crisis. Since 1945 successive governments have operated an expanding prison policy whereby as fast as new prisons are built they fill up, and the places available always lag behind the rising numbers of the convicted. Some correlation exists between building and sentencing policies: once built, prisons must be filled, and so they are. The prison crisis is exacerbated by the prison officers' dispute with their employers, the Home Office. Meanwhile, the crime-rate soars, and prison, if it does any good, cannot be seen to be doing so. The system works habitually and by nature in secrecy and shuns publicity. Whether or not society creates its criminal class, at any rate it nurtures and perpetuates it — perhaps it needs to — and its motto is *imprison and forget*. And once caught up in imprisonment, the circle is hard to break.

As to the rest of us, those fortunate or smug enough to think we will never enter the closed world of prison, how shall we know whether they work on our behalf as deterrents? These are *our* prisons. Police, judges and prison officers are all hired and paid by us, and work in our name. The vast closed machinery of imprisonment operates to separate off from ourselves those we convict and whom we consider dangerous. Its functions are to confine, to punish, to give miscreants pause for reflection, but most of all to keep them securely from the rest of us, under tight supervision. Their security is in reality ours. Yet prisoners are part of us in their humanity, not least because most of them return to the world, and how they are on re-entry should be part of our concern. Whether as bitter, frightened men or hardened bullies or improved villains, they will be with us again. Criminals are with us always. They are our shadows, inhabitants of the dark submerged half of ourselves we barely understand and therefore fear and forget. Our problem is that by mythologizing the criminal, who is not always the same figure as the prisoner, we dehumanise him. We fail to see our own capacities for crime, for violence, for response to pressure in a sudden and tragic loss of control. We are more vulnerable thereby, and stand in danger of becoming victims. Those who commit crimes and go to prison were formerly among us, are now, and will be so again. They are no different from us.

In the meantime, they are in prison, in a world apart with its own savage style, its own manners, its own lingo, invisible to the rest of us, although even here life goes on somehow. Rod Caird in *A Good and Useful Life* describes the initial sense of being cut off from the world, inhabiting a special zone: 'I was now directly under the control of the Prison Department and it acted as a buffer between me and reality. All my friends were physically insulated from me, and could have little influence on events my side of this new barrier. I was now in a different world, with its own rules and norms, and even language, and a population of total strangers.' If the sense of separation is what's keenest felt, survival inside is measured by adjustment to the nether world, to life in limbo land, and this invariably involves numbing the senses, suppressing feeling, withdrawal. If he connected crime and punishment in the first place, the prisoner, concentrated on his own condition, soon begins to separate the two. If he feels contrition for the victim, this blurs inside his own grim routine. On a long stretch, the crime recedes into the past, fades into memory and history, or becomes the occasion of lame excuses (*I was young; I was foolish; I was drunk; I was led; I was crazy, about her, about him* . . . .). Inevitably, not the crime but its retribution is ever present. The day-to-day realities of prison life become the focus of attention, and the enemy — authority — unchanged, the inmates' attitude unchanged. This is the department of hurry up and wait. There's every opportunity and much encouragement to be harsh, tough, unjust or cruel, to withhold, to wind up. Within the mass, the prisoner is made to feel alone, yet never private. He is cut off from the world, and yet cannot enjoy his own company. As Jimmy Boyle has put it, he is a private man who enjoys solitude, but solitude imposed is loneliness.

So what is prison like and does the system work? And how would we cope, should we find ourselves mystified inmates in a dangerous place at Her Majesty's Pleasure? And there are other questions to which there may be no answers, though we go on asking them. Prison is a great mystery — to those in the system as well as those outside. And maybe its force as a deterrent is determined by its mystery, the dire tales, scarcely believable, that come back from beyond the frontier of imprisonment. Here are some of them.

Ken Smith
*August 1988*

# DARK SHADOW

# 1
# ARRIVAL

I came to Wormwood Scrubs in 1985 in answer to a newspaper advertisement for a Writer in Residence, to work with anyone in the prison community of officers, inmates and families, who wrote or wanted to. I needed a job, though above all I needed to be absorbed in something serious. Amongst 1400 prisoners and 500 staff, and an undefinable number amongst the families, it was assumed I'd find clients, people who wrote, and so I did, though I soon gave up the thought of the families, whether of staff or inmates. I could scarcely walk up to the visitors' queue and ask if anyone had written a sonnet, and for many reasons — from the administration's, the inmates' and my own point of view — I didn't seriously try to contact the families of men in prison. No inmate asked me to. As to the officers, they had their duties, and they were serious men little given to introspection and less to its exposition on paper. Again, I didn't see much prospect in enquiring whether an officer wrote stories or songs or poems, or was interested in writing his memoirs. Those who spoke of it thought they might write what they knew later, beyond retirement and their pensions.

I concentrated therefore on the prisoners, and worked at first with remands and short-sentence men, finding that often at the beginning of a sentence, or on remand, men were likely to be introspective and drawn to writing. Thereafter, as prison inures them to itself, they harden and withdraw; most go numb, and as the wire tightens on the imagination's sources they begin to atrophy. At length, I concentrated mostly on the lifers, perhaps the greatest challenge, but in any case on D Wing there was the continuity of contact they afforded over the two years I was there. Remand and local prisoners are always on the move from prison to prison, but the lifers' stay in the Scrubs is lengthy.

It may be said that prisoners do not deserve such attentions, and the roast them-in-hell school will no doubt go on saying it. That the prisoner brings his condition on himself by committing the crime or by being caught for it, is true but is not the whole of it, however. Crime, prison, and the continuing boom in both, are far more complex, and we are all potential victims. When I came here I was, like most outsiders, quite naive; when I left two years later I knew little more. The criminal as monster, the criminal as hero, and the criminal as victim, none of these is a working image. Prisoners are as different from one another as any other set of individuals. Society, which makes high demands and is content with low expectations, creates its prisons out of its own failures, and inside, where so little achievement is possible, failure becomes the expected norm, and *good* a highly relative term. There is nothing romantic about prisons, or prisoners; nothing romantic at all about killers, rapists, bullies, pushers, strung-out druggies, armed robbers, sexual deviants who prey on others, baby burglars, sneaks.

For prisoners, the blunt fact of confinement dominates their attention all the time, even asleep. They wish they could talk and think of something else, and though they at times succeed, the perennial reminders of prison soon claim them back. With them the theme *Prison* is the only subject of debate; it conditions all communication, it is the baseline of all conversation when not its whole preoccupation, and it clouds over whatever survives of the memory. Teaching Bridge, or French, Computer Studies or Soft Toys, may provide a neutral ground, but Writing engages thinking and feeling, and what is most on the mind and deepest-felt surfaces early. I came to think about the problems of writing in prison where there's only ever one subject. Crime may be the topic, the law or the police, the outside or the family, writing, or the weather, or sex, or God, but the subtext of everything is the same: prison. I found there was no way I could talk about writing without working through the medium of a language of constant complaint and frequent hatred, where the verbs were threats and the moods sarcasm and longing and the adverbs probably insane. All this, I decided, would not go away, so I let prison cast its shadow over every encounter, and took matters from there. Each prisoner must tell his tale in his own way, and poetry stirs the dreams and the ghosts.

To begin with, I was afraid, though not for long, and once equipped with a bunch of keys I was soon busy working with prisoners, three days a week. I came to feel safer inside than I did out. Mostly I worked on the hoof, figuring out where men were, in the hospital, or cleaning on the wing, or locked up, and going to them. A few I met in their cells, others in interview rooms, the Education cell, or in the glass-sided 'fishbowls' on the wings. Most men preferred one-to-one conversations, and where I met with groups there was always some reserve. My working day had to be fitted around hours of unlock; at noon and during the exercise hour I met men hurriedly, sometimes talking with three at once, all in a mad scramble that would suddenly, at lock-up, turn silent.

I found men who wrote: poems, tales, children's stories, their memoirs, music, songs, novels, science-fiction and horror, escapist doodles, statements about their case or their appeal. They needed some kind of help, sometimes criticism, sometimes none, sometimes just an ear, an audience if only of one, briefly. It was often tricky ground, a minefield that felt and sounded hostile even where it was not, a terrain for which I had no maps. Much of it ended in failure. 'Prison,' said the young AG responsible for hiring me, 'is the place of failure. In prison, unfortunately, no one expects much else.' I came to redefine what I was doing when I realized how difficult it was for some men merely to write a letter, even to talk; describing the inside to the outside world is difficult, akin to writing from a foreign country to someone who's never been abroad.

Some were trying to write to families who had turned their backs on them in disgust, or to their children whose mothers they had murdered. I came to think in terms of minimal results and counted as an unexpected initial victory an article a man wrote about his life in prison and his crime. For him, the world had closed after his conviction for murder; his wife had since divorced him and taken away their son: his mother mourned him as dead, and said she had no son. He had no visitors and little correspondence with the outside, and was adrift inside prison. He sent the article to his parish priest, who printed it in his magazine. His mother read it and wrote to him. He wrote back. I considered it a breakthrough. So did he.

In letters, inmates try to stay in touch with the world, to do their business, organize something they need, to begin, develop or prolong a love affair, a friendship, family life, a conversation. That the censor reads their mail, and the replies, is a source of resentment and caution, but a fact of life in any case. We were all of us on candid camera, always watched, almost always within earshot. They were used to it, more or less. I grew to be, more or less.

In any case, the problem defined itself as trying to keep the imagination alive, where any stimulus to the starved prison self might be a starting-point, where language was always charged and meaningful, mercilessly so, and where men somehow survived to tell their tales, and where my task was to encourage them to talk, to write, to remember, to think, to keep the mind alive. Because I believe in growth, and the possibility of growth even amongst the damned, and because I believe that writing is a progression of thinking out loud, I therefore worked on the principle that the men I worked with were seeking help in figuring out who they were, their crimes, how they came here, and considered that they in any case were their own starting-points, and mine. Whoever they were, they knew things I did not, and had no wish to know directly: the experience of having (many of them) committed violent crime; the experience of long imprisonment and the prospect of longer, perhaps indefinitely, till death. Their names and pseudonyms are here, in sundry guises: nicknames that are names used in the nick. Changing names, I immediately entered into fiction, but where Bob is John and John is Jack, someone is always one or the other. To all those who gave me access to them and to the prison, I am grateful – and to Greater London Arts and ILEA, who funded my time there. I have singled out the work of only one man, Dave Wait, whose name came from a dream he had in which, finally released from prison and walking at last to the gate, someone called after him: 'Dave. Wait. Wait a minute.' And he turned back a moment, knowing that it was not over. A fifth part of this book is his, and to his criticism and advice and inside knowledge I owe much of the rest. A lifer in prison for murder, his writing illuminates those parts of the labyrinth I cannot reach, and I regard this book as an attempt to build a bridge from his end and from mine across the gulf between the inside and the outside.

So here is where I am in the Scrubs, talking exclusively about men in prison. Whatever little I may presume to know about men in prison, I know nothing about women's experience of it. I didn't meet any women prisoners.

Though the fact and agony of confinement is surely similar for both sexes, I make no further assumptions. Apart from some civilian staff, and one or two lady governors, there aren't any women in the Scrubs. Their absence is the first complaint of the prisoners.

I was privileged to enter a forbidden place, with my keys and a pass to say who I was, talking to men I would never otherwise have met. I was a writer, self-taught in the eye and the ear and the memory, given to eavesdropping and overhearing, forever noting asides and noises off, always piecing things together into some pattern, and often wrong about half of it. Here was much that was said between the lines and beneath the breath, and perhaps as a writer I have always been something of a thief. Here was material enough for several lifetimes of books, and I grew tired of answering the same questions on the outside and was beginning to opt for silence in the matter, as most people who work in prisons find it expedient to do. Outside, it seemed there were two sorts of opinion, both of them useless: either prisons shouldn't exist or they should be even harsher, and either way no one should work there. I came to consider silence unproductive. I began to write a book, about the imprisoned imagination, about prison, about the Scrubs, and this is the result.

# 2

# YOUR JOURNEY CAN END HERE

The Scrubs. The Scabs. Many journeys end here.

The largest maximum security prison in Europe, HMP Wormwood Scrubs is considered the flagship of the British prison system. It consists of four long wings on four landings, housing remand and local prisons, the lifers' and long-term dispersal prison, and the hospital wing, plus outbuildings and workshops, the administration block, kitchens, gym, a new (unopened, said to be unusable) hospital, the education building known as The College, and around the whole of it the security fence and the wall. A century of silence and misery has gone by in here. 'It ought to be a museum,' one Governor said. A former Governor, leaving the Scrubs in 1982, denounced it as a 'penal dustbin'.

When it was built in the 1870s it was considered a model prison, one of a number built to the requirements of what was then current thinking on penal reform. The direction, then, was towards segregation, silence, isolation, and therefore the cells were built for single occupation in separate confinement, the women's cells of D Wing, for whatever reason, slightly smaller than the cells for men. The cells were without toilets. Its builder, Du Cane, naively believed that when locked up, the prisoners would ring their bells to go to the lavatory. He seems not to have been familiar with his officers' prevailing attitudes; they are but slowly summoned by their prisoners' bells. Therefore to Edmund Du Cane, first chairman of the Prison Commission and author of the new harsh policies of hard labour and separation whose legacy this place is, every prisoner today owes his slop bucket.

Out on what was scrubland at the then city's edge, the Victorian reformers set aside land to build the prison. Prisoners from the Millbank were marched over, their first task to build their quarters; their further tasks, says legend, to dig the clay, make bricks and assemble them into the four great toothy hulks that are the four wings of the Scrubs, bristling with turrets and chimneys, long echoing galleries and winding stairways at the ends of landings, iron windows and doors and double gates within gates and the whole enclosed within a continuous wall in which one gate, *the gate*, opens to admit or release. Within the wall, the further continuum of the security fence, seventeen feet high and topped with razor wire.

The Victorians' investment is still in intensive use. For a few years during the Second World War, the buildings were taken out of the prison system, and used by the secret services. D Wing housed captured German agents, who were turned around here, and rumour has it some were shot. There are stories of other executions, against the north wall, of conscientious objectors in the First World War. History is vague here, and meshed with apocrypha. The only notable changes in a hundred years are that the women's prison in D Wing is now the men's life wing, the young offenders of B Wing have gone elsewhere, the cat and the birch and the hood have gone, as have the further sanctions of the treadwheel, penal servitude and the noose, hopefully forever. There was neither treadwheel nor topping shed in the Scrubs. The regime has modified its harshest edges, and now only long imprisonment itself remains the toughest punishment society can impose. Otherwise the plant's still operating. The diet is described as 'adequate', the provision of exercise and sanitation and diversion minimal. The prison's century-and-more of use has seen the introduction of more barriers, more locks, the security fence, constant camera surveillance within and without, and the coils of razor wire capping every barrier like the frosting on some barbarous birthday cake. As more buildings have gone up, there's less space within the space within the wall, and as the prison population has risen and the crime statistics soared, the same gaol houses many more bodies than it was built for.

Outside, the city's thickened and quickened, and London's leapt west where the traffic goes and the trains glimpsed across the scrubs pick up speed for Bristol, Cardiff, Plymouth and Penzance. The motorways and interchanges spin across industrial estates and railway yards, and everywhere is Ballard country on the Heathrow flightpath, and there is no centre to any of it. The towns and villages have blurred under the press of population, with intermittent attempts at planning, and anonymous west London flickers past the windows of the tube, light industry and housing, the warehousing and workshops of the city's lengthening perimeters. At the East Acton stop, down the steps and under the train bridge where the underground is overground, by the ticket gate there's a blackboard chalked with the primary colours of another landscape, a stirring Highland scene you might see from a train 500 miles away, and beneath it directions to Wormwood Scrubs.

On one side of the prison lies Hammersmith Hospital, behind it the open flats and playing-fields of the scrubs, where the bitter wormwood plant that gave the waste its name no longer grows. The locals were said to make beer from it. The ground has been cleared and graded into playing-fields, except for token patches of fenced-off scrubby bush, and though the name of the place is still the name of a local amenity, it seems a name always fashioned for a prison.

The area consists of council housing, streets and crescents of solid brick, a municipal estate long settled down in trees and gardens, much of it now privately owned, a working-class domesticated district of family houses and second-hand cars, a street called Henchman. Across the roof-tops rear the long grey sheds of the prison, and there are little streets that end against the prison wall. No one seems to look that way. The prison sits amongst its neighbours, and its neighbours look inwards at themselves as if the prison were not there, and in a sense, perhaps, it isn't. I can prove nothing, but sense in the streets around the prison an averting of the gaze, a sort of jump in the landscape. Along Du Cane Road the gaunt window spaces of the prison hostel stare back. Watching pedestrians passing the prison, I notice that most of them look straight ahead, or sideways into the traffic, choosing not to see — though sometimes furtively glancing at the prison. It's for the most part hidden behind the hostel, a place apart that no one approaches except with purpose. In any case, from the road there isn't much to look at: the gate, the uniformed officers on duty, the wall that's featureless and continuous and inflexible. The inside is hidden, a world apart, another city, a grey glimpse of yard and stone in the gate's brief opening.

It is grimly familiar, this gate. We have seen it before in movies and on television as the setting for the beginning or the end of a man's sentence: in the brown wooden gate that slides open for traffic, a brown wooden door opens. It is a man's size, but seems tiny in so much varnished wood, in so much brick, diminishing whoever steps through it. In the film it is probably raining, and early on a weekday morning, and the plane-trees along the street are shedding, and when the prison door opens a man steps out wearing clothes he has grown unfamiliar with, carrying a suitcase or a paper parcel, going out into the world again on the day he has dreamed of, and feared, maybe for years. In some movie scenes, he turns to his jailor in the peaked cap and the crow-blue uniform with the crown on all the buttons and shakes hands; in others he walks off, his step skipping from prison slouch to the rhythms of the city, and never so much as glances behind him. Our protagonist is free, lost in the crowd. In a *Minder* episode on television, Max Wall comes out here, with his caged budgie which he frees on Parliament Hill. In a London Transport TV advertisement a bus drives in through the lifted barber's-pole traffic boom and through the gate, taking its fare-dodging passengers with it. And on the tubes the gate appears on a poster warning against assault on the staff, a simple message in a photograph of tall bricks with white stone facings in an upright checkerboard, a blunt round Saxon arch, and either side the watching reliefs of the reformers Fry and Howard. The poster's legend spells *Your journey can end here.*

Prisoners enter this gate in the white meat waggons the Met use to ferry their charges to prison, and whatever they see of the foregoing they see through the dark side windows of the van, each man handcuffed in his cubicle snatching his last glimpses of normality, the world of work and women, children, gardens, street furniture. The wooden gate slides open and shut, closing its shadow behind the newcomers, and then a metal gate and then another gate and then another gate admit them, and they are taken to reception, where they become names and numbers and paperwork, and quickly memorize their new address in W12.

Entering the prison, the world outside is suddenly the other side of the wall, remote, mysterious, tantalizing in the sounds that penetrate: traffic, tube trains, barks and children's cries from the streets beyond, the distant milky throbbing of police-car sirens, the drone of airplane engines coming in from distant places. Now everywhere is distant, even the air immediately over the wall, and everything is difficult, prison the norm, time indefinitely suspended, and nothing very certain. The wall has interposed its solemnity, its solid, brickish fact.

Inside, more walls, more locks, more bars. There are many smaller prisons within the main prison: the lifers' dispersal wing, the short-termers' (serving up to four years) local prison, the remand wing, the Seg Unit, the special unit called The Annexe, the 43 Unit, and then the prison within which each prisoner is alone, with others, in a crowd. In here, the ethos is industrial, regimented, under the tyranny of the clock, like the early factory system to which it is related, though there's little industry. Because those who invent penal systems believe work is a great straightener, prisoners must engage in it, but then there's never enough work to go round, and then contrarily we say their work must not be productive or interesting or prejudice external industrial arrangements. So for the most part prison work is repetitive, boring, mind-numbing. For a while there was a braille unit, where men translated books into reading-material for the blind, and felt useful thereby, and some became inventive with shapes and tackled illustrations. It was closed down in the eternal internal shufflings of power between departments, suddenly discerned as non-union labour. The men working there were reassigned, the officer in charge resigned in disgust.

In the main, such work as there is involves maintaining the fabric — working in the laundry or kitchens or cleaning on the wings, painting or gardening, or working in the shops. It is tedious and done sluggishly. Prison is utterly boring, and everyone conspires to make it so. Prison industries are largely unprofitable, producing goods at twice their cost, and in 1984 they were the subject of great scandal, when 25 million pounds was unaccounted for in losses and bad debts. Other vast sums have gone missing. In consequence in 1986 a further 54 workshops were closed, and various officials were charged, but so far all have been acquitted. As a result prison industries have become further restricted, and the result of that is more bang-up.

Prisons produce articles for prison use; some are factories providing uniforms or furniture, plastic cutlery, manuals, workshops in the huge semi-secret state that is prison. In Coldingley they produce traffic-signs for places they can't go to, and work laundries serving NHS hospitals and the Army. In Wakefield, it's said, they make hydraulic jacks used to prise off cell doors prisoners have barricaded. Otherwise prison itself is an industry without a product. In the Scrubs' workshops, they make prison overalls out of brown cloth, and aluminium window frames. It seems an odd choice: strips of sharpened metal make ready knives, and tailors' shops contain scissors and the makings of ropes. The Scrubs' black museum testifies to the uses put to such industrial artefacts. Often in prison, it seems, temptation is never completely excluded. There seems to be a cat and mouse game under way, designed to tantalize and test the ingenuities of men locked up. This is all regarded as part of the general wind-up.

In here, the air's desultory. This is the anti-world, set in the normality of the suburbs. Lassitude pervades everything and everyone inside, where hoping and dreaming are the same activities, and many men have come to the end of both. In here, there's nothing much to dream or hope for: a visit or a letter is all that will break the routine, connecting the inside with the outside and its news. Anything else is hope in magic or in miracles: men dream of winning their appeals, of amnesty, of civil commotion, of a breakthrough or new evidence in their cases, which, like them, are filed away and gathering dust. Little else disturbs the rituals of prison, exceptions frequent enough to become part of the routine: a fight, a fire, a punishment, a slagging, a death, a ghosting, the large defeats and meagre victories in the war between authority and inmates. The rest is gossip, filling time, and the elaboration of stories.

# 3

# HORNS AND BLUE LIGHTS

By two p.m. the visitors are queuing at the side gate. The prison lets them in, efficiently and impersonally and without humour, and lets them know they are outsiders entering a forbidden zone, a country in the permanent grip of supervision so absolute the language to describe it buckles up. This is a border that sets the teeth on edge, with the suspicious formalities of a hostile frontier, and where familiar objects are suddenly highlighted: a woman carrying a paperback novel, *Never Love a Stranger*, a child who's playing with a toy gun and a pair of plastic handcuffs. There is no compromise with comfort. A busted shelter by the garbage skips has been put up by the Women's Royal Voluntary Service, who also run the tea and biscuits inside in the visiting area. Outside, preoccupied, indifferent, officers go about their business, inhabitants of some other planet, ignoring the visitors so long as they stay in line. They do.

For the man inside anticipating his visit, he'll make the best he can of what he has: a haircut, shave, the best blue denim with the striped shirt pressed. For her, the visitor, if she thinks about it at all, there's the question should she dress up, put on her best feathers and strut, or should she go in looking dowdy and fraught? Which would least or most upset him? Most men inside don't know either. There's status in a visit from an attractive woman. Women are rare and distant and always forbidden, impossible as angels, their scents, soaps, powders and aromas noticed and savoured. Some men welcome a wind-up, storing such imagery for hours, days, years, a beauty real or imagined or remembered, movies in the mind played out to solitary intercourse. What legitimate little can be brought in from the outside is mostly imagery, contact with the world, however slight, however fleeting, pictures in the head that ultimately lull or drive off sleep. Prisoners long for company, for women, for sex, for love; all this preoccupies them. But on visits it is difficult to express much across the tabletops these guests share with their unwilling hosts, where both arrive at the frontiers of the separate self.

Outside the gate a busted guitar lies beside the shelter. A girl walks out of the visitors' door, weeping openly, supported on either side by two of her mates. 'He shouldn't be in there, Sharon.' Inside, the glassed-in officer staring impassively explains that his VO is out of date to an old wrinkled black man with a scribbled fuzz of white hair and a baggy suit who is protesting he can't get in to see his son. 'Liberty,' the old man cries in a loud voice. 'Liberty, Liberty, Liberty.'

Beyond the gate, in the prison's numbed normality, the first sight, just as he originally intended, is of Du Cane's stone church. Inside, it is a great soaring barn of quiet, its altar semi-circled by portraits of the saints a prisoner painted long ago. St Jude, patron saint of lost causes, has been attacked, the canvas bashed about by a blunt instrument. The conversation-piece for visitors in here is the grand piano, given to the prison by Ivor Novello, who did a stretch for black market petrol in the early Forties. 'We'll gather lilacs in the spring again.' The prison authorities would like to get rid of the church and use its space, but the preservation order on it prevents them.

Inside: prison, voices calling like whips, the edges of several conversations together, and the hum cut from time to time by shouts, thumps, clang of gates, hissing of steam pipes, snatches of birdsong. Bits of dialogue, screw talk and con talk, overlap each other, men shout to one another along the outsides of the remand wing, their messages shortened to news of bail aps and appearances, briefs, visits. Men walk in subdued circles round the yards, there is an air of rigorous ecclesiasticism, where the dogs bark in their compound and CB radios chatter their messages. And everything is suddenly significant.

Outside the security fence there's a parked van from Rentokil. *Pest Control* the sign on the side says, provoking obvious passing comment as to the need for it round here what with the cockroaches and the rats and some that are two-legged pests the world has put away from itself. Inside the fence all efforts are bent towards that normality defined as *good order and discipline*, the measured-out routine of prison life. Some men, on gardening detail, are digging along the verges, planting wallflowers. Others move in small accompanied parties to and from the library, the hospital, the gym, the church, the weekly film. Two yard officers are stringing new razor wire along the wall's top. The Pettibone hoist is working down the side of D Wing, cleaning guttering, inspecting bars, pulling mops and parcels and rubbish from where they've been dumped out, fluttering little flags of angry static. Above, a plane passes down its flight path, and there are birds — pigeons, crows, and sparrows that hide in amongst the razor wire from the sparrow-hawks.

Everything is normal.

Today, my text will be *serendipity*: the discovery of the unexpected, by accident, the capacity for surprise, a word coined by Horace Walpole to describe this faculty in *The Three Princes of Serendip*. Who says a word can't be made up? In prison words are made up all the time, and a word can be made to mean anything, and meaning is in any case forever relative. As in all embattled cultures, words can be used to divert meaning. Language is code.

Yet so little to find, in a place where what little a man has he hangs on to. Entering prison, a man begins with nothing but the regulation issue and must work his way towards whatever small comforts he requires: an extra shelf, a small cupboard, a radio, a bit of hardboard to pin a postcard to, a mug to call his own, these must be gifted in or traded on the wing or somehow earned, or ripped off. There's a great commerce in mundane objects. Significance overpowers the meanest items: 'the absolute tyranny of a piece of soap,' a man says, staring at it over the sink.

For some the luxury of a watch. For all the priority of a radio, however pieced together, and wherever possible wired out to little speaker boxes, enough for the small space of a cell. And the worry about batteries, keeping the supply going. Duracell are banned, for some reason best known to God and a few of his chosen angels. Ageing batteries, even, are some sort of trade; they can be warmed on the heating pipe to enough life for a little more radio, the other side of the tape. Tape players are allowed. Recorders aren't.

Some inherit things from men going out. Some scavenge in the garbage, where there's precious little to find. Some, with money on the outside, can afford some comforts, but even that little presupposes much: outside there must be relatives or someone who cares enough or owes him sufficient to transfer money to him on the inside, to his prison account, or an accountant or a brief ordering his business, and in these transactions some are cheated easily of their money. At any rate he'll pay over the odds and his deal will be taxed. The prisoner is soon rendered into the victim. Often his relatives use his crime to justify their greed in helping themselves to his property. So it's still difficult. And men with money are envied and resented by those without; the subject of who has what in their monies or outside is part of the general undertow of speculation and jealousy and gossip here in the beehive. This prison of enforced living together has all the features of a bad marriage.

A man guards his bits and pieces — books, pictures, spare clothing, pen and paper, slippers. Things that would elsewhere be useless matter here — bits of wood and card, old magazines, dog-ends, paper-clips and drawing pins, matchsticks and casual detritus, containers of any kind, games and time-fillers, and anything sharp. Trade, mostly in barter, flourishes; given the striker from a gas lighter and a bit of plug chain, a scrap of wood and a length of mop rope, a man can make himself a lighter. With access to a shop, he can make a metal lighter, parts for a model Harley Davidson a bloke he knows on the threes is building, a screwdriver for tinkering with a radio. All this, naturally, by sleight of hand, bearing in mind regular and impromptu body searches and cell searches. Some of this trade, kept quiet, edges into the making of weapons or escape equipment. Everyone knows there's no way out of here, not since George Blake in 1966. But they still talk about him. An officer claims in all seriousness that Blake had a mate with a goldfish, and used the goldfish food to weaken the bars he broke through. Another says, 'Blake was clever. He was very good at being where he was supposed to be, so when he wasn't, at first he wasn't missed. And then he'd gone.' Everyone dreams of escape, and some try. In the Scrubs' black museum there's makeshift ropes and ladders, fake guns, knives made of metal and glass, nailed sticks, slingshots, catapults. And from somewhere the Palestinian must have got the key they found in his cell, the reason they ghosted him.

See how soon the mundane dives under. In here everything is heavy, or soon becomes it. Every thought. The fact is, life is lived here on a subsistence level. It is a bee's life, every moment outside the cell spent scavenging for swaps and scraps and bits of information, and where there's not a lot of anything but all of it gets used. Paints and other materials can be got from Education, and paintings can be traded legit on or off the wing, where scenes of other places, other landscapes, light up gloomy cells. Matchsticks make models and rags make soft toys. Used stamps go in a box for charity. An old newspaper with an unfinished crossword is worth having, and in here the news is somehow never stale. And yet always is. The old cliché that in prison tobacco is currency isn't quite true; *everything* in here is currency, tobacco more often what currency can buy.

Whatever skills a man might have, these too can be traded. A man who can cut hair will always find hair to cut. A man who can write a good letter finds work in the black economy of human need; a man who can write a poem may rent it to another to send out to his wife or his girlfriend, expressing what he himself cannot of love and hope and grieving. Some, with nothing else to trade, sell sex. In prison, which is all waste, nothing is wasted.

But garbage is genuine garbage in these parts, much like the stock of second-hand shops in the poorest parts of town — lids for leaky saucepans, handles for broken cups, an assortment of worn socks, somebody else's false teeth, old glasses. Of certain commodities there's no shortage, so one common mark of prisoners' contempt for their keepers is bread, thrown about between the buildings, flat, thin Wonderloaf slices skimmed like frisbees out of cell windows, rain-soggy buns dumped out to the birds. And shit. Sometimes it's wrapped in the same see-through family loaf plastic, or in a loose newspaper dumped from a high cell window at noon. Anything to be rid of it: the bomb, the parcel from the man who can't or won't wait till unlock and slop-out and won't use his bucket and sit with it. He can't see why he should, and nor can I. Prison is not a place to get diarrhoea. Despite the millions being invested in rebuildings and modernisation, there'll still be thousands of prisoners slopping out till the end of the century at least.

My theme is bread and shit, then, since this is what there's most of in the detritus of prison, but the scraps in the yards are barely worth noticing. Anything of any use is quickly picked up. Men make use of any stub of pencil, scrap of card, nail, pin, twist of wire, bit of string.

Between the cleaning squads on their ways around the wings the wayside junk is more predictable: torn Rizla packets, mostly green, tiny rollup butts, grey balled-up prison socks with two green bands around the top, a toothbrush or two, bits of broken plastic, plastic plates, plastic cutlery, plastic mugs, plastic razors, a plastic medicine cup, a broken cassette's spilled tape that will never again be music. Around the remand wing rubbish is thicker; remand is always overcrowded, prisoners twoed up or threed up or foured. Its population is younger, more contemptuous of prison and many of them new to its rigours and not for the most part inclined to treat the place as home. Rather the opposite.

Along C Wing's sides the shabby garbage drifts in and out of the skips — empty cartons, newspapers, empty cans. Steam rises from breaks in the heating pipes between the wings, the drains block up and are continually being dredged and dug out. Between C Wing and the kitchens grease spills out and coats the stones.

Elsewhere, caught in the wires around the wings, there are towels, socks, underwear, mops, blue-and-white striped prison shirts, rags. Gaol rubbish is necessarily pathetic, and symbolic. What's thrown away often expresses anger, frustration, defiance, pathos. Waste has its own eloquence. Occasionally there are rare finds: a man writes in his best longhand the story of his arrest, which turns into the story of his life; he drops it from his high window, perhaps convinced by writing it of his story's hopelessness; I pick it up. The bits of a torn letter rolling in the wind turn over the words *love, want, need, goodbye,* scattering them around the many feet walking the yard. Such words can't get out, and flap against the fence with last year's leaves. Graffiti is etched into doors and corners, simple words expressing boredom, hate, desire. *I'm always here* it says, high up on the wall of a cell. And on the corrugated cardboard table of a punishment-block cell someone has written, with the slow, patient sincerity of a man realizing at last all its possibilities of meaning:

> *Time* is what it is.
> Time *is* what it is.
> Time is *what* it is.
> Time is what *it* is.
> Time is what it *is*.
> Time *is* what it *is*.

Etc. Whoever wrote it no doubt considered it carefully and said it to himself aloud in all its permutations, for a long while, in solitude. Like everything in this place, it is a sentence already and immediately overloaded with too much meaning, and with none, part of the huge anti-joke of prison: irony in the dust.

These I have found:

*Item*: a playing-card, face down, by the south gate out of reception where men come through escorted to allocation, with their permitted possessions, the rest in storage. Dropped, or thrown away? Perhaps the first of many such cards, to be found all over the prison, that would make a set and furnish a running royal flush, if anyone knew where to find them, or any of the rules of the game. Turned up, it is a Joker.

*Item*: again in the reception area, a small plastic toy submarine, the sort that comes in bits in a package with the cornflakes, and clips together into a little puzzle. It is a yellow submarine. Not a red cement truck or a blue boat or an orange bulldozer or a green jet fighter. A yellow submarine.

*Item*: a piece of sky on a bit of a jigsaw, a tiny cloud-flecked piece of the great blue open sky, across which bars or railings: a lost piece of a puzzle that seems to be itself a puzzle picture of prison. There must be other pieces hereabouts, in the sanitised area where men come and go, in transit with their gear, harried and chivvied and cuffed up. Boxes break and parcels split, there may not have been time or materials to make a decent package of an improvised suitcase, and the handling not too gentle, and things shake loose on the road. The puzzle's lost one piece. Men lose things all the time. Things fall apart.

So someone has a pack without a Joker, and someone has a jigsaw with a fragment of the barred sky missing, and the time-filling trinket of the yellow submarine assembly that might otherwise have started a conversation or whiled away solitude beyond the point of absolute boredom has gone absent without leave. It all looks like junk anyway, the things men hang on to, and if they're treated with contempt, then their goods are treated with contempt, and some treat their own gear the same. What a man values may look like a dog-eared photo of an old bag to someone else, but to him it's the only picture he has of his mother, wife, sister, a woman he once knew, someone he loved and who maybe loved him, someone of whom he still dreams and wishes he were with.

Beyond simple commerce, there's other trade in items more exotic: yeast and brown sugar and fruit or peel for hooch, favours sexual and otherwise, dope. Inside, dope doubles its street price and usually goes in little five-quid deals, a couple of spliffs' worth, I'm told. *The Daily Mirror* thinks the price is double again. The dope dealers have taken over from the old tobacco bosses, and hooch is now less prevalent than gear, I'm told. The wing heavies run the traffic, the same heavy villains from the outside. Scraps of such information come my way, along with tales of heavy kickings, cuttings, beatings and boilings — hints, but nothing anyone would swear to, and everything discourages further enquiry. The principals are quickly hurried off — to the hospital, to the block, to the 43s, ghosted to another prison. Sometimes hashish adds its heavy piquance to the stew of prison smells — the sharp fetor of sweat, piss, feet, food, decayed brickwork, damp, shit, sperm, disinfectant. The screws tolerate it, men say. It keeps prisoners quiet, especially the blacks, they say. In 1986 there were 2,300 drug finds in British prisons, according to Home Office Minister John Patten. In 1987, in a speech to the POA annual conference in Southport, POA assistant general secretary Phil Hornsby claimed that 'Over half the prison population is now involved in drug abuse in one way or another. That means 25,000 prisoners using, holding, or dealing in drugs.' (*The Guardian*, 21 May 1987). Predicting anarchy as prisons turned into drug centres, the delegates unanimously called on the Home Office to ban food brought in from outside in an effort to stop the traffic. This ban has now been implemented. Whatever the true figures, there's a lot of big talk in prison. The fact is that among men already convicted of terrible crimes, the misdemeanour of possession counts for little: 'What they going to do? Put me in prison? I am in prison.' The POA needs the figures to increase its numbers, but if there's as much as they claim coming in, the wonder is by what route. To press their case they have to say they're not doing their job fully. Packed oranges and loaded kisses at visiting time can't account for so much, if the figures accurately reflect reality. There are some inmates, a man explained, who are just never searched coming back from a visit. He left it at that. There's trade, and here on the wing where everything has already happened, such matters, along with most of the structure of law, don't count for much. It's claimed that hereabouts anything can be obtained for the right price, and maybe it's so, but some things would take a lot of arranging and many things will never happen. As for hooch, there are ways and means, and the joke one day was on the Wing PO who, certain that a man who'd thrown a banana skin in his piss bucket was making hooch, dipped the ladle in and tasted it.

Another man, found with two buckets of hooch under his bed and put on report, went down for adjudication in the morning. The seized buckets had been kept in a cupboard on the ones overnight. The man persuaded a civvy he was a cleaner, and needed a broom from the cupboard, got it unlocked, and drank all the evidence. On adjudication, though he was pissed out of his mind, there was nothing to charge him with.

But I know nothing. I pick up tales and small lost items, scraps of language, bits of apocrypha, edges of information, the faint punchlines of jokes receding into silence. 'There's a thief around here,' a man says, looking for his matches. 'This place is full of crooks.' It's never much of a joke. Whoever said jokes were made up in prison was just plain wrong. The punchlines are often corny, the jokes dated. Inventiveness comes out in speech, in quick rejoinders, often in the put-down. 'We call him Bungalow,' one man says of another, 'cos he's got no top storey.'

'That screw, he goes all the way to the far end of the wing, turns round and stands there scratching his arse, and then walks all the way back to the other end, and has a cigarette. Every fifteen minutes. I've timed it.'

And other tales. And other objects, other words, other speeches delivered in the dark brewhouse of prison, the discovery of men with names like Headbutt, Werewolf, Odd Job, Wavyline, Trotter, Marsbar, Littlelegs, the Blob, the Fat Man, Beak and Bulletproof and the Professor, Sago, Cyclops, Foxy and the Captain. And everywhere other bits of other puzzles, the Queen of Hearts, the Ace of Spades, a card on which someone has written the one word *happy*. In a cupboard in a classroom in the college an old teaching-aid card simply says DOOR, another LAKE RIVER AND FISH, alongside a cardboard cutout of a sewage plant. And by the door to the admin. block, crumpled in the dirt, a lettered metal blue strip fallen from the control panel of a Met meat waggon that spells out

HORNS AND BLUE LIGHTS

# 4

# INNOCENT TILL PROVEN

*If ever there was a time there was,*
*a time there was is now*
*But if ever there was a time*
*Now was the time too late*

—Alun S.

Remand is worst. Most of those who accept guilt or at any rate the likelihood of a sentence, settle reluctantly to the waiting game, hoping that regular prison will be more relaxed. Sentenced, a man settles to the routine, and — unless it's life — he has a release date to focus on, however distant. Remand is indefinite, a limbo of rumour and uncertainty, where communication is tortuously difficult and the regime stricter, harsher, abrupter, and to the newcomer a great shock. On remand, there's no association; any society, most conversations but the cellmates', must be furtive. Prisoners years on in the system remember this first impact of prison vividly; some say if it had stopped with this then maybe they'd have straightened out. It is the wearing away of the initial shock into grim routine that takes the edge off prison.

Remand *is* worse, the old hands say, meaning worse than the lot of the convicted, though remand in prison is preferable to remand in police custody. Throughout 1987 and 1988 between 500 to 1700 people awaiting trial have been held in abominable conditions in police cells all over the country, some hundreds of miles away from home and the scene of the alleged crimes. And there are convicted prisoners serving their time in police cells also. Despite repeated Government promises to end the practice of remanding into police custody, the numbers grow, both as the consequence of overcrowding, and of industrial action by the POA. According to NACRO, in 1986 the cost of keeping a prisoner in a police cell stood at £170 per night, cost the police £2.5m a year, and took up the largest proportion of their time. Conditions in police cells are often worse even than the minimum standards of prison.

A remand prisoner is one who cannot get bail, held by the prison or the police to be produced in court to answer charges, or who is refused bail because of the nature of the charges or police opposition. Some 22 per cent of all defendants committed for trial are remanded, and this proportion has tripled since the 1950s, and doubled since the 1976 Bail Act which was intended to have the opposite effect. Traditionally, magistrates remanded for periods of only eight days, when the prisoner must reappear in court, but since 1983 a prisoner need only appear once every fourth hearing. Sometimes, due to manning problems or disputes, the prison fails to produce him, and his case is put further back. According to Home Office figures, the average time spent on remand in 1986 was 57 days; according to NACRO, 16 weeks —over 100 days— is the current average a prisoner might spend in prison between committal and conviction in London, most of it in 23-hour bang-up. Fifty per cent of all of them are acquitted, or get a non-custodial sentence. According to NAPO, more than 2000 people a year are remanded and subsequently acquitted, and there's no compensation. A Home Office report published in 1986 finds there are some 68,000 unproductive remand hearings a year, and that officer escort duties for them take up 38,000 man hours per year. Remand prisoners account for over 21 per cent of the prison inmate population, most of them concentrated in older prisons and remand centres. Around the country wide differences are apparent in the proportions of those granted bail and those remanded; from the beginning it is all something of a lottery. And the proportion of remands to convicted is growing fast.

Compared to conditions in police cells, C Wing is a better bed and breakfast. Compared to living on Broadwater Farm, a young man just brought in after the riots there in 1985 remarked, there's not a whole lot of difference. Some who are found not guilty of the main charge find themselves strung out on a lesser one or a technicality, and are sentenced to what they've already served less remission plus one day; it means they walk home. But they have still been in prison for months, and taken on its ambience. Only those found guilty and imprisoned benefit from remand time credited against sentence. For those acquitted, there is no compensation, and only by initiating a civil action for wrongful detention can any be obtained. The thing to know about prison is that it mostly doesn't work, and remand especially is counter-productive and largely unjust. The remand prison is overcrowded and run as a tight ship. Men are banged up with a slop bucket and each other for company most of the day and night, unlocked only for meals and exercise, maybe a film once a week, a bath once a week, a visit or an interview. Some who can't cope are sent to the block; they have a sentence before they have been convicted. Some are or go crazy; the prison can't cope with them and sends them on the muffin run to Brixton, where there's a facility for the mentally disturbed. In normal circumstances it's hard to do any business from prison, harder still from the remand wing, hardest of all for the first-timer, newly arrested and fresh off the waggon. Remand prisoners wear browns, or their own clothes, and can have more frequent visits, though they can no longer receive food and drink from outside. All the same, they are treated strictly as prisoners, mixed in with the guilty and the innocent, professional with amateur, the lags with the baby burglars, the violent with the meek. Their extra privileges are often cancelled or curtailed due to staff shortages and manning levels. Contact with the world through visits is often suspended, often abruptly. The incidence of suicide on remand, and all that such figures conceal, indites the remand system.

On remand, a prisoner is theoretically not yet proven guilty, but in effect he is a prisoner and treated as guilty; his warders have no training in how to deal with him otherwise, and with some 500 men locked up on the wing, any man's plea, however urgent, is soon swallowed up. The ambience is villainy, because many of the inmates are villains, and so they are all largely regarded by governors and staff. If a man gets off, he's thought lucky. Here a man must learn fast, adapting to his new conditions, frustrated in his efforts to deal with his life outside, where he will lose work, reputation, contact with his family, self-respect, a condition that might last up to a year, with dire consequences for his family and for the rest of his life. And if, when tried, a man is acquitted, then he is merely free again, freedom being sufficient of a prize in itelf from both the perspective of the law and of the inside. But he goes out a prisoner, with the habits and attitudes he has learned in order to get by in prison. He has absorbed prison's ways, its sleight of hand and sideways looks, its lingo and its cunning, its air of sarcasm and complaint, its secrecy, its pallor. Innocent or not, he's learned the culture of criminals. As one prisoner said: 'I'll never get rid of it, the stink of jail. It's in me, in my skin, in my hair, in my gear. Anyone I meet will know it and smell it. I'll never get shut.'

Remands are crowded and packed in together among too many unknown quantities, banged up most of the time, glad of any chance to get out of the cell, to talk to anyone, to be out even on the dangerous spaces of the wing. Communication outwards is slow and difficult; it involves getting applications in by 8.00 a.m., starting with the landing officer, and from there up the ladder of authority requesting a visit, a phone-call, the Governor, the doctor, welfare, education, probation, brief or priest, and all this pressing business grinding exceeding slow through the mills of the bureaucracies. After remand from court and the ride in the meat waggon and passing through reception, there's an initial interview next morning with the wing governor: the prisoner is marched in Army style and formally identified, his charge and plea and remanding court specified, he signs for possessions and money he came into prison with. He's offered work within the prison if he wants it, though by and large beyond feeding and cleaning the wing there isn't any. Workshops are for convicted prisoners, in the Scrubs mostly for lifers, short-timers in the kitchens. But if he accepts, it's the same as saying he's available for work, and he'll get paid. Finally he's given an envelope and letter to write to whom he will to tell them where he is, and the prison franks it. All else he must learn for himself: how to fiddle, spin out time, scam, lie, give a good account of himself, survive here. The only way to release the monotony of the long bang-up and one hour exercise a day is to work, which means working for *them*, the enemy, but cleaners get around, and tea-makers gather information, and painters and canteen crew are out some of the day on the wing, and get to go out of the building as far as the kitchens. In prison, freedom is a relative affair, and mobility, however circumscribed, is what counts. Out on the wing, objects and information get lost and found and exchanged along the way. And there's the matter of time, and passing it.

And for this, when it happens, he will be charged the poll tax.

*Don't let the Crown get you down.*

I meet the Chileans, a roving international band of expert pickpockets, ten in all, described by the police who arrested them at Victoria as 'a gang of locusts, absolute professionals'. One of them is Italian and writes poetry. Another, from Chile, knows no English, but he knows Neruda. There is a squad of Ghurkas, soliders in the British Army, nabbed bringing back black Nepalese from leave in their mountain kingdom, blinking in the yellow light. From their bearing they are still in the Army, in a barracks where there are no parades and their knives have been taken away. There are foreigners of all sorts and natives of the streets, scooped up all over London. There are sad Nigerians busted at Heathrow, the dumb couriers of drugs. They are among those whose experience of this country will be only of its gaols; sentenced, they will serve their time and be deported.

On the remand wing the men I meet are mostly those who have the bottle to get out and about for a while. Some are on real or invented business, others work there, cleaning or painting or in the kitchens. They have work that gets them about, and therefore because they're painting in the many colours, mostly yellow, mostly blue, of the wing, I keep meeting painters and decorators who write poetry. Or say they do. Jeff's one such, his outside skills employed on the inside. He's got some poetry, he says, in his cell. He leans down from his ladder, brush in hand, watching the screws. Like the Forth Bridge, the wings are always being painted, but the wonder of it is that so many of the painters write. Outside they're anyone, some but not all criminal, many without much education, most with more than a fair share of crisis and trauma. Either they are men with sufficient initiative on coming into prison to put down a trade that gets them around, or because they are imaginative enough to think of such things, therefore they write. Some are just kidding. Sometimes a prisoner says he writes, but has nothing to show, or maybe he's borrowed something from his cellmate. Or from a book. One day a man recites *The Windhover* as his own. Others mean it. At any rate, they are men with inner lives in which no one takes much interest.

As on the inside, so on the out. Many people write, whether in secret or merely as an activity they keep to themselves. Sometimes it is no more than a diary, sometimes it's letters, though more often than we think, it's poetry. Sometimes it's something written years ago, kept since, or written for an anniversary. Some men have journals they keep only in prison, picking up where they left off on the last sentence. Sometimes the poem is for a particular occasion, for a particular person, or the only handle on a crisis. Trauma, and the thought of loved ones who can't be reached, and time in which to reflect, all come together in prison. Writing poetry is not considered odd at all in here.

With Jeff and others we meet from time to time in one of the interview cells. We think we ought to write a play, but talking about it is all we ever do. Perhaps we think we've written it by talking about it. So many bizarre events take place all the time in C Wing; they should be collected, we agree, connected up as dialogue and made into a play about the nether world. But we'll not make it.

There's no place to move about, to rehearse or put it on, and it wouldn't be allowed, and no one here is about to take on the bureaucracy. Just to meet is difficult enough, and discussion is constantly interrupted. Here all is random in a rigidly controlled chaos, and everyone is subject to lassitude and mood swings, and next week these men won't be the same group, just as they're not the same from last week, when we looked at haiku and discussed the real problems of writing even a letter from prison. We are always at the beginning. Everything but the subject of prison is fleeting. Nothing stays the same where everything remains the same, and only the feverish population changes. Letting off steam is what these men want. In each other's presence their concern is not to lose face, and each is separately focused on his individual fate.

'My cellmate says he went out last night. He says some people came and took him away down the West End. "Nice place," he said, a pub, he couldn't remember its name or where it was but he described what it looked like, and what he drank and who he met. "Funny thing was," he said, "they were all wearing yellow trousers." '

Monk's suddenly become a Catholic. He had put down C of E but then he heard that with the Catholics he'd get an hour and a half of solitude, down at the RC Chapel every Sunday morning, the only space and time to himself in any week of his indefinite wait. 'Who would have thought it,' he says of himself. 'My pick of the week is the RC Chapel.' And he gets to see a bloke he knows on remand on B Wing, picks up scraps of gossip, and other items. His wife's coming on a visit. His head is stuffed with thoughts of her, with urgent messages to pass to her, not least of which is that he loves her and hopes she's not legging it with some other bloke. Now, interrupted by his incarceration, their marriage has its history, is his implication, and that right colourful. He doesn't trust her. He's hoping for a truce for the duration. He wants to know how he looks. He's shaved and scrubbed himself as best he can, and pressed his denims.

'And that one. The Chelsea supporter. Fat Man. He knows what he's getting. Headlines in *The Sun. She* wants him. When he came in he was talking about bail. Then he talked to his brief. Now he's not talking at all. He's just worrying. He's thinking about life.'

Bob's written a whole page of haiku. He kept his cell-mate up late, and himself sleepless, letting words fall into patterns of syllables in his mind, and wrote them down.

*In the pre-dawn dark*
*A blackbird sits, the sun is*
*Just a song away.*

Jimmy's had a visit from his wife. She's brought him cigarettes and a large melon, and he is more interested in canteloupe than in haiku. He shares it out among the others. It's a hot day on C Wing and melon never tasted better.

*The fox ran swiftly*
*Over winter's frozen ground*
*While the moon looked on.*

The melon's sliced and gone. Jimmy scrapes the last flesh from the skins, sucks them dry and dumps them out the window. Now he fishes out a full pack of twenty, and lights up. He hands them round. It's been a good visit.

*I feel loneliness.*
*It's standing strong inside me*
*Like some statued stone.*

Jeff's miserable. He likes the haiku well enough, and he'll give it a crack himself, later. Just now his mind is too much on where he is, again, for the same daft reasons, only this time it's the end of the line, the end of a long line of bars and petty nickings to afford them. He's heard from her and she's through with him, she's told him don't come back, and he's lost the kids. Time and again, his verses say, she's stood by him and he's let her down, and this time she's not concerned with what he gets or when he comes out. 'Just don't come back again,' she says. He's sent her the poems he's written but she won't read them. She tore them up. He stole his brother-in-law's video and stereo to pay for drink; her brother, who'd already had enough of Jeff. He stole from his own. He speculates maybe he'll just die, and then she'll be sent his things and his notebook. Then she'll read his poems to her. Then she'll know how he feels. He's going down, and knows it. He wants to. He wants to be out of the way, forgotten, where he can get on with despising himself thoroughly. He's expecting a sentence of two and a half. He gets it.

*Will I fall in love?*
*Will the wind echo my name?*

Bob can't finish it, and thinks to leave it as it is. Stone says he ought to finish it, it has to be a three-liner. Stone seems to like a rule to keep, Bob a rule he can break. Stone's another painter and decorator. Stone by name, stone by nature, he's an easy sort of man, a merchant seaman, a 50-year-old drinker and junkie. Once, he says, in the Tonkin Gulf, early one dawn because he'd got up to take a leak over the side, he'd spotted a mine strapped to the stern of the boat he was a deckie on, raised the alarm, saved some thirty lives, got a medal, the Purple Heart. Somehow he feels the medal ought to count against the daft list of petty crimes he's been caught out in, all his life, to pay for his bad habits.

Jimmy licks his fingers for the last of the melon, offers Stone and Monk a cigarette. The others turn him down, determined with their rollups. Monk's another junkie, vague about what he's charged with, though it sounds like smuggling. There was something he was importing, something legit, inside of which, etcetera, the customs found coke. Nothing to do with him, he says, half-heartedly, expecting no one to believe it. He knows he's going down. It's only a question of how long. And whether his missus will stand by him. He thinks she won't. As it turns out, she doesn't.

As for Jem, his dealing days on the King's Road are over, he's been here for months, and the henna in his hair is growing out. He doesn't say much. His tipple is sulphate, for dealing in which he's pretty sure he'll go down. He was holding the sulph, the plastic bags, a pair of brass apothecary's scales. He knows a bloke who was done for just the scales.

*Boy wants to be man.*
*He so wishes time to fly,*
*Chasing the dragon.*

Jack describes his bust: the heavy mob with sledgehammers. He'd have opened the door, but they didn't wait. They smashed up everything, which was mostly the stereo. Meanwhile, he was high on best bush and saw it all in superscope, and couldn't quite take anything seriously, and took a fit of the giggles. What struck him was they were so serious about their business. And then, charged and the business over till court, about three a.m. in the cop-shop he was straight again, listening to the constables discussing their private lives, the what's-for-dinner and what-the-wife-says business, as they brought him a cup of tea, and he was struck by their ordinariness, these men who'd raged through his life with sledgehammers and baseball bats a couple of hours before. The fact that they were human after all he found difficult to cope with.

Stone describes the misery of heroin: on it highs like no other, off it lows like no other. His writing is junkie script — discontinuous, uncentred, a string of striking images. 'Stronger than God,' he says of junk.'Than sex or drink or religion.' He says he's a slave to it, and despises himself for it. But if he were let out of here this afternoon, he says, the first thing he'd do would be to score. Monk looks up. 'I'm with you,' he says. 'I'm going with him.'

*This prison window,*
*And the moon's bright silver rays*
*At night in the gloom.*

Adge is writing a story, which he shares as it develops with other men about the wing. He has it spread through three prison exercise-books. It fair cracks along and he's keen to get on with it, in between the kitchen work. He's a small, wiry northerner, in for some difficult-to-grasp computer fraud, and Adge says he doesn't mind too much what they give him, he's still got the money, and measured off in months he's well ahead. The money's a few thou, a lot to him, sod-all to the banks, and will be there when he comes out. He's tough and he can do it on his head; he estimates, accurately as it happens, he'll draw a two, less remand, less remission, can just about predict his release date. Adge is cheerful and practical about it all, and to pass the time there's his story, based on his adventures the previous year, a young man free and footloose around the

Mediterranean. Between the lines he's the shy protagonist hitching rides with not much money, taking chances, hanging in. The tale begins in Monte Carlo and proceeds up and down the Riviera, mostly in fast cars. The heroine is beautiful but unable to speak, struck dumb in childhood by some psychic shock (brought about by her villainous father, it turns out, the gangster and nonce). But she's rich because her father turns out to be a big-time crook, a sadist and a villain, about which she, at the beginning, of course, knows nothing. It's a fast rattling yarn, and there's lots of adventure and teetering climaxes; there's innocence, love, sex, danger, villainy thwarted, much of it graphically detailed, and Adge promises a happy ending, and the beauty released into speech by love, when he gets there. The length of the story depends on when his case comes to court. Expecting to be sentenced soon, he'll be gone to another prison. He just wants to get on with it. His chief problem at the moment is remembering details of romantic foreign places he'd buzzed through a year back, where their names are on maps in relation to each other, and ways they connect. He needs maps. And railway timetables, and basic research to make his tale authentic.

But I give him no maps, no timetables, not knowing what he's about. Maybe he has some elaborate escape in mind, and needs to plan his route across Europe from Victoria. We concentrate on the story, on its shape and pace, on questions of syntax and likelihood. Me, I have a suspicious mind. Perhaps I always had. I've no great faith Adge will finish the story, and now he has them stranded in the Alps, newly lovers with several police forces and the bad guys and the girl's father all after them at once, and no ideas how to get them out of it. Somehow he wants to get them to Hong Kong, another place he's been about in, and wonders if I can get him any brochures. When he's sentenced and settles to his bird wherever he's sent, he'll either write the tale or put it aside, or start another. He's thinking now of just writing porn, erotic masturbation tracts, prison for the use of, another form of currency. Adge is already disappearing.

Moving through these spirals of the inferno, I note that here as everywhere, some men are wallies, some are fools, some are plain evil, though most are merely desperate, and in prison desperation makes men dangerous. Some, like Monk without the junk, are mates of like feather, strange to see in here. Sharing a birthday, we are shadows of each other, another pair of ghost brothers, each of whom might have turned out to be the other.

All the same I am as ever circumspect, suspicious, paranoid, probing into hidden motive, careful. I get a callup slip from a man on remand on B Wing. He's written his name, his number, his cell and landing, and asks to see Ken Barlow, *poet of this prison, thanking you Guv*, and adds along the bottom that he always watches *Coronation Street*. When I see him in the probation cell he finds himself out for a while, blinking, gathering his wits, with someone to tell his tale to. But he has no writing, no ideas about writing, no interest in writing, no need of paper or pen, no desire for dictionary or books or poems or any of the few things I can legitimately get for him. There's nothing much to do therefore but get quickly to the point: his scheme.

In short, he's on remand, been here a month, although he's innocent, he says. He's never been inside before and only wants out, where he's a tradesman, an electrician with a job, a life, home, people, mates, girlfriends, a child by one of them. In short, would I, a famous actor in the endless saga of *Coronation Street*, stand bail for him? One unreality is intruding on another. He's thought this up in his cell, connecting some rumour of my being here and having been on TV with a character in a fiction.

*It'll never happen, John. I don't know you, do I? I'd have to go to court and say I knew you, when I've only met you here. That's perjury, John.* And if he skipped I'd be well out, and I figure nowhere in the job description can I fit in John's request. I couldn't speak for Barlow, but I shook my head. He grinned briefly and shrugged, annoyed and disappointed. *Nice try, John.* The charge was rape. What he described between himself and a woman he'd done some wiring for was debatable perhaps; in the proceedings there was a knife, his, but that was for shredding cable, he claimed. Sex there had been, and a fundamental misunderstanding as to consent on one side or the other, but in court he wouldn't have a whisker of a chance. It didn't look good from where I was sitting. *No chance, John.*

Monk says, 'My cell-mate thinks I'm crazy. He says he'll change his plea just to get away from me. All he does is stare out of the window and there's nothing to see, and make up daft little verses like:

> *Mary had a little lamb,*
> *She milked it with a spanner.*
> *She made the cheese between her knees*
> *And sold it for a tanner.*

And he says I'm daft.'

# 5

# IN THE ANNEXE

Jack, Blue, Quick, Sly, Nob, Dark: six men eventually appear in response to the officer's call of 'Any more for poetry?' along the two landings. We meet for an hour in the cell used for such meetings, the lock on the spring and the pale bare walls hung with black lettered AA cards: *Think. One day at a time*. This is not a group, in the sense that these men use the word here, the focus of fierce rivalries and loyalties, much grief and much anger.

What's in the box? On a winding road, far from here, on a good day of sun and wind and birds in the trees and not much to do but turn the long curve through the woods: you find a large wooden box in the middle of the highway. You walk up to it. You lift the lid. What's inside?

Jack: 'A snake.' Blue: 'A dead pigeon.' Quick: 'Cancelled cheques.' Sly: 'Second-hand clothes.' Dark: 'Nothing. Nothing at all.' And Nob: 'A stiff. A woman.'

'Does it smell of anything, this box? Is there a label, a stencil, a number, the dust of something?'

'Nothing.'

The Annexe is another prison, sealed up within the main prison, apart, a quiet island. It has a therapeutic air, a calm tension all its own, where men move about in a strange, unreal quiet. Here they and their officers perhaps only seem more relaxed, and they talk in a language the inmates call theraspeak of their hangups and traumas and crises. The serious business of this unit is 24-hour intensive wrap-around therapy, a rare attempt at rehabilitation, whose intent is to bring men to understand themselves and how they came to be criminals, in the hope that such knowledge will lead to their changing. In such therapy self-projected images (which are often a tissue of lies) and ego-defensive barriers are broken down through a process of intensive question-and -answer sessions, and like peeling the layers of an onion, the idea is to arrive at the truth, the core of the personality. Inmates are called 'patients', and patients undergoing psychoanalysis and group therapy gain insight into themselves. They begin to understand what makes them tick. A by-product of group therapy is an awareness of others and of the need for social skills. Many prisoners on group therapy learn, for the first time in their lives, how others see them. The feedback is a valuable tool in modifying behaviour.

'We don't claim to cure anyone,' one of the shrinks says. 'We work in areas of doubt. We deal with doubt, and work with it. We take it into account, and turn it about. We refract it. And by the way,' he says, 'you're fishing in the cesspool. This is the dustbin of mankind. What are you looking for?'

In here all are volunteers, the officers in some defiance of their blunter deterrent-minded brothers, the inmates from regular prison, many of them recidivists. Some come initially to escape the routines of Pentonville and Wandsworth thinking anything must be better, some in hopes of the softer option it turns out not to be, some merely filling out their time. Some exclaim that, in years of prison life they've never had this chance to figure themselves out before, and wonder at the waste of themselves, of others. Some are changed. Some go through the motions. Ideally, these men have to want to change, and find the going rough; here they are obliged to think about themselves and their crimes and their victims. It isn't easy. They are pushed and rooted and shamed beyond whingeing into recognition of themselves, and urged to do something about it, if only to sidestep the repetitive grim circus of prison. Most of them are re-offenders again and again whose habits are a repeating spiral of violent offences and gaol, their crimes distinctly anti-social, drink or drug related, or sexual. Some are prematurely aged through drugs. Some have sold their bodies for junk money. Some have ulcerative sores, permanently swollen hands and undernourished bodies. One has had a hand amputated through infections caused by injecting. They speak another language of addictive personalities: 'staying clean', 'a smack habit' or just 'a habit', 'using', 'a works', 'a crank', 'N.A.', 'Boots the chemist', 'Palf,' 'Physeptone', 'a ten pound bag', 'Turkish', 'Chinese', 'pharmaceutical', 'half a grain', 'sepsis'. They all meet each day in therapy groups where their task is to talk, exhaustively and however painfully, about their offences, habits, patterns, dependencies, weaknesses, their beginnings often in a life of perversity and fury. It turns out many who began in deprivation turn into the next generation of gaolbirds and villains. In their turn abused children grow up twisted into abusers of children; incest begets incest, cruelty more cruelty, and we breed our own lethal malcontents.

I suspect few secrets are kept in here, in the glass-sided room called the Wendy House where these meetings take place. And these men know that after being here their files will be thicker and their excuses thinner. In here men whose crimes repel even other criminals are brought together and exposed to each other in the withering light of disclosure: the child molester and the rapist, the incestuous and the sadistic, the hetero and the homo, the violent drunk and the junkie who steals to run his habit, the defrocked priest and the fallen angels, the bold and the timid, all sit in confrontation with each other and their therapists, and no one escapes inner scrutiny. Some pull out. Some fail. Some play games and some are good at it. Some men are broken here, and fail again, and go back to the familiar routine of the main prison. Some are changed, although the Met says there's no difference in the re-offender figures for men released from the Annexe. But a rare and genuine attempt to understand and change — to rehabilitate — is being made here. As an outpost in the prevailing tide of deterrers and lockers-up, the unit is embattled, fiercely enclosed within itself within the prison, guarded in what it gives out about itself. Officers who work here have to believe in something more than counting and turning keys, and they are not popular amongst their colleagues. From the feedback the therapy is fearless, and men who graduate from here remain in touch; there's aftercare. On their staying straight the unit's survival depends, they are aware. Amongst the invisible statistics of success are some who make it and who never come back.

We few who are not a group meet to talk about words, and words are loaded and difficult here. Their stories are often horrific and often true. The six of them stare back at me, checking me out, checking each other. Some are new and I'm a softie. We run through the poem somebody always knows — Burns or Kipling or *The Raven*, and other verses anonymous, and someone's poem about the birds in the prison yard. 'Pepper,' I say to Quick, who's played this game before. 'Hot,' he says, and nudges Blue, who throws in 'Pot' and then the others spin it into 'Pot, smoke, gear, change, loose, booze, noose, clothes, naked' and we're away. Nob brings it back to sex, always. That's how he got his name. He's a leering sort of bloke, with a one-track mind, a rapist.

In here, Sly points out, he's served longer than he would have. He's been on four days' home leave, and will be out in a few weeks. He's sitting things out, scornful of the therapy here, insisting he can get better in his home town. He acknowledges he has a problem. It's little boys and he's the fallen schoolmaster. As a teacher his tastes are classical and rigorously traditional, his manner one that contemplates no argument with what he knows. We don't much like each other, Sly and I. Today, Sly's out to spread disaffection. The others are defensive, vigorous on the Annexe's behalf. Dark says that by encouraging honesty, by requiring it, the system leaves the individual open to repercussion, in here, outside, or later in another prison on another sentence. Here men are expected to protect the unit, to report on other inmates as to drugs or hooch, and by doing so break the eleventh commandment: *Thou shalt not grass*. It is this imperative, central to prison survival, they must be weaned from; their solidarity with other prisoners. They are aware of conflict in the dual role of officer as warder and nurse. Dark says he'd rather do more time and come out straight than go round and round the system for ever. Sure, he says, a man who admits in his group to fantasies of rape or violence is talking himself out of parole. There was the man who foolishly admitted he fancied his young lady probation officer. He didn't get parole either. Statistically, they have a better chance in the anonymity of the larger prison; here they're focused on, analysed, minutely observed; they are encouraged to add to their own files. 'You have to say,' Dark says, 'that you want to stay to get cured. But what you want is to get out, to go home.'

Jack talks about a dream he's had. In it he's drowning, he's been thrown a lifebelt, but instead of saving him it drags him under. It sinks and he drowns. 'The drowning man fights back, and drowns his rescuer,' he says. 'It's this place.' The others grunt agreement. No one much likes Jack. He winds them all up with a poem he's written that he fishes out next, and reads. It's a prayer to his daughter, full of admirable sentiments, asking Mother Mary to bring them together again. He's sent it out to her. But everyone knows he's in here for incest with the same daughter, and the prayer just makes everyone sick. Jack, on the other hand, despises everyone else. Of Blue, who was caught in a burglary by the woman of the house, knocked her down, poured petrol on her and burned her alive, he says 'disgusting'.

And Quick. He's been in prison all over the planet, been involved with drugs and guns and prostitution, but his main activity for which he's now doing time has been pornography. He makes blue movies. He's written his story, all in a rush and a rage, cramped into a prison exercise-book. For over twenty years on and off he has been in various prisons, beginning with a childhood blighted in a Japanese concentration camp and continuing through prisons in several countries and sundry deportations and years on the run. No one wants him around. On every page his autobiography expresses hatred. Throughout it he betrays and is betrayed, robs and is robbed, his life a complex bisexual conundrum to which he attributes his hatred of authority, a tally of shootings and knifings and brutal punch-ups, the flicker picture narrative of a desperate creature surviving in the world somehow, dodging through the huge anarchy of events: a thief, cheat, pimp, fraudster, kyter, pornographer and on down into darker shades of pale. He's an intelligent man, blind to himself, yet coming to some self-realization that at any rate thus far his life has been a waste.

There's the makings of half a dozen novels, but none of them he'll write. It's all synopsis; as biography it's almost not unusual, though dreadful. Like Quick, some men are legends, for their defiance, for their cunning, for resistance. But nothing redeems the unremitting hatred he feels for everyone he's ever met, through pages of ranting fury, written in a purging as he found himself, yet again, in a cell in Pentonville — watching through the window the cockroaches feeding on the garbage and the crows feeding on the cockroaches and the rats feeding on anything.

So can he write it? He shakes his head. He's not a man with leisure to write his life story, as he might on a long sentence. He's going out soon, and we'll not meet again, and we've no time to talk much further. What he needs is time, and out there will be none to spare, for he'll be back on the hustle as soon as he's out. Or he needs a ghost to write it. But it's all hate. Like him, it isn't going anywhere.

Sad for Quick, and for anyone he meets on the outside. His rage chokes his writing as it chokes him. For him everyone else is the enemy. He scorns and despises everyone: his distant and long dead parents, his fellow crooks and prisoners, the police and the judiciary who he says conspire against the criminal. The *uniformed brutes* who arrested him, the *benched bewigged perverts* who sentenced him, and the screws whose task is to confine him, all fall under his scathing lash. His only active principle is loathing; his writing, his voice and tone and his cold, steady gaze constantly assert it. His air is one of misunderstood innocence, his offences minimized, his woundings all in self-defence, all that was done to him motiveless malice. He readily admits to bias. Reading him, I am afraid of him.

In here he's been invited to feel guilt, rather than despair, to connect his feelings with his actions. That's difficult for him. His hatred, expressed in the way he tells the tale of his life to himself, constantly intrudes. He thinks he understands himself well enough already, and implies that this is just an easier bit of bird for him. But the shrink has suggested three things to him, he says, and none of these has he taken lightly, nor without resentment, but the shrink's got him thinking. He's learned, he says incredulously, counting off on his fingers, that he's 'invented' his father, that he's always anxious to be in charge and therefore manipulates what others think of him, and thirdly that he's just plain afraid of sex. This last really upsets him, and him in the flesh trade. Could it mean, he wonders, that fear of sex is what put him behind the camera? It's got him thinking.

As for Dark, his may be a success story. For weeks we've met and talked, discussing his poems, his long record of violence and confinement, his dwindling hopes of a future. Still in his early thirties, he is a bully, thug, rapist, a persistent offender with a long, violent record. In the Annexe he's come to think about why, and voices a determination to change, to go straight. Shy, he has the manner of a man who still finds it difficult to talk of himself, but talks anyway, needs to. He says he's come to realize he worries constantly what others think of him. Underneath what people say, he is forever detecting hostility, he says, finding it in his own inner thoughts, deducing it in theirs. If his head is full of such suppressed snarling, everyone else's must be, he reasons. Always on a short fuse, there were a lot of fights. Drunk, he was a terror. He came to see his view of women was distorted, that when what he wanted was love he would repel it, out of fear of failure. Living with a woman he'd get drunk and pick a fight, rather than sleep with her, fucking in anger, never making love. 'All I ever wanted was love, and that I was unable to give.' In the end, he said, what he wanted was to end all that, to curb his violence, to open up, to find someone who could love him, though he feared it was now too late. After all, who would trust him with his record? Who'd take him on? Or would he lie and not mention it? He thinks all this out loud, resolving to cut the string. When released he wouldn't go back anywhere he'd lived before, wouldn't go back to his family; he'd cut the long ribbon of guilt spilling after them, and start anew with better understanding of himself. Suddenly he withdrew into himself. Men said he was just staying behind his door, he was under heavy pressure, and when we met, briefly, he wore a worried look as his release date approached. Then he was gone, back to Pentonville at his own request to do the last six weeks of his sentence there. A brief message came back on the grapevine. He said he thought he ought to start again from there, from real prison, to remind himself how sick he was of it all.

'Here,' Quick says. 'I had this dream I was dead. Thing is when you die you get a choice of hell or heaven, but they're both pretty much the same. It's like reception but they tell you you can make one phone call back to your nearest and dearest to tell them you've arrived. But in hell the phone doesn't work and in heaven nobody has a ten-pence piece, and the queue stretches away to infinity. That's why you never hear anything back.'

Jack, Blue, Quick, Sly, Nob, Dark: six men.

# 6
# NONCE

Coming out of the inside gate to the visitors', just inside the security fence, two inmates are being returned to their cells. The two inmates walk ahead of the officer escorting them, separately from each other, he walking distinctly apart from them. One is a young man, tall and powerfully built, wearing a new blouson and jeans — his own clothes, so he is on remand. His is an embarrassed air, his walk uncertain, not yet economized into a brisk, tight prison walk, nor slurred into the mocking slouch of those who are used to it. He is crestfallen but far from crushed, with a hesitant bravado, still crisp, and his walk has not yet lost its spring. He's new to it. The other man is a slight wisp in crumpled prison blue, walking well ahead of the young man and the escort. He knows the way. He wants to get back as quickly as he can, and he walks nervously, as if expecting attack from any direction at any moment. He seems to merely drift over the yard, like a quick ball of dust.

The officer, tall, confident, efficient, swings the visitors' gate shut, sends the lock home and pockets his keys all in one smooth easy movement. He moves in a series of graceful arcs, a dancer in some satanic ballet. As he swings round and turns to harry his charges, his eye catches the eye of another officer coming along in a parallel direction. He nods.

'43s,' he says, making an open face expression, his eyes swivelling to indicate these two and back again. He does not look at them, but notes them, pointing with his eyes, merely glancing at their heels, clocking them. He means: *These two are going back to the 43 Unit. They're going your way. Please take them for me.*

'Shit,' says the second officer, and grimaces. He nods back. His expressions run through a mimicry that says (1) he'll do it though (2) it's distasteful and anyway (3) he's in charge now. Then he barrels out his chest and shouts after the two inmates still running on ahead, for no one has told them to stop or wait, and these transactions, though brief and efficiently done, have slowed down their keepers. 'Heel,' he snarls. It is a tone that utterly excludes them, is barely intended for them, part of the joke he shares with his fellow officer. He is now in control, but the two inmates don't know it yet so they still haven't stopped, each at his different pace.

The first officer, meanwhile, has reopened and stepped back behind the gate, his face leaning briefly out. 'You have to use their names,' he says. 'The first one's Henrietta. I think the other one's called Joan.'

The second officer goes after them. 'I said "heel",' he barks. 'It means stop.' They stop.

These two are nonces, men who live in segregation under Rule 43, on the 43 Unit. There, they are separate from other prisoners, though not from each other, and as with these two, the principle of keeping apart convicted and remand has been waived. As nonces, they may or may not be sex offenders or child molesters. They may be there for any of a number of reasons, decided for them or at their own request. They are kept apart for their own protection, with only the company of other 43s. Theirs is a particularly difficult corner to be in.

A prisoner can be unpopular, a pest, a scrounger, a loony, a dog-end man, a whiner, a bully, a paranoid schizophrenic, a brown tongue, a backroom lawyer, a thief or even a bit of a grass, but the worst he can be — here or anywhere — is a nonce. The fact is a prisoner can also be a decent human being but, irrespective of character, a man's life in prison often depends on where he stands in the rigid hierarchy of prison values that descends downwards to the nonce. The top end of this scale is subject to discussion; for most it is the lifer, usually a murderer, and at the pinnacle the *crime passionnel*, the domestic, thereafter shading into degrees of guilt at what might have been manslaughter, self-defence, unthinking bravado, drink, stupidity. In a parallel hierarchy the aristocrats are the professional villains, cracksmen and kyters and heisters and heavies, craftsmen with particular skills looking down on lesser fry, on mere domestics, whom they consider unprofessional. Thus everyone but the nonce gets to look down on someone else. Most have some resort in the measures of human value, some real or imaginary claim to self-respect, however much a funkhole. A man who enjoys torturing cats can't understand a man who sticks needles in his arm and steals to pay for it. In his own eyes, a man might see himself as *an honest thief*, expressing contempt for muggers and dippers. Or he may point to the crimes of the rich, rarely discovered, rarely punished by imprisonment. Baby burglars and first timers aren't really taken seriously. Victimless and non-violent crime is sometimes not regarded as crime at all. But rapists and sex offenders are way down any value system. At the very foot of the ladder, well down into the muck, there is the nonce, at any rate the nonce as the media sees him, the butt and scapegoat of other criminals. In fact this is not universally so. The prevalence of violent sexual crime in recent years reflects its own growth in the prison population, so much so that in D Wing they are half the crowd they don't stand out in, and only the most shocking might be got at, and they move to the 43 Unit. In such numbers they are perversely unremarkable, each other's company. Hatred of the nonce is more often expressed as an idea, a threat, a displacement. Some, in time, manage to transcend their reputations, eventually settling to life on the wing, dismissed forever as 'an old nonce'. One such on D, a child murderer so long ago his crimes have faded into history, lives unmolested, at home where he has been for forty years. The more obvious nonce is a shambler, out on the wing a lone figure because no one wants anything to do with him, sometimes the image of the beast. One, slow and ageing after twenty years inside, drools continually as he talks, which is mostly to claim how much he helped the boys he corrupted. Another, standing at his door on the ones, peers through pebble specs, slouched and beaten; '32 counts of buggery on little boys' another man says of him, turning away, his shoulders rising briefly, pleased for a moment to be but a common murderer. Another, permanently unshaven, scruffy, picks his way carefully down the wing, avoiding others. On this wing, where the rapists barely count as nonces, this man qualifies. The woman he brutally attacked had to quit work, gave up her career, lives in permanent fear, can't go out, can't hope for a relationship with anyone, her life permanently blighted. It's said that when the cops got him they broke his arm in three places, and visibly it's badly put back together. He raped a nurse, so who would fix it for him? There's no one here who feels sorry for him, or condemns the cops. He is a complete nonce.

In the nether environment of prison, where society expresses its contempt for them, constantly questioning their worth, constantly insulting their humanity, inmates largely adhere to this system of values. In it and through it each man finds his place in the fiercely critical regard of his companions; his self-respect, founded on values true or false or some place in between, depends on establishing where he stands. He is distinguished from other men in this, chiefly expressed as a negative (*I'm not a thief, I'm not a rapist, I never cut nobody*). But above all, he distinguishes himself from the nonce, the pits, beyond which no form of life is less.

In this way prisoners are divided from one another, so the value system suits the management's intentions, and is to some degree reinforced by them. Management itself has its own rigid hierarchies of governors and officers, head office and region, gentlemen and others, dividing authority between the POA and its branches in different prisons, miscellaneous interests and petty fiefdoms, sundry prison departments, and beyond the remote mysteries of the Home Office, Civil Service and Government. Despite the current programme to unify officers and governors in the same service with the same uniform and structure, the governors have recently formed their own association to negotiate for them, to Government enthusiasm. And in the background, it's rumoured, the Masons, with their grades and circles and secrets and funny handshakes, connect across the systems. Down here, in the lower reaches at the sticky end of several chains of being, such other heights are only dimly glimpsed.

Beneath them all, at the bottom of the world: the nonce. Nonce meaning a nothing, a nonsense, a no one, a non-thing, a phenomenon existing somewhere between noun and verb, between the most terrible acts and the dreadful words for them: pervert, child molester, sex offender, monster, beast. Its use signifies contempt, hatred, and it is only rarely ever used in jest. The nonce is the game in an ever open season. He can be cut, stabbed, thumped, scalded, burned, marked, or killed; he is the eternal target. Men who express their hatred of authority, police and prison, discharge their hatred on the nonce, and other men applaud and reward them. The nonce lives always in fear.

And even nonces have their hierarchy. Properly, the nonce is a sex offender, a child molester. The first might spit on the second, and both on the child killer, and he on the perverted killer, the torturer. The ultimate pariah is no doubt the child-torturer and murderer Ian Brady, twenty-six years in prison, and Brady's prison career has accordingly been one of close protection. He appears in the late sixties in McVicar's account of life on Durham's E Wing, set up for troublesome prisoners, a despised and distant figure keeping to his own space, living in fear of the violent contempt of his fellow prisoners. In his time at the Scrubs it was said his safety could not be guaranteed anywhere, on the 43 Unit or the block or in the proposed control unit. In the early seventies he was moved to Parkhurst block, where for almost ten years till his move to Gartree in 1983 he never once went on exercise, and the only time he went outside the block was when Lord Longford visited him. For most of his sentence, Brady has typed braille texts for the Royal National Institute for the Blind, an activity he began in the Scrubs with the encouragement of the Catholic nuns, who saw such work as reparation for his crimes.

Up (or down) from Brady are others convicted of cruelty towards children, all of them looked down on by other kinds of nonce — the grass, the squealer, or the prisoner who was once a cop or a screw. Some go to the 43 Unit for debts run up on the wing, where interest on a loan is 100 per cent, or to escape some old vengeance that has followed them into prison. Inside, there're plenty of other ways to get into trouble; there's gambling, drugs, hooch, homosexuality. One man who elected to go there jumped a nonce at supper time. With a bit of sharp metal brought in from the shop he made as if to stab the man over and over, taking care to keep the tray and the man's dinner between blade and victim. He made it look good, but did no damage. In reality he was in debt, and wanted out, and his mark was an available target. Usually it's enough to say threats have been made, and there are many reasons why a prisoner might prefer the 43 Unit to the hazards of the wing. There are many ways to wind up a man. 'Nonces,' one said, 'serve two sentences.'

Out on the wings, the nonce's lot may be constant fear of assault, of threats and verbals, the casually well aimed shove into the soup, trip down the stairs, the blow or the blade that strikes in silence out of the crowd and carries no need of further explanation. And it comes from everywhere. 43 Units aren't always well sited. In Brixton the remand 43 on A Wing lies below three landings of normal remands, and gravity does the rest. On normal location on the landings and the stairways are opportunities for a push, a passing swipe, a kicking or a stomping. Because he is a criminal who gives other criminals a bad name, the Yorkshire Ripper, attacked with a broken glass jar in Parkhurst, was an obvious target. But the general belief that nonces are given a hell of a time inside is often illusory. Some manage to conceal their offences from their peers, passing as 'honest' criminals. Others are all too ordinary. On D Wing Peter Cook, the Cambridge rapist, lives on normal location, and no one bothers him; he's tolerated, dotty, indifferent to anyone's opinion. To all appearances, he has accepted prison. Others do less well, especially where children were involved, and here the grade of nonce is most vulnerable. In Scrubs' D Wing, Price, who got life for starving his child to death, left his shoes in the recess one noon bang-up. The story was that when he came back for them they'd been shat in; he simply put them on and sloshed back to his peter. 'No one at home,' they said of him. 'No point in baiting him. He doesn't get it.' Soon after he went to the 43 Unit, and since then, he's been sectioned off. Nonces get no help from anyone. If a nonce were bleeding, he'd beg for a bandage. They get spat and shat on. They endure the hissing and threats of other men, in passing, through their doors, at night through the walls. They get scalded and burnt. They get beaten. They get buckets of water or piss tipped under their doors, salt or sugar tipped into food brought into them from outside, their food spat in or otherwise interfered with on the way over from the kitchens. They face a constant barrage of abuse and threat, and live in constant fear behind their doors, not associating, dreading exercise.

Segregation is another system within the system, a prison far into the interior. Currently there are some 2,000 inmates on Rule 43 in prisons in England and Wales, and the number is growing. And even here they may not be safe. There is a pecking order even here. A 43 inmate persuaded his cellmate that he ought to kill himself, and watched him try to hang himself. He failed, but had a stroke and now he's paralysed down one side. And he's still in prison, a nonce for whom no one cares, the *persona non grata* of other nonces.

At the end of one wing, behind a plain brown painted door like any other prison door, with no attention drawn to it, there is another door into the block and next to it a spiral iron staircase up to the 43 Unit. For men on this wing on short-term location, this door opens into mysteries, horrors, beasts, the inhabitants of two other prisons. The block's door is a forbidding slab of metal, broken only by a flat observation slot, opening on the inside, and a sign saying to telephone first. In there men lie beyond the reach of anyone but the trilogy of law, medicine and the church, and but remotely even then. 'Here be monsters,' says the wing movements officer. He lets in the small grey nun but my man, whose callup slip he's carefully examining, will have to wait, he says, till he comes out of the black hole, when he'll probably be ghosted, so we'll never meet. Dire tales come back from that place: there are too many tales for some not to be true. A dark and ill-lit place, the block's apocryphal, though some regard it as a lie-down, a break from the hell of the wing, some solitude. Behind this door the cells are strengthened, the bedframes cemented to the floor and welded together, the furniture a chair and table made of corrugated cardboard. In here also are the strip cells, with double doors, and nothing but a raised wooden bench for sleeping on, where the prisoner wears only a space-suit.

And at the top of the staircase behind a further door, the 43 Unit. It's a light blue sort of place, the two upper landing sections of part of a wing where the high windows thin out the light through glazed panes. On the 43s live some of the worst men in the world, men for whom few can find any compassion. The unit has the same old smell of prison, piss and disinfectant and rotting brain cells, though here it's cleaner and sweeter, its air softly abrasive, languid, lethargic. 43s live in a cocoon of fear and loathing. Within, all is quiet, efficient, routine. During association there's TV, darts and board-games, tea. Men grow lazy here, where there's no work, and they participate in few prison activities. Unlocked, most men stay behind their doors. There's one man who doesn't know where he is, in which prison.There's John Steed, the M4 rapist, who has huge fat thighs from taking steroids, in for three violent rapes and a murder. Others are just lumps. Some spend the years growing fatter and duller and lazier. They're all wary of each other, even here, though close little groups form, tight cliques and intense hothouse relationships. It is a hushed sort of place, where men move without bravado, almost apologetically. Only on exercise or in church sitting in the nonces' pew, or on their way to the library or a visit, can other men get to them, well guarded as they are. Most merely jeer from safe distance.

One, an old man of 79 with many previous convictions back to 1945 for sex offences and violent assaults, complains of a journalist who's written up his case. He had savagely murdered a child and dumped her body in a dustbin. At his trial he had expressed his hatred of everyone; he'd said, 'I hate men and I hate women. I hate boys and I hate girls. But most of all I hate coppers.' He's vague and confused. He has the newspaper to show, but he's already cut the piece, and lost it, whining that the press has no right to write about him. Then the man I've come to see comes up and hisses into the old man's ear, 'Fuck off, nonce. They can write anything they like about you. For ten pence I'd cut off your head.'

He's got an idea for a scifi novel. I've got him to draft it and it's now into Chapter 3, where he's stuck. In the story, a future test pilot blasts off from Cape Canaveral, the first to break the speed of light. Next thing is he's crashed, and he wakes in a locked room, from which he is occasionally taken for questioning. Those who have charge of him have their own arguments with each other, and aren't much interested in him, and he doesn't speak their language. What he figures out is that they are the gods, engaged in their own power struggles with each other, and what else he doesn't know is that the Earth is surrounded and protected by a membrane which — by hitting the speed of light — he's punctured. The gods' only interest in him is to figure out how he did it and how to repair the puncture. By setting out not to write about prison he's arrived at a metaphor for his own condition: locked up by disinterested gods whose language he doesn't speak and whose questions he can't answer. That's why, I suspect, he can get no further with it.

And Yannis. He's here on remand, to do with Special Branch and arrested under the Prevention of Terrorism Act, and therefore *sub judice*, but opted for the 43 rather than the remand wing, where all he'd had to say was there had been threats, and he was moved here. He's not a sex offender or any kind of nonce, and claims to be an innocent bystander in the wrong place at the wrong time. The officer who's sent him my way was probably doing him a favour by finding him someone to talk to. Yannis is fiercely intelligent, and claims to be a businessman, a doctor, novelist, lateral thinker. Arrested with him, all his family are on remand, his wife in a police holding-cell, and all of them regarded as conspirators. In the remand wing he says he was in pain, requesting attention to his eye, and rang his bell repeatedly, though warned not to by the screws. As a result he was charged and put some time in on the block. So now without being convicted of anything he has a record of indiscipline. His case is mysterious, impenetrable, and barely reported in the press. He's writing down everything he can.

Another, a pale sliver of a man, explains the pecking order. He had murdered a young girl, in what seemed casual horseplay, an insane and cruel game. He'd put a rope around her neck and hung her. He is three years in on a minimum recommendation of twenty. Three things he loves, he says: Elvis Presley, Arsenal and his daughter; he's changed his name by deed to include his hero in it: Something Something Elvis Presley Something. He's writing a book. Clearly disturbed, he hastens to point out he'd not interfered with the victim. In his own eyes he's no nonce, but he's here because as the killer of a juvenile other prisoners on the wing had made his life difficult. At the beginning, on reception into prison on remand just after his arrest, in Brixton, another inmate had recognized him. While he was changing into prison clothes in a cubicle, a prisoner had thrown a razor blade in to him.

'Do yourself a favour,' he'd said. 'End it all now.'

# 7

# ALEXANDER

Alexander dreams of the outside. From his safe, 34 on the fours, he has a view west, 'a good view', he says. He watches the planes appearing over his head out of the east from distant and utterly unknown destinations levelling out for Heathrow. He watches the sunsets, 'often quite glorious, especially in the autumn', in the exhausted haze that is the air over the motorways. He watches the corner of the scrubs that he can see beyond the north wall: the whole of one plane-tree, a patch of bushy plants and saplings in which lurk the mysterious outlines of the wooden climbing frames of an adventure playground. He watches the houses across the way. He sees people going in and out, jogging, walking, perhaps occasionally across the flats the corner kick in a football game. And birds, the crows and rooks, magpies, hawks, pigeons, starlings. Like most prisoners, he understands irony, and is intrigued by birds.

His air is one of utter hopelessness, though he's not without humour. He is usually painting. He paints cells, walls, pipes, and doors, either in the thick dark blue gloss or the thick light blue gloss or the baby-crap yellow that are the colours of this particular sector of purgatory. Alexander is here because of drink. He's had a lifetime of it and its consequences — a lifetime of assault and battery when out of his head. He is tall, stooped, gaunt, ageing, thin and sandy on top, with the ashen look of a man long out of the sun. His face is leathery and looks much beaten. He'd not be a man to meet on the wrong side of the river. He is a straightforward sort of man, and he writes poetry.

'It passes the time,' he says, both of the poetry and paint. 'It helps me think.' As for the painting, he takes care and pride in it. That's his job. That's what he does outside, yet another painter and decorator, a man maintaining his trade inside and out. But there's not a lot he can do here with two shades of blue and one of yellow but get it on even and straight and not make a mess. As we talk he's slowly cleaning paint out of his skin with a rag. He's painting with his shaving-brush, and says they have no other. And besides, he can grow a beard, can't he?

'Look at this,' he says, folding up the rag. He starts a cigarette. His hands are always stained blue, and his rollups come out blue. The bits of paper he writes his poems on are splashed and dabbed blue by his fingers. 'I have just this one little cap of turpentine to clean up with.' He holds up the plastic cap with its spoonful of turps. 'They're scared I'll drink it's what it is,' he says, and puts the cap down. 'As if I'd bother.' It is a slow Scottish burr, declining on the ends of sentences, inward as he adapts his continuing inner monologue into mournful speech. His thoughts swim up, disjointed, surfacing from his gloomy interior. He's a man in his late fifties. His eyes and the face are those of a hard man, yet the eyes are always on the edge of tears. His face and voice are thoughtful, sad, yet both break from time to time into a wide slash of smile across his grizzled face.

He's done twenty-two years inside, on and off, in bits. 'Twenty-two years,' he says, in disbelief. The realization surprises him. 'And all for little stuff. Mean things. Burglary. Robbery. Assault. Affray. GBH. ABH. Drunk and disorderly.' He pauses, studying his rollup again, lighting it from the smouldering rope of his lighter. 'And it's all the drink.' And he leans back. He's not satisfied with that, and his face winces. His face says he is making himself remember this, forming the thought by saying it: 'No. That's not true either. It's not the drink. It's me. The problem's not in the glass or the bottle. The problem's in me.' He describes a lifetime of booze. 'With it,' he says, 'I thought I was God's gift to women. I wasn't.' And he laughs. Last time out he'd met a woman, lived with her for a while. She was an alky, but for a time he resisted and stayed on the waggon. 'She had all the right parts in all the right places and proportions, but in bed she was a wet fish. It was horrible. When I was sober I realized that was me when I was drunk. I saw myself. It was horrible.'

'The paint gets into everything,' he says. His poems are poems traditionally written in prison, conventional ballads and lyrics rhyming *hell* with *cell* and *jail* with *fail*, expressing remorse and foolishness, short on the line and wide on abstraction, but they poignantly describe Alexander's unhappiness, his regret and his shame for a life wasted and too late realized. He thinks that, if he could help someone else he could best help himself, but who would trust him with any responsibility? He's already failed one post-release rehabilitation programme. For a moment he thinks he might contact the brother he's not seen in thirty years, and then reflects he'd already done that, years ago, and got no reply. He understands. He has no family by now. Out there is a hostile and unfriendly universe. Somewhere back in the distance there was a wife and a child, a daughter. He'd abandoned both, lost in a lake of heavy and whisky; the child had been born malformed, and therein lay his rejection of her, and now he laments that time when he couldn't see the child's need for a father: her humanity, in the denial of which he denied his own. Now, like many prisoners come too late to reflection, he's trying to reach through his walls to the world's mess and cruelty. His poems are mostly prayers for peace, within and without, either side of the bed of knives that is Alexander's mind. Struggling to understand himself, his mind clouded by years of booze, he scowls into his hands.

He sighs. 'The last time I was out I was in a hostel in Battersea, with the Salvation Army. I had a job. I was three months without a drink. I was doing all right. Then I met the woman, she wanted me to move in with her, but the hostel wanted me to stay. I said I was cured. They said I wasn't. They were right. I wasn't cured. I moved out. She drank. So I drank. She was an alcoholic like me, so of course I drank because she drank, and here I am again.

'Twenty-two years. I've been painting the insides of prisons for twenty-two years. So I've thought: there must be something else I can do besides paint prisons. There ought to be something useful.

'I drink you see. I drink for the same reason everyone drinks, to forget. So I get drunk, I forget things, then I forget myself. Then I do something stupid. I'm a very bad man when I'm drunk. I'm very aggressive.'

He was going out soon, to another hostel. The Sally Army would meet him at the gate, on release, and stay with him all the way to Plymouth, to the hostel. Again, he'd face the impossibilites of getting work, of living in a hostel on the dole, of starting again at his age, alone, and staying away from drink, 'This time,' he says. 'This time I'm not coming back.'

He's joined Alcoholics Anonymous. He's found religion. In Coldingley prison he says he underwent a religious conversion and an exorcism; what he describes is sweating terror in a cell night after night, weeping and gnashing of teeth and sackcloth and ashes, long hours of praying on his knees. Another prisoner, a former priest, had convinced him he was full of devils, and conducted the exorcism. He describes devils being cast out of him, emerging with great hideous cries from his throat and almost throttling him, leaving his throat raw and his body exhausted long after. The nuns had given him crucifixes, and he'd slept surrounded by them. He'd lain awake so long clutching one in either hand that the profile of the dying body of his saviour had dug into each of his palms, and there were calluses he held out to show me. 'Stigmata,' he called them. Where his palms had healed little lines and etchings of blue paint had formed in the creases and healed into the skin.

'The paint gets into everything.'

# 8

# THE QUIET MAN

He says simply 'I'm here for the resorts.'

The resorts? Last resorts?

'The beaches. You know, the bombs on the beaches, after the Brighton business.'

Donal, by trade a carpenter from Donegal, formerly of the IRA, complete romantic, complete anti-hero, on remand awaiting trial with five others for conspiracy to plant bombs in hotels and on beaches, is in the prison hospital under close observation. He looks very young, dark, tousled, very Irish. He is 28. Before his arrest he'd resigned from the IRA, but from the British Government's viewpoint he's a terrorist. From the crucifix and rosary and open Bible he's a devout man, or now he is. They call him *the quiet man*. He writes poetry.

*Stalked the blackbird to her nest.*
*Beauty within smiled interest.*

He explains quickly that he suffers from depression, is sometimes manic, has been diagnosed manic-depressive. They have him on lithium to stabilize him and even out his swings. He has a history of mental illness that is seasonal, following the highs and lows of spring and winter. He has been in a mental hospital. He puts it down to the drink. Back in Donegal he had just been discharged from a psychiatric hospital when Patrick Magee, known to him as Tom, recruited him to the IRA.

*In flight we flew,*
*Swan of grace in poetry,*
*Dove of peace virginity.*

Following the arrest in a Glasgow flat on 22 June 1985 of three men and two women forming an IRA active service unit, Donal, who had been their runner, was arrested in London. He says he gave himself up. The group, led by Patrick Magee (who also writes poetry), were a prime catch for the police and security forces, and a widespread and indiscriminate terrorist threat was averted. Magee and Gerard MacDonnell were seasoned bombers of many years active service, and Magee was said to have had a hand in the Harrods' bombing while Peter Sherry, also arrested and subsequently convicted, was a leading IRA sniper and an expert with the Kalashnikov. All five were convicted and sentenced for plotting to plant bombs in four London hotels and on beaches in twelve English resorts, and Magee additionally for the Brighton bombing of the Conservative Party Conference in October 1984. It was his palm-print on the registration card of the Grand Hotel, where he had stayed a month previously in the room where the bomb went off, killing five people. In all, Magee drew eight life sentences.

*Alas the hawk in fiery flight.*
*We dropped the bomb with deathly might.*

When arrested, MacDonnell was carrying a Browning automatic, £10,000 in cash, and various documents. Amongst these was a list, the 'Bomb Calendar', itemizing targets marked H or B (for *hotel* or *beach*) in Brighton, Blackpool, Bournemouth, Dover, Eastbourne, Folkestone, Great Yarmouth, Margate, Ramsgate, Southampton, Southend and Torquay. According to the list, sixteen highly accurate time-delay bombs were to explode on consecutive days between 19 July and 5 August. Nine were on 24-day timers, the other seven on a 48-day lapse. For the police the pressing question was whether the bombs were in place; Donal, dog's body, couldn't tell them, and the others wouldn't. Under interrogation, the group were unco-operative, as they were trained to be. The panic was to find the bombs. The next day, 23 June, police in London defused a five-pound booby trapped bomb planted in a room in the Rubens Hotel in Buckingham Palace Road, its timer set to mid July. Thereafter for almost two weeks full-scale bomb alerts were set up in all twelve resorts, and there were bomb scares in Great Yarmouth, Torquay, Dover and Ramsgate. Many suspects were picked up for questioning. No bombs were found in any of the listed targets, but in Glasgow, three miles from the flat in which the group were arrested, police uncovered an arms dump of explosives, detonators, timers, batteries, switches, booby trap and anti-tilt devices, weapons, together with hotel brochures and timetables for English coastal towns, a street map of Hereford (HQ of the SAS), and other documents pointing to specific military targets and personnel. The scare was off.

As an ETA tactic, planting bombs in the sand of beaches is directed at the tourist industry, and thereby the State. As an IRA tactic in its war with the British State the resorts campaign spread fear and, had it come off, would have caused slaughter and mayhem amongst civilians. Ruthless as the scheme was, it was nevertheless to have been a series of sideshows. It would have created havoc, stretching the police and Army throughout the country, and this was the campaign's intention. From the presence in the group of the gunman, Sherry, the security forces inferred that the resorts and hotels were merely initial targets, diversionary tactics that would stretch the police and clear the decks elsewhere for the assassination of prominent political and military figures. As a campaign it was a very thorough attack upon the British State.

Explaining himself, Donal is matter-of-fact, at times apologetic, self accusing, at times incredulous. 'There were 27 bombs,' he says, amazed at it all, 'packaged and ready to go.' He has a tone of one unable to believe he ever took part in such horrors, or even contemplated them, almost as if another Donal had been the fixer for the group. As such he was incompetent, and says so, ruefully. Sometimes he laughs at himself. When he'd met Tom he'd said he wanted *to do something*. Recruited only months before the arrest of Magee and the others and he then just out of a mental home, he was sworn into the Provisional IRA in February that year. With no criminal record, he was a useful recruit. He describes a ritual of masked men followed by an IRA crash-course he was put through. In a darkened house with mattresses to the windows they slept by day and trained by night. Most of this training consisted of prowling about without being seen, siphoning petrol, hijacking cars, and studying maps and diagrams of weapons. He was taught to set a mine and to handle automatics, but never got to fire or set anything. He says it was all ludicrous, and seems to him now like a daft game of soldiers. He describes his instructor pointing his weapon at gas cylinders in the house, forgetting he had bullets in the spout.

He was given £500 and sent over the water to England to arrange transport and safe houses for the team, without knowing what the plan was or the involvement of Magee. In Glasgow he met Magee whose instructions were to rent a flat in London and buy a get-away car. He soon cocked that up. The flat he rented in Glasgow in which the five were arrested had only one entrance and exit, the car was a two-door saloon. Provided by the IRA with false vehicle documents and a false Irish driving licence, he wrote his real name and address instead of his *nom-de-guerre*, and gave his own name again when renting the flat. He says he was out of his depth by then, and beginning to realize what the real purpose of his mission was. By then he was beginning to be afraid, and wrote his own name in the hope he'd be found wanting and sent home. In London he began drinking heavily, and on a mission north to Carlisle to collect Magee, he drove down a one-way street on the outskirts of Manchester and was stopped and breathalysed. He got away with that, and fled back to London without meeting Magee. He apologised profusely for all his mistakes, he quarrelled with MacDonnell, and feeling the pressure from all sides, he drank more and more. Everyone in the unit criticized him and came to distrust him. Meanwhile, he had met a girl and fallen in love, and began to fear he'd be arrested and would lose her. Finally, he wrote to Magee resigning from the IRA. The letter was later found amongst Magee's possessions, and Donal traced through it.

*Alas the hawk in fiery flight.*
*We dropped the bomb with deathly might.*

Resigned or not, he's down for trial with the rest of the gang, though, unlike them, pleading guilty to conspiracy. He has already admitted his part, though in his mind he believes himself not guilty when faced with the scale and gravity of the plan: yes, he did this and this; no, he had not thought out the likely outcome of working with Magee and the others. When he realized what was happening he did his best to get out. When the game was up he co-operated. The prosecution make no claim he placed or made the bombs. He is still a Republican and a Nationalist, but he has changed his mind about the methods. The thought of bombing civilians makes him shudder now, and he's relieved it never happened. Besides, he points out, if he pleads not guilty there's still the evidence he's given, which implicates the others. He's in a tricky situation.

He thinks that on their expectations of life sentences he'll go back-to-back with them for a ten to fifteen, the lowest man on the totem pole. 'But I won't recognize it,' he says. 'I'll be up there. I'll still be Donal. You'll still know me, but I'll be climbing those bars.' He blames everything on his illness, on his youth and impressionability, on his romanticism. He's wise after the event, is Donal. And disenchanted. He denounces violence, and calls a plague on both houses: 'They're as bad as each other, they've become the same as their enemy.' As for himself, he expects a sentence, though his hope is for an asylum, and commitment for treatment. His lawyers are pleading mental incompetence, pointing up his mistakes, and his defence is separate from the others, who understandably want nothing to do with him. They say he grassed on them, and at any rate they despise him for co-operating with the police in the search for bombs.

And yet he's cheerful betimes, week to week following out some pattern of his highs and lows, tempered now by prison and the expectation of a long sentence, and however affected by the drugs he's prescribed. Some days he's so low I can't rouse a word out of him. In between, there's Yeats and poems Donal's written, holy pictures and the beads and the frequent visits of the priests, photographs of his girlfriend — the girl he met in London — who has stuck by him, of his family and of Donegal, rainswept bracken and thatched single storey houses tiny in a landscape that brings tears to his eyes. He longs to go home. On other days he's frenetic, talking fast, telling a story and breaking off to tell another, filling the small cell with words from books and memory. 'I want to go home,' he'll say, meaning 'out of prison', following that up with something repeated from another tale about a Belfast man he knew who'd been on hunger strike in the Maze: 'He said that wasn't yesterday that was my twin brother. Give me my bowl. Don't you know I'm a schizophrenic? Don't you know I'm paranoid?' He repeats it again, trying it out on himself. One day he says he's been talking to a squaddie, also in prison, also in the hospital, who's been over there. He is amazed to find how much they have in common, how well they get on together.

Confused as he may have been to begin with, the lithium's side-effects no doubt confuse him further and account for his sluggish days. Even so, he doesn't sit for long. However dulled his anxieties, he's still a worried man. He checks the door and the landing frequently, and speaks to men he knows along the wing. Through all its up and downs and diversions his tale holds straight and fits the story brought out later in court and in the press. He was misguided. He was a fool, he says. 'I am a fool,' he says.

*Pigeons call within my sight,*
*Confuse my inners, what is right?*

He got himself into the mess. He'd resigned, but resignation from the IRA isn't easy. He couldn't walk away then, and can't now. His girlfriend had persuaded him to give himself up. Interrogated by the police at Paddington Green, he was put under heavy pressure; he understands, he says; they were desperate to find more bombs or whether any more had been planted. They flew him up to Glasgow to identify the flat. By then, he says, the explosives had been moved to the cellar three miles away where they were later found. Though he had told them the truth about all he knew, which was little, they weren't to know he wasn't lying or holding something back. At that point they didn't know whether bombs were 'down'; they had the bomb calendar and the targets, but so far only one bomb in the Rubens Hotel. 'They were desperate. There were innocent civilians involved,' he says now. They took him back to London. Somewhere in there he says they took him to a hospital for an ECG test on his heart. He was supposed to have one every six months and he was due, though it's strange his interrogators would break off for such a diversion. Perhaps they feared for his heart. At any rate he is convinced he was given an ECT, several jolts of high voltage through the brain, which could have been appropriate for schizophrenia. He says the police then whisked him back to Paddington Green and locked him up for a while with paper and pen, then took away what he'd written. He sang. He wrote reams, all he knew, though that was all he'd already told them, the truth as much as he knew it. He had no more to give them. Thereafter they charged him, and here he is. 'But I don't blame them. They were desperate.'

In time Donal's trial came up, though he barely appeared at it. His co-accused, found guilty, were sentenced at the Old Bailey to umpteen lifes. Donal's sentencing was held back for consideration, and he lingered on in the hospital while the court considered what to do with him. Then he was sent to Wandsworth and vanished into the oblivion of JR, where even his brief couldn't see him because all legal visits were already taken up there. I heard from him along the grapevine, one last message as he disappeared: he was OK. He was reading, hoping, praying with his fingers crossed. Later I read he'd got four years. Described in court as 'a foolish servant', he'd been sent for treatment to a secure mental hospital. He wasn't going home but he'd got most of his wish.

*Adieu I bid, all you that glance.*
*The beauty birds hold me in trance.*

# 9

# RECORDS

They are what the police consult when rounding up the usual suspects. They are what follow a man from prison to prison, like ghosts he cannot shake off or ever see. They pursue him and are added to from office to office, from offence to offence, through suspicion, arrest, trial, conviction and beyond into prison, and then from prison to prison. They are the visible parts of his life, as the law and the State see him. Released at last, a man's records go back to Head Office, and come out if he's jailed again. With time, they fatten in their manila folders, and with each document the inerasable record grows. Each addition, from whatever source, is stamped and bears the man's number that stands for him throughout his career, his life. He dies with it.

Some files, thicker than the rest, are the *curriculum vitae* of professional villains, recidivists, men variously but forever at war with the world. Others describe lives of utter misery, bad fortune from the start, sheer poverty of the body and the mind and the soul. Or of the imagination. Some whose careers seem only the tracks of fools or hunting wolves read as biographies of how not to be, scripts for actors hired to demonstrate absurdity, how not to do it, and doing it very well, disastrously. Some, without extenuating circumstances or any sign of vindication, seem to be truly evil. Some men have records thicker than their arms, parcels of paperwork and reports on officially numbered forms, shadowing them from approved school to remand home, to Borstal, to youth custody, to local prison, down the snakes and down the ladders all the way to long-term maximum security and the life-dispersal system. Reports spawn more reports, most of them confirming the original. So it goes on. The record that is his file details anything of note on the prisoner: complaints, illness, correspondence, trouble, disciplinary offences and disputes with officers, anything remarkable or unremarkable, however insignificant, or any sign of whatever might be taken here for progress. Since prisoners are convicted, they are *per se* always on the wrong side of any issue, and of almost anyone who makes an entry in the files. McVicar records how, when they got into their own records in a disturbance at Durham, many entries mystified them as remote from reality, but what most interested them was to find reports made by chaplains whose knowledge was confessional. In general, each entry in the file carries forward the judgements of the previous entries. A balanced record is a record that coheres, that confirms itself in all its parts. In their own way, they are narratives. They are the records of the ways the guilty do not win. Those that are caught.

And they are all considered objective, the truth of the matter in hand. They are further compounded by continual rewriting. All the aforesaid, together with school reports, probation reports, police reports, are written, most of them, by writers with similar viewpoints who have read previous reports, their shared perspective that they all work with criminals. The most cogent prison observations, naturally, are made by the wing landing officers, who work at the face. They may be biased or not, as individuals, but in any case they are trained to look for quirks of behaviour, indications of acquiescence or rebellion. But their position is man-management and their skills are deployed to spot trouble before it happens, and in the main they are not in sympathy with their charges. They can't be, and can't afford to be. On the landings, neutrality is an impossible balancing act. So much then for objectivity. In the end, reports are written by professionals, committee sitters, receivers of salaries, wearers of suits and uniforms, those trained in linear thought and the assembly of agendas, who are also hopers for promotion, potential pensioners of whichever branch of the law or the civil or social services, and whatever gold may gleam in their hearts, they are not risk takers. They follow precedent, more often than not. There is a mighty system within which they work, and it is not accustomed to dissent. And since it comes to questions as to when to let a once violent man, possibly a psychopath, back into the world, if ever, neither the grey suits nor the blue ranks, nor we, can afford to take risks or follow hunches. The prisoner never gets the benefit of the doubt.

Some with no previous record enter the prison system abruptly, and their records are brief and perfunctory. For men on the life wing there's a summary of a page or so of detail, the report of the reception committee that interviewed the prisoner soon after his arrival on the wing, whether sentenced for the first time and therefore new to prison, or transferred from elsewhere and more or less inured to it. It is the first assessment of a man just weighed off on a long sentence, listing those present as officers and civilians who form the man's board that will oversee him through his years at the Scrubs. They will meet from time to time to reassess him, adding more reports from landing and workshop officers, supervisors, Probation, Education, Welfare, outside agencies and social services, the Chaplain perhaps. Even I, the resident mystery, can put in reports when asked.

And the record is always there, a lengthening shadow. I learn that the existence of this great freight of information always being added to, is one reason for not writing anything. As under any dictatorship, everyone has a file; writers add material to their own dossiers. A man explains: he'd like to write, indeed he does write sometimes, and eventually he shows me some simple and very moving love poems, to someone he doesn't name. At any rate it's not the woman he loved and whom he killed for her faithlessness. But he doesn't want to write about prison. 'I had a life before, I plan to have a life after.' As to sending it out, as to publishing it, there's the records to consider, and what the censor might take out or security might choose to include in his file. He has to think about his parole, about his EDR, about getting out of here, and then the conditions of his licence. 'The Sword of Damocles,' he says, his hand over his head. 'It's there all the time. When they arrest you and tell you "Anything you say may be taken down and used in evidence against you", that doesn't stop with your trial. They can still take it down. They can still use it against me.'

The summaries, the minutes of these meetings, are rich in narrative irony, and meticulously kept. In a police state the files would look like this. Here the stranger labyrinths of the human psyche are neatly typed and photocopied, with a mugshot photograph, the bare bones of dangerous biographies, all in alphabetical order.

Here's Jones, for instance, who is no one, who is someone, who is one of many.

re: B12345 Jones, John DOB xx/yy/zz

Jones was received in D Hall from Hospital on aa/bb/cc. He was sentenced to life imprisonment x 3 at the Central Criminal Court on dd/ee/ff for the offences of murder and rape x 2. He says he will not be appealing.

The first six months and full induction programme were explained to him. Facts of case are not available at this time and have been sent for. We have newspaper cuttings, and social and probation enquiry reports from a previous sentence. Jones was born in Leeds. At the age of 7 he was placed in care, his mother having deserted the family. There were two older children and a younger, a baby, said by Jones senior to be by a different father. Mr Jones continued to work and look after all the children until he was evicted for non-payment of rent, and at this time the children were split up into different Children's Homes. An attempt at fostering Jones failed after two months, as did three further attempts, and there followed a succession of homes with the four children variously split up. Eventually the mother, now Mrs Dawson, succeeded in having all four children released into her custody, but after a few months this arrangement broke down, and the children were again taken into care.

In February 1973 Jones again returned to live with his mother. In October of that year Jones was in trouble at school (theft). Mr and Mrs Dawson were finding conditions impossible, and Jones was again placed in care to await proceedings regarding the theft. He appeared in Juvenile Court the next year and was made the subject of a Care Order. He was placed in a Children's Home with his brother, where he seemed to settle down. A year later he was placed with foster parents, but it seemed the family expected too much of Jones academically and he ran away and was returned to the Home School to finish his education. He left the school and moved in with his sister where he remained until his arrest in 1979. He was arrested for stabbing his sister fifteen times. It seems to have been an attack without any particular motive. He was sentenced to five years imprisonment, most of which he served at HM Prison Y. We have reports from his time there in his file.

Jones says he was released in October 1982, having served thirty-eight months. He returned to live with his parents, and then went abroad for about a year. He got a series of jobs from washer-up to fruit picker and barman that enabled him to stay away for about two years. He appears to have had some trouble with the police in the Mediterranean, and decided to come home. He again lived with the Dawsons and remained there until his arrest for the present offences.

In August 1985 he was working away from home. He says that he was staying in a hotel getting legless every night after working all day. On the night of the first offence he says he went drinking till around midnight, and left the hotel, he says, to steal a car to go driving in. He was in the car park looking through a Rover when he saw that he had been seen by a woman out walking her dogs. He says his intention was to threaten her into not reporting him, but he raped the woman and strangled her. He describes dressing the body and hiding it on a construction site at the bottom of the car park. He went back to the hotel and went to bed. The next day, after work, he went drinking as usual, and returned to the scene of the crime. He tells me the police were stopping people so he volunteered as a witness saying he had seen the dogs running loose the night before. The police seemed content with his statements, and interviewed him several times, and he was used in a reconstruction. The police accused the woman's boyfriend. Jones remained in the area until his work was over, and returned to the Dawsons.

Three months later, he was arrested committing a burglary near his home, and for this he was fined. Three months after this he was still drinking heavily and was going home one night when he saw a young girl walking the same route home as himself. He describes attacking her, threatening her, and raping her. Afterwards he walked her to the end of her road, and went home to bed. The next day he was arrested and made a full statement concerning the young girl. On remand for this in Brixton he heard that the police were on their way to interview him for the murder offence. He then says he owned up to it.

This man shows no sign of remorse, and seems cold and calculating. Words come to mind like 'callous', 'ruthless', 'uncaring'. Much of what he says here is described with a wry smile, as if he is amused at some private joke.

I foresee no control or discipline problems within the prison, though he is decidedly an unpleasant young man, and dangerous to women, and likely to remain so for the forseeable future. His personal case officer will be . . . . .

Officer/Life Induction Unit:

Date:......................

# 10

# KEEPERS

They are called screws after the screw in the crank which prisoners turned in the last century, uselessly, thousands of times a day in their cells; the turnkey could tighten or loosen the screw, according to whim, making the job easier or harder. In this way he could *wind-up* a prisoner. Their other names are *keepers, kangas, kangaroos, roos, warders, wardens, jailers, custodians, turnkeys,* though to each other and to their faces they are *officers*. Behind their backs and to all prisoners they are *screws*.

Basically they are custodians, keepers of the convicted, their routine tasks to contain, to count, to lock and unlock, to watch and report. Many of them are specialists in the trades of imprisoning, but all are in the business of control. That is what is at issue here: control of others, of the self, symbolized by the key, the chain, the block, the truncheon. Close, they form their own fraternity, with their own ranks and organizations, their own clubs and sporting events, and most of them keep to their own society. Many of them are ex-Army. To prevent them forming too close an association with a prison or particular prisoners, they are moved about the system with little choice in their postings, so that many spend long periods of their duty living in prison towns, like Princeton on Dartmoor, or in prison housing estates or hostels. Like the police, whom they envy and despise, their relationships are largely formed within their own ghettos. They keep their distance from outsiders, as do outsiders from them; many of them complain of feeling ostracized, taking the view that they do a task society requires, and get few thanks for it, and this happens to be true. Though they play up the pressures and dangers of their work to advance their case for special treatment — demanding pay parity with the police, for instance — there are assaults, and they deal on intimate and daily terms with dangerous or difficult prisoners, some deranged. Officers have been attacked both inside and outside prison, and so they draw closer to their own kind, clubbing together for safety and reassurance. Out one night with his missus an officer from Scrubs' D Wing found himself in a nightclub where the bouncer was an ex-inmate, and took a heavy beating for it. And for no reason at all an officer in the hospital wing was stabbed in the eye with a pencil by a highly disturbed prisoner from D Wing, now sectioned away. Such incidents are common, particularly on the more volatile remand wings. Officers have good reasons to keep themselves apart, but it renders them less open and less considerate. They are first of all disciplinarians, and they are, as the 1979 May enquiry into the prison crisis as it then was noted, *a somewhat inward-looking group*.

It must be said many officers are affable, josh their charges along, share a joke, relax with them a little, can be got to do a small favour. These are usually older men; the younger officers tend to stick by the book, and can sometimes be seen marching along military style and barking orders while escorting a group of inmates moving in several variations of the prison slouch. There are officers who are well-intentioned and take what they do seriously, working at the thin end of the seam of hope: officers at the beleaguered special unit in Barlinnie, for instance, and in the Scrubs Annexe; others nurse the sick or find some niche within the system running a little workshop or a library. Some who begin as idealists soon get beaten by the overriding ambience, and are pushed out. Among the governor grades there seems to be frequent interchange between the Prison Service and the priesthood. Some become disillusioned and turn cynical; some question their role and their task. For those with any sensitivity, looking for long into the heart of horror sours them. All face pressure to conform to the status quo.

And some are chancers, tempted by so much opportunity to exploit the system and their charges; some go bent and bring unauthorized things into prison and, in time, are grassed on and sacked. Some are caught and, to their terror, imprisoned themselves. Theft of one kind or another from prison establishments is common enough and forms its own dimension of non-crime, where prisons are for the most part no-go for the police. Between officers and police there's no love lost, the popular belief being that most officers failed the entrance exam to the police force. Whatever the case, prison officers feel their lower status, and are looked down on by the police, known locally to officers at the Scrubs as *Shepherd's Bush Boots*. They receive the prisoners after the police are through with them, and they see what they see. In any case they complain that the police treat them in any investigation as potential suspects. Officers still complain that after the 1979 D Wing riots when the police came in to investigate their putting it down (it was eventually established that 53 inmates had been injured), the police treated them as the criminals.

So there's a siege mentality, and the truth is as ever difficult to come by; allegations of all kinds are made, few are investigated, most come to nothing. The truth is that most of the prisoners they deal with want to get on with their sentence and get it over, and are as bored with the proceedings as they are. Of necessity the work involves a lot of standing about, waiting, watching, filling the hours between the hours of the prison clock. Chiefly it's boring work, and prisoners mock them for their job, for its tedium, and for the fact that most of them will get out long before their keepers do.

By the nature of their task, prison officers are secretive, and as an industrial group they work and often live apart from the outside world. Their work brings them in daily contact not with society at large but with criminals, and they may rightly claim they see the worst of human behaviour, though few of them would acknowledge their part in it. Whatever their vision of the world, it is coloured by this contact, by their isolation as a group and their consequent cohesion, and by the prevailing military temper of the service. They will certainly cohere and unite in any confrontation with prisoners, but away from them they can be very bitchy and childish. And not only prisoners inform on each other. Screws inform on each other in and out of prison.

Individually they are often defensive, to the point of aggression, and theirs is often the short answer. They are not given to argument or discussion with their charges, though with each other and with Head Office they are militant and quarrelsome, particularly through their association, the POA. With them, discussion turns into dead ends; one young officer, studying penal history for an O.U. degree, asserted his research proved that in the old days men used to beg to work the treadwheel. As in military life, there is a theme composed of constant grumbling, aggressiveness, character assassination, heavy expletives, cruel jokes, schemes and skives and covering yourself. They live a life divided between authority on the one hand and anarchy on the other, and that in some isolation from the rest of society. Their families suffer for it, as I suspect do many of them individually, in the prison of the prison officer. Their job is to repress, and many of them seem as individuals themselves repressed.

They are a taciturn lot, and conversation with most of them harder than pulling teeth. Some said they could, would or should write a book, but they'd wait till retirement. Everyone here has a pension to lose. Mostly they're bluff, and their tone and its context soon sends any conversation into unreality. In a mood of comic bathos I spent an hour with an officer on the hospital wing on an essay for his O.U. paper, giving in effect amongst the bells and buzzers and banging iron a tutorial on John Donne's *A Valediction: Forbidding Mourning*, hoping my descriptions of metaphor and metaphysics made sense in the circumstances, half of me the fly on the wall. Another, a great hulk of an officer, talked about his art, pyrography — drawing in wood with a red-hot poker — and explained how he was working on a series of the 'Flower Fairies'. Did I know the 'Flower Fairies'? With most, contact was all official business, and officers no doubt find it difficult to switch from giving orders to normal speech, in or out the prison. Often they complained — that prisoners got a better deal, or better shoes, or more attention, than they. With some there was conversation beyond the endless subject. Joe, a workshop officer, told how on escort duty he and his partner had stood for hours by a mass X-ray machine, an example of the unquestioning obedience expected by the service, but there was not a lot of conversation beyond time of day and technicalities and banter. Such as there was began reluctantly. Some hinted at dark secrets and a whimsical but inflexible hierarchy in the regions above them, and trailed off or were interrupted by the job. For the most part contact was formal and brief.

'I've seen a ghost,' an officer says. 'I'm not saying I believe in ghosts, but I've seen one. I was on B Wing, night shift, about 3.00 in the morning, on my own, doing the paperwork, sitting at the desk. Suddenly I had the feeling somebody was standing behind me, just to my right shoulder, looking over what I was doing, and I really didn't think anything of it till I thought: "Eyup, I'm here on my own. Everyone else is locked up. So who the hell is this?" I looked behind me, and he was still there, looking over my shoulder. It wasn't like I just glimpsed him out of a corner of my eye. I looked back and he was still there. Short, thin, a prisoner. He almost had his head on my shoulder. All I saw up close was the face, and it seemed to me like a whiteness with two black coals for eyes and one black slash for the mouth, and then he disappeared. Maybe he was hooded, the way they used to be. I went to see the Chaplain, and what he said was it was no harm. "He just wanted to know what you were doing," he said, "so he was looking over your shoulder. It happens." He said it was normal. There's people here, officers, hard men, not dreamers, and they know certain parts of this place there's just a feeling they have. Something's there. The dogs know it and won't go near it.'

And most talk is macho, tough, brutal. There's much humour of that kind, usually at someone's expense, mostly prisoners. Racism in prisons is often openly expressed, and the National Front claim membership amongst officers in many prisons, including the Scrubs. In some prisons they are said to stick a marmalade golliwog sticker on the doors of black prisoners so the morning shift will know, and some are said to carry membership pins behind their lapels. Their military ambience is authoritarian and largely right-wing. But whatever its cast, the humour is usually vicious. Rousing a man from his cell, a man with only one eye, the landing officer addressed him as *Cyclops*, with a snigger he and I were expected to share. Their manner with prisoners is usually brusque, sometimes callous. Officers embroider their own legends and tales of prison: of the man who went to the MO to ask for something for his falling hair, and the MO instructed the escorting officer to issue him with a paper bag; of the man who went sick with 'auditory hallucinations', though what he didn't know was that an officer rode his bicycle about the wing on the nightshift, and what kept the inmate awake was the bike bell; of the dead 'roach screwed into a bit of loose tobacco in a tin ash-tray so that some man would come along and find the makings, and smoke it.

Some clearly enjoy their power to bully, to sneak, to boss others about, to watch and make reports, to betray. Some delight in searches and finding. In otherwise tedious work with no job satisfaction some clearly enjoy the duties society endows them with: to punish on society's behalf, adding to the punishment of confinement. The opportunities to withhold, to refuse, or to wind up are endless. For some, there are opportunities to beat other men up systematically, and that this happens is as undeniable as that officers are assaulted too. Society is at war with itself in this place, and these soldiers think of themselves as on the front line of the containment of disorder, and sometimes give way (as the official HO enquiry into the 1976 Hull disturbances found) to *excess of zeal*. Later, after police enquiries led to eight officers being found guilty of conspiring with others to assault and beat inmates at Hull, a Home Office spokesman termed them *a mob trying to control a mob*. Even this only came about because of pressure from MPs and from PROP. The 1979 Scrubs disturbances came about as a sit-down demonstration against the suspension of education (wind-up) and resulted in suppression by the MUFTI squad (pay-off). All this, when asked about, is quickly dismissed: civilians on the wing caused all the trouble.

And yet so long as there are prisons, there must be jailors, men and women willing to trade boredom and a closed lifestyle and each other's society for some security in a hard world, and who must be variously affected by the work they do. Even so, they are all volunteers, who must be over 5′6″, and pass a rigorous medical examination, a simple Civil Service test in English, arithmetic and general intelligence, and an interview. Thereafter their training consists of four weeks' acclimatization working in a prison, eight weeks at the OTS prison schools in Wakefield or Leyhill learning self-defence, radio telecommunication and security. They are trained in finding hiding-places within the prison, in what to look for, such as hacksaw blades, home-made jacks for bending bars, and how to search a cell, how to look for drugs or recognize a drug-taker. They are taught adjudication procedure, how to vocalise reports to the Governor, how to write them. They are taught basic judo and MUFTI training, and interpersonal skills involving engaging the prisoner in conversation and then writing a report of it with an emphasis on the prisoner's response. They are given outline courses in theories of criminology and psychology, and then a week's orientation in their first posting. Largely, however, the job is learned on the job, from senior officers whose style of doing things characterizes each prison, and through whom the disciplinary mode is transmitted. Theirs is not a popular profession, as the continuing difficulties in recruiting sufficient of their numbers show. In 1986 they were said to be 3000 officers short, and with Fresh Start there are now complaints that the promised increase in recruits has not materialized. Despite the rising prison population, the Government wants less officers to do more work, and so they are locked in dispute with their employers. Essentially the argument, as exemplified in the 1988 Holloway dispute, is over manning and safety levels; the Home Office want two officers present when a landing is unlocked, the POA wants three. But this amounts to a struggle for control. All the same, in recent years their numbers have increased in greater proportion to the increase in inmates, and as a group they are in a unique position to put their case.

Many are specialists, and though in any day an officer might perform several tasks within or without the prison, each task is closely defined. There are yard officers, men who failed the exam to be a fully-fledged officer, whose duties are limited to the opening and closing of a single gate. From the chief down, command passes to the POs in charge of wings, the SOs in charge of sections, then to the bulk (2/3) of basic grade officers. Laterally their trades divide them into security (invariably Welsh, and known as the Tafia) in charge of gates, control rooms, and the perimeter; hospital officers who are part nurse, part warder; workshop officers; trade officers on work services around the prison; PE instructors; catering officers; training officers. All these, in addition to their other functions, supervise prisoners. Basic grade officers are worked with great flexibility around and outside the prison: on duty in workshops or classrooms or on escorts, as landing officers, or on routine disciplinary work. Block screws are regarded with the greatest loathing, and in the block the darkest secrets remain unravelled. One explained a shit protest: five men went on it, of whom three quit in a few days, one went for 53 days, another for 70. Food was pushed in under the door. 'There was shit piled on shit,' he said. Another officer had, on separate occasions, five buckets of it thrown over him.

Apart from the specialists, however, the basic work is counting, locking, unlocking, counting, entering totals in pencil into the paperwork, tallying, keeping the books straight and the miscreants in. All day they count, silently or aloud, soldiers still numbering their square-bashing routines. In the morning before unlock the men are counted in their cells, the numbers shouted down the landings. After unlock and slop out and breakfast, inmates are counted out to work and into workshops. With the men off the wing, the officers supervise cleaning and maintenance of the wing and its disciplinary procedures. All day their cry is heard: 'One on, Sir'; 'One off, Sir'. Lunch brings the men back, counted in, fed, locked, counted, unlocked, and so on through the afternoon and evening through exercise and association, till bang-up comes, early, by 8 o'clock. Such a task can only be routine, mind-numbing.

They operate almost as a class of their own, the guardians of the awful. 'When I go to work in the morning,' a landing officer remarked, 'I don't go to Mars. But you'd think I did.' They operate in a special world, hierarchical and military, a zone from which the press and public are excluded. Most find it better not to talk about their work outside the prison, adopting silence.

Here there's a uniform, a clearly defined ladder of authority, pay and allowances and a pension at the distant finish, and some prospect of promotion, if very slow. The majority of recruits to the prison service are from the armed forces and bring with them a defined view of the world; their work is considered a *service*. Many wear military tattoos. Therefore the prevailing ambience is military, each layer of authority excluding information from the rank below; tasks and authorities are clearly defined, senior officers are addressed as *Sir*, and there is a general deference towards authority. At work there is a defined chain of command and a bluntly expressed scheme of shared values, there are orders to be carried out unquestioned, procedures for absolutely everything. The doctor is the MO. Disciplinary hearings are military style, the prisoner marched in under escort to be charged, assessed, punished, marched out, and offences are commonly defined as *against good order and discipline*. In their ranks they range from the infantry of basic grade officers, through Senior, Principal and Chief, the latter the Company Sergeant Major in charge of all the officers in one prison. Above them range the real officer class of AGs, DGs, Governor IVs and No. 1 Governor and beyond again the heights of regional HQ, the Home Office and Civil Service all the way to the Home Secretary, with all of whom they are in continuing dispute. In prison towns their living quarters resemble, and often formerly were, military camps. Their attitude to non-uniformed staff defines everyone who isn't a prisoner or governor as an outsider, a *civilian*. Largely they are sceptical, often cynical, terse and practically minded. Their attitude and tone towards authority is in stark contrast to their attitude to prisoners, and forms a species of bilingualism. Even in their militancy they are rebellious soldiers arguing their pay, conditions and status.

As custodians they have shaped and ordered the prison system's daily running according to their own expectations and attitudes, whatever penal theory may propose. A recent report shows that, despite the trend in prison building to reflect current prison policy to house men in small flexible and interacting groups of no more than thirty, the result is the same where prisoners are simply banged-up as usual, at the convenience of staff who need only claim shortage of their numbers. Most attempts at other sorts of regime than endless bang-up are thwarted right here, so men are locked up anyway whether in large units or small. Officers occupy a position to block reforms or any reorganization, and, cynical of them as they are, are able to predict the results. Their claims to want to undertake welfare and rehabilitative training work in addition to the role of custodian is belied by their history as the latter. It was in commenting on that expressed wish that the 1979 May enquiry found them to be inward looking, unsuited to the role of counsellor. Between the deterrers and the rehabilitators there is less and less swing to the prison pendulum. At one end the liberals and do-gooders of the nineteenth century, and in the twentieth the social and welfare and educational and psychology professionals; at the other the consistent collective and individual deadweight of those who put policies into effect, working at the face, where ideas fail in practice. Largely sceptical of theories and the opinions of outsiders, as a group officers have shaped the system to suit themselves, and the continuing prison crisis is, as Mrs Thatcher has said, nothing less than a struggle for the right of management to manage. It is a moot question who is in control here, and who is the prisoner.

The fact is the officers are in control, if beleaguered. Caught as they are between Government policies to expand the prison population while restricting spending, prison officers have become increasingly militant over the last fifteen years, often vociferously through their union, the POA. For it is they who run the prisons day to day, and what they do not want to happen does not. In the fight over control of prisons, and all the infighting over working practices, there is hostility on all sides with the prisoner in the middle, the pawn. Governors are seen as rubber stamps, an ultimate authority and repository of theoretical responsibility, who don't in the end count for much. Beyond are the bureaucrats, the enemy, and everyone here has a file. In recent years prison officers have not neglected to remind the public of their role, and they have been engaged in a many cornered industrial struggle, at times with their own POA executive. In this fight their hold over the prison system has provided them with a wide range of industrial options. On the grounds that prisons are overcrowded and understaffed, they can and frequently do refuse to take in prisoners over the prison's official capacity, and refuse to escort prisoners on remand to or from court or act as dock officers. Within the prisons they restrict legal and regular visits and interviews with police, probation, welfare, psychology; they restrict and periodically close down education, association, exercise, bathing, letters, laundry. These practices become more frequent as the crisis deepens. In all these areas officers can exercise arbitrary authority to which the prisoner is vulnerable. It is the power of the petty, in this case used to advance a struggle for control and enhanced status.

The POA represents the majority of prison officers, some 25,000 members. Individual POA branches operate largely autonomously within each prison, and are actively engaged in deciding day-to-day policies over manning levels and admissions and transfers. Enquiries following the 1979 riots on D Wing at the Scrubs revealed that it was the POA branch rather than the Governor that in practice made many such decisions, the outcome of their ability to withhold their services in any of a number of areas.

For years prisons were run on overtime. Faced with shortages of staff, governors stretched their budgets to pay for it, and the result was a mass of complex allowances and bonuses, rest days and compensatory payments, housing and uniform and superannuation allowances. In the organization and manning of work-rosters, the need for massive overtime gave the officers power, and the Government's attempts, apart from cutting costs, have been to re-establish the authority of prison governors to govern. Through overtime and other wangles officers came to rely on a higher standard of living. Some, assigned a prison house, let it out for profit; others invest their money, and some apparently are wealthy as a result. In 1986, before Fresh Start, the Home Office claimed some 30 per cent of an average prison officer's earnings of £15,000 depended on overtime working, at an average of 16 hours a week, meaning a typical prison officer working a fifty-three hour week. For this to be an average, many must work even longer hours. In one London prison, according to *The Guardian* in 1986, one officer was earning £27,000 per year for an eighty hour week. In 1985 the Home Office spent £81.6m on overtime working, an increase of 137 per cent since 1980. That this was possible has come about through many concessions made over the years, and if prison officers by and large have an inferiority complex, they have proved adept at compensating themselves for it. By coming in for two hours on a rest day an officer could earn eight hours pay, and the manipulation of rosters has become the bone of contention, the so-called *Spanish practices*. Because of them in April 1986 the Home Secretary, urging new manning practices, was able to claim that 15 to 20 per cent of resources in the prison system was being wasted annually.

In an effort to sweep all this away and cut out overtime, the Government's Fresh Start package has since been gradually introduced, its aim to cut down overtime to zero over the next five years, restricting the working week to forty-eight hours for a basic salary of £15,000. Other parts of the package intend — optimistically — to unify the governor and officer grades into a common structure, and to improve prison conditions as a result of changing working practices to small unit and section work in an effort to spread responsibility downwards through the ranks. In response, the officers, much as they may complain about overtime, are eager to protect themselves. A suspicious lot, their attitude stems from years of Home Office chicanery, and is not without cause. Their employers want a productivity deal, but the POA points out that with less hours worked and the existing system stretched to breaking point, more recruits must be found to increase their numbers and maintain control. This the Government has failed to do, and recruitment lags, while new cash limits have been introduced. Each prison is now individually budgeted, and must stay within its limits. And there is the prospect of privatising some parts of the prison service in remand and low security prisons, to which the POA are strongly opposed. The main effect of Fresh Start has been to increase pay so that a basic grade officer on £15,000 is a more attractive proposition, but recruits are still not flocking to the colours, and it seems great reliance on overtime will continue. Within the prisons nothing much has changed, however, and the immediate effect of introducing the package has been to restrict manpower so that for lack of it in October 1987 four prisons and a wing of a new prison had to be closed, and other work or training programmes cut down. As a result of these closures 600 prison places were lost.

On the night of 30 April 1986 prison riots broke out in several prisons across the country, the direct result of local overtime bans by the officers, resulting in £4.5m in damage and the loss of 800 prison places. The POA had successfully balloted their members to suspend all overtime. As a result they were under strength in some prisons. The resulting destruction and extensive press coverage demonstrated their power. Over the next few days there were disturbances at over forty prisons. Extensive damage was sustained at six prisons, and Northeye in Sussex was burned to the ground. At Gloucester, when officers coming on duty refused to implement the Governor's new working practices, they were locked out, and prisoners later staged a roof-top protest. Later there were allegations by prisoners and a report by the Prison Reform Trust, hotly denied as unprofessional by the POA, claiming incitement of prisoners to riot at Northeye and Gloucester and other prisons; the allegations suggested some officers used the prisoners in their charge to advance their own cause, and these allegations have become the subject of yet another enquiry by the Inspectorate of Prisons. The riots were a convincing demonstration of the power officers have in the withdrawal or restriction of their labour and though they soon suspended their industrial action, they had proved the point of their indispensability.

Two years later, in 1988, the system's still on the boil, with riots at Haverigg (twice) and Lindholme (twice), and tension high throughout the system. Overcrowding continues, and Fresh Start is becoming a creature of the past, as the same old wrangling continues between the Home Office and the POA over manning levels. Army camps have been opened up as prisons, with Army guards, and the Government's plans to privatise remand and escorts, if carried through, will breach some of the power of the POA. In August officers struck at Holloway over manning levels, and the supporting lockout policy carried out at other London and regional prisons has stacked up the numbers held in police cells. What's evident in all of this is that the Government is going for a showdown with the POA and that, pushing inmates in at one end and restricting officers at the other, they are moving towards confrontation. Further explosions are expected.

# 11

# POTTED HISTORY

With pressure at both ends, the prison crisis grows daily worse. Currently the prison population of well over 50,000 prisoners is packed into cells and dormitories originally designed for 41,000. The majority of these are twoed up or threed up sharing a slop bucket, locked up for 23 hours out of 24. They lack sunlight and calcium, and many develop physical and psychological problems as a result. Continuing neglect, despite bouts of enthusiastic prison building such as at present, lies at the heart of this dark corner of the state. Many buildings are old, crumbling, insanitary. In 1987 the Scrubs' Board of Visitors' annual report described the regime there as *desolate and purposeless*, the prison as a place *where it is both difficult and often unpleasant to work,* and criticized the lack of activity for prisoners, the overcrowding and staff shortages, the perfunctory medical services and the number of mentally ill prisoners held there. The Annexe, the only light of any hope in the prison system in the whole of England and Wales, was said to be in danger of *dying from attrition.*

Such a picture is typical of many British prisons. According to a report from the Commons Home Affairs Select Committee, *The State and Use of Prisons (1987)*, one problem is that two-thirds of inmates are crammed into one-third of the buildings. The report goes on: *It is disgusting and unacceptable that over 20,000 prisoners are likely to be slopping out for the rest of this century.*

The current £1B prison building programme that began in 1980 to meet the expected rise in crime can't keep pace with rising numbers. Initially the Government were hoping for a match between places and prisoners by 1991. Instead, on current trends the 1987 shortfall of 4,900 places will rise to 6,700 by then, or as much as 8,200, depending on whose estimate of expected increases we are using. Even by 1995 the shortfall will be a minimum of 2,500. At present the Home Secretary is planning twenty-six new prisons and 6,600 new places in renovated old prisons, with a programme to add some 12,000 new places to the existing 41,000 by the mid 1990s. This would bring the space available to about what the prison population is now, but a study published in 1987 by Dr Robert Matthews of the Middlesex Polytechnic Centre for Criminology forecasts a fifty per cent increase in crime in the next five years, and a prison population of 70,000 by 1995, as against the Home Office's predicted 60,000. The report predicts an extra 500,000 burglaries, a doubling of robberies and an extra 30,000 acts of violence by 1992, and while making no link between crime and unemployment, it argues that *when unemployment is combined with a strong sense of relative deprivation it is likely to be a precursor to increases in crime.*

So the writing is on the wall for yet another hike in the crime rate which, even with a 35 per cent (and falling) police clear-up rate, will result in a further expansion of the prison population. Even on the Home Office figures there will be an expected rise in the prison population by 1995, and despite the building and refurbishment programme, there is no hope of the Government fulfilling its promise to end overcrowding by the early 1990s, nor even by the end of the century. To achieve this, yet another ten prisons would have to be built. The end of the century seems to be a cut-off point in our thinking; beyond that we dare not think. It seems reasonable to assume that so long as large-scale unemployment continues, crime will increase, and that despite warnings about sentencing policy, the number of prisoners will rise to exceed the number of places available, just as it always has. Recently, more hopeful indications have been emanating from the Home Secretary's office; efforts are being encouraged to find alternatives to prison; there are signs the problem has been perceived.

Nevertheless, one of the few growth areas in Government spending is on prisons, expenditure on which went up by 8 per cent in 1985 and in 1988 reached £700m. In the first five years of the present administration, prison spending went up by 85 per cent, including a 400 per cent increase in prison building. Each new prison place created costs £45,000, and the cost of keeping each prisoner is running at £13,000 per year per head: £250 per week. For all that, overcrowding inside continues, and on the outside the crime figures continue to soar. Nothing much has been changed by all this spending; according to the Howard League, 75 per cent of the costs goes on labour, 3 per cent on education; according to the Home Secretary 20 per cent of the costs are wasted in Spanish practices; according to a Home Office consultative document, *Remands in Custody*, there are an estimated 68,000 unproductive remand hearings every year, taking up — in escort duties — 38,000 working hours a year, depleting other services within the prisons. Remand prisoners, half of whom are eventually acquitted, currently account for 22 per cent of prisoners. In addition, there is a massive courts building programme currently running at £130m to build two hundred Crown Courts, sixteen High Courts, and fifty County Courts.

Meanwhile, the Government is restricting prison spending in existing prisons and the resulting shrinkage in budgets has alienated the prison officers. The riots and disturbances in over forty prisons in early 1986 sent shock-horror waves through the media, but the outbreaks were themselves the result of internal pressure from overcrowding, a warm April, and the withdrawal of overtime by the POA. This itself resulted from new cost-accounting procedures imposed individually on prison governors, and the ensuing struggle for control. As the numbers continue to grow and the budgets to shrink, intermittent warfare between officers and their employers continues. The condition of the prisoner, pig-in-the-middle, remains the same, or worsens.

Since April 1987 the Home Office has been gradually introducing a new pay and productivity package, Fresh Start. It seems destined to go the way of all good intentions as to prisons. Squeezed tighter and tighter, the system under more and more stress as officers and prisoners are switched around the country at each temporary stopgap, warnings of another explosion come regularly and are as regularly set aside. Reports and enquiries and investigations come and go, their recommendations put partially into effect or ignored, their conclusions often over-cautious. A year into Fresh Start, the POA was threatening a national strike. The crisis continues.

Our problem is crime. Prisons, as the cliché has it, breed crime; the high recidivism rates in almost all categories of crime suggest that for many offenders prison, deterrent or not, drags them further into itself, whether they will or not. It produces more crime, and creates more problems than it solves. Amongst adults the rate is now running at well over a 50 per cent return within two years of release. Dr Matthews calls this a 'recycling effect'. As the experiment with the short, sharp shock regime showed, harsh regimes breed resentment and harden offenders. Some 70% of young people so detained reoffend; punishment has been found to be counter-productive, and as a result the number of short, sharp shock centres has been reduced from fourteen to eight. Returning to society on release is often difficult; friendships, family and neighbourhood ties may be broken or severely strained; housing and work are even harder to come by. Restriction of social and local government budgets, and reductions of funds available for community work as alternatives to prison, despite pious words to the contrary, mean that, for many, crime and a return to prison become a never ending spiral.

In locking up a hundred people per hundred thousand of our population we imprison more of our citizens than almost any other country in Western Europe, as many as does Turkey. Only the Scottish system exceeds ours. We do this because we do not know what else to do. Like all contemporary societies, we lock up our dissidents, deviants, criminals, psychopaths, even the insane, and disregard how we who are society produce our own malcontents. We drag our criminal shadows along with us through history, postponing the inevitable. Most criminals come out again, and many are worse for the experience of prison. All we are doing is temporarily burying our waste, like so much toxic overflow that re-emerges elsewhere. Some we simply don't know what else to do with, and don't much care about — the violent, the murderers, the rapists, the armed robbers, the terrorists. If nothing else they are off the streets, and we feel the safer for it. Since we have no death penalty and no means of banishment, secure detention for life is our only alternative for disposing of the dangerous. But these, the ones who poke through our nightmares, are the minority of prisoners. Lifers at present number some 2,000 inmates; in 1957 at the abolition of the death penalty there were 140. These long-term prisoners accumulate within the system, but they are hardly the cause of its overcrowding. Again, it is a matter of whose figures: according to the Home Office, 45 per cent of all inmates are in prison for non-violent minor offences; according to NACRO, this figure is nearer 70 per cent of sentenced prisoners, usually involving theft and burglary. According to the Home Secretary, of 3.8 million offences on the books in 1986 only 0.2 per cent involved crimes endangering life. Whatever the case, the majority of prisoners are in for short-term sentences for minor offences, and the rise in recorded crimes against the person is far slower than the rise in crimes against property.

Debtors and defaulters, fiddlers, teenagers who turn over parking meters, many in on petty offences to whom prison teaches nothing but crime and the system, fill up the prisons and account for massive sums in public expenditure, not with the aim of reformation, but as a deterrent, which can be said at best to only half work. In the prison service the most enlightened regimes are at most pragmatic; generally speaking, the idea of reclaiming the criminal has long gone. Official policy remains one of fitting the punishment and treatment to the offender, rather than to the crime, but in practice this barely happens; prison consists of punishment and detention, segregation from society. These days little effort goes into attempting to train the offender for release, and such 'training' as exists consists of bang-up, minimal exercise, some association (i.e. mingling with other prisoners) and, for the lucky, associated labour.

Since in two centuries of penal theory and experiment we seem no further along, and as society more and more restricts personal freedom, the problem is likely to remain with us. We need to investigate and adopt alternative sentencing policies, not merely to cut down the prison population for its own sake but for our own, to cut back on the widening spiral of crime in which we are caught. We need to think about the difference between violent and non-violent offenders, to focus less on crimes against property and more on crimes against the person, and to reconsider prison as a place of absolute last resort. We need to study even the hardened and the brutal, for whom confinement is the only option. We need to know much more about the effects of imprisonment, to weigh its usefulness. We need, no doubt, to link the offender to the victim (where there is one), which prison signally fails to do. Prison, if it provokes remorse in the prisoner, largely promotes it for himself, and the point is easily forgotten inside. Out here, we need a more enlightened defence against violence.

Since the abolition of the death penalty, the alternative, life imprisonment, has accumulated a rising lifer prison population. There is an understanding that the minimum term for life has recently quietly been extended from fifteen to twenty years. Little is known about the effect of long-term incarceration. The boredom is mind-boggling. Few lifers, when they do come out, are dangerous. Some 30 per cent of murderers commit suicide. Most are broken by long years of confinement. We do not need to return to the death penalty, which is irrelevant to murder. We do need to understand something of what causes men and women to kill or commit crimes of violence, and to understand something of the effects of long-term imprisonment.

Banishment, the other alternative, went out when there were no longer colonies willing to take our convicts. The British prison system came into being after the loss of the American colonies. As a deterrent there was still then, at the end of the eighteenth century, frequent public hanging for a whole range of offences, though crime did not seem the less because of it. Indeed, in the nineteenth century, growing public revulsion at hanging led, in this century, to its abolition, and as an option it is — hopefully — now obsolete. Lesser offenders went to local and county prisons, debtors' prisons, private prisons, but the main alternative to death had long been transportation, and with the loss of the American War of Independence and until the opening of penal colonies in Australia, there was a need to do something with those who would formerly have been sent abroad, sentenced to long terms of servitude. Two alternatives were found — the hulks, privately owned, which put men and boys in irons the length of their sentence and set them to hard labour in chain-gangs in appalling conditions; and after the 1779 Act authorizing the building of a state prison, the Millbank, the first in a series of 'model' prisons intended to answer the problem.

The Act of 1779 marks the first adventure of the State as jailor, responsible directly for housing criminals, and drawn thereby into these considerations of reform and deterrence. Millbank, opened in1812, was considered reformative, its intention to rehabilitate selected prisoners thought capable of responding to a chance to reform. It was regarded as a religious institution, its regime a mix of religious instruction and hard labour and seclusion. Prisoners worked alone in their cells, and were kept apart from other prisoners. With this in mind they were provided with toilets, a facility withdrawn later in the century. The question of seclusion or separation (solitary) was crucial, and remains at the centre of the question of prison. The reformer John Howard considered it a necessity to avoid contamination of the inexperienced by the seasoned criminals, but what he had in mind was classification and selection into small groups who would associate. We have come back to this idea in current thinking about prison regimes and prison design two centuries later.

The Millbank was the first failed experiment. Though flogging had at first been excluded, it was eventually introduced, with solitary confinement, and the intentions of the regime became indistinguishable from repression. Within thirty years the Government admitted the prison was an 'entire failure', and it became a reception centre for prisoners awaiting transportation or transfer to the hulks or locals. 'Training' here consisted now of preparing prisoners for life in the Australian settlements — training for more imprisonment. At the same time that the Government was planning to send all convicts there, transportation was becoming unpopular in the colonies, and in another decade was to cease entirely. Nevertheless, in an effort to placate the colonies' complaints at being dumped with the Mother Country's criminals, it was determined that all transportees should be 'reformed' before going there.

'In a crisis put out a colony', said the Greeks. In the presence of a crisis and the absence of a colony, build a prison. The answer again was a new model prison, Pentonville, opened in 1842. Here, for those inmates selected for training and transportation seclusion became separate confinement; complete solitary was imposed for eighteen months before they were shipped out. In consequence there was much insanity and suicide, and after the experience most of the prisoners were found to be quite daft. Despite the fact that prisoners had been selected for their stamina, all the Pentonville 'experiment' proved was that solitary destroys the mind. By the middle of the century, with the end of transportation, separate confinement became the lot of all prisoners, and with the introduction of the crank, the treadwheel and penal servitude, prison regimes grew harsher in response to what was identified as the recalcitrance of prisoners. The only concession in these years was the introduction of associated labour, to be abolished in the 1870s by Du Cane in favour of the principle of separation and non-contamination.

In 1877 (again another thirty years) the prisons were to be unified into a single State-run service doling out a unified regime to all prisoners. Du Cane, the prison service's first commissioner, was its architect, and though regarded as a reformer, his regime differed little from what went before it: a reformative discipline of solitary labour, seclusion, and religious instruction. If anything it was harder. More prisons were built, this time to his 'model': Wakefield, Reading, Wandsworth, Wormwood Scrubs. In them he introduced some innovations, such as the idea of gradation, but he abolished cell toilets (the ones in Pentonville were removed) and closed the prisons to the press and public. Prisoners, so that they might not associate at all, were required to turn their faces to the wall when out of their cells, or wear masks, and subjected to the rule of absolute silence. Solitary, bread and water diets, the dark cell and flogging were the usual punishments, and the severity of this regime was to last into the present century. Separate confinement was eventually abolished in 1922, and various forms of association reintroduced. Clearly, regimes are lighter today, though at every stage the theme of being soft on crime has been heard, but the prisons we have now are the result of this potted history of experiment, partial fulfilment, and tinkering. We are still using most of the original 'model' prisons, though we now talk of showcase examples such as Long Lartin. What we are left with still is a long succession of locked doors and day-to-day stopgaps and a deep resistance on the part of the custodians to change.

Perhaps there are only new sorts of crime and more refined means of punishment. Men believe it is psychological torture and mental cruelty they are now subjected to, in place of the lash, but there's no shortage of physical punishment either. Men speak of their experience of new prisons, where doors and gates open and close electronically, describing them as 'electronic tombs'. Technology creates more thorough supervision — and more isolation. The central dilemmas remain the same: the system is in crisis; what to do about crime, what kind of prison regime, the problems of association versus seclusion, the debate between the rehabilitators and the lockers-up. In this latter debate it's clear the punitive lobby are on top, and not much thought or effort has been given in recent years to rehabilitation or to the means of 'training'. Among prisoners and officers rehabilitation is a joke. The training prisons, such as Wandsworth, train inmates for other satellite prisons of the mother prison. The gap between intention and reality remains as wide as ever.

# LIVING IN MY HEAD

## BY DAVE WAIT

Dave Wait is currently serving a life sentence for murder.

# 12

# BANG-UP: THE DOOR

'Behind your doors, behind your doors,' the screws shout. Always twice. Everything twice. They always slam cell doors and gates. Some, to rub salt in, show by gesture — waiting at the cell door twirling their key chain — that the act of locking the door is, for them, a meaningful gesture loaded with job satisfaction.

As part of the Government's rebuilding programme, old cell doors are being replaced by new ones. The old doors are thick wooden panels, morticed together and overlapped with metal straps which are bolted through from each side, and attached to the door-frame by three large hinges. Sometimes they literally tear away from the wooden frame. The new doors are blocks of wood encased in $\frac{1}{8}''$ steel sheeting which is welded to the corners. They weigh about two hundred-weight and so are fastened with heavy-duty hinges onto steel door-frames.

All the old doors are also bolted. Cat.A cells have two bolts. Almost gone now is the judas spy-hole with its pear-shaped flap that the screw would swing across, count the body, and in the morning if it was dark, flick the outside light on and off in rhythm with the count. Where they still exist, the judas covers have a tiny hole in the centre. From inside it's usually possible to see through this hole. It's a design fault — the watched can watch the watchers.

The new doors have an observation strip an inch wide and fourteen inches long. The screw looks through toughened perspex. On the inside, to widen the scope of vision, an oblong part of the door is bevelled inwards. A hinged flap covers the observation strip on the outside, although some have to make do with cardboard taped to the door.

A source of worry and concern to the screws has always been the old doors with no glass in the judas. To look through properly, the screw has to get near the door. From the inside an eye belonging to a screw, suddenly appearing at a hole in the door, is a tempting target for the maimed and mistreated, bitter or twisted. At this point some screws have been pissed on, a bull's eye for the body inside.

Both types of door, the old and the new, except in prisons that have electronic locks, have the same type of locking mechanism. The morticed bolt is spring-loaded, so that when the brass handle is depressed downwards, the bolt is drawn back from the door-frame and clicks into place. The door is then open.

To lock the door, it has to be brought into contact with the door-frame where a little toggle is depressed, releasing the bolt which shoots into the frame. Hence 'banged up'.

Chubb locksmiths manufacture the locks and keys in all prisons. As a part of their contract they provide security advice to prison staff who have that responsibility.

The key, the historic symbol of imprisonment, is the screw's power over the imprisoned. The hell of imprisonment radiates from the key like an evil force. In newer prisons where the cell doors are electronically locked, the screws still have their bunch of keys. These doors can be locked by the key and also by a key-word typed into a computer. In time, the computer will lock us into our cells by a signal spoken by another computer. In these electronic prisons we, the prisoners, have a cell-door key, either a brass Chubb or a Yale type key. When we go outside we lock the door because we distrust each other. It's strange that they have given us the means to express our distrust of each other. At first it's weird locking a door, a reminder of the way people behave outside.

So here I am, the prisoner behind the door, in my banged-up solitude. I spend this time in a variety of ways. There's sleep, of course, although it's fitful and nightmarish at times and always ends where it started. I am imprisoned even in my sleep. My dreams are the stuff of imprisonment. This is my condition.

# 13
# IN THE SWEAT-BOX

Big blue or white vans, mobile prisons with small cell windows. Inside it's all sheet metal. A door at the back, narrow like the passageway between the rows of tiny cubicles on either side, and locked by a brass key from the outside. The cubicle doors are just as narrow, opening outwards, always one at a time. A mesh grill in the cubicle door designed to frustrate vision: sometimes a glimpse of someone outside in the passageway, the screw checking the numbers, another prisoner being off-loaded when we stop at a magistrate's court or at a prison. On the other side, a small window about seven inches by five inches, double glazed. At the bottom, between the two sheets of unbreakable glass, a clear tube about as thick as a straw and as long, lying horizontally. In the tube pink crystals, and what looks like cotton blocking each end. Mysterious. It's probably, in fact it's almost certainly, a little gizmo to stop condensation. But I've heard all kinds of stories about the little tubes. It's rumoured that it's nerve gas, there in case the van crashes and the occupant of the cubicle tries to escape.

My feet rest on a floor of shiny rippled metal. Inside the cubicles there's just enough room for the average person to stand up or sit down. Seats are bare metal, part of the van's structure, and they all face forwards. The engine's vibration goes through the sheet metal and our bodies. Looking through the outside window, unless we stop in traffic next to a bus, we could be invisible. People in buses look our way, doing what we are doing, looking at the world through a glass window. For all the rest, the world we're taken from passes by, going about its lawful business.

On this run we're off to Ashford, a prison for 17 to 21 years old. We've stopped at a couple of magistrates' courts, picking up remands. There's a few black kids who seem to know each other. One, who's a few cubicles in front of me, is the loudest. Between themselves they shout above the rattle of the van, every other word a bloodclot or a raasclot or a fuckhole.

A cockney voice behind me shouts, 'Shut your nigger mouths, you shitheads!' It goes quiet for a moment. Then the black in front of me starts shouting a burst of dire threats: 'I'll rip your bloodclot.' The cockney provokes him some more: 'Go on, you stinking shit rapist.' Now they are all shouting about throats being cut.

Now the black kid is going berserk, banging on his door and shouting incoherently. The screw comes along banging the doors with his truncheon:

'Shut that fucking racket . . . Shut the noise up!'

We're coming into a large police station, a stop-off point for the screws to have a tea-break. All this racket is going on as we drive into the yard. It's attracted other screws who have been waiting by other vans. Now there's whistles being blown. Cops and screws are rushing up. I see them waving their truncheons and jostling to get on our van.

Inside, it's all noise. Doors are unlocked. Looking out of the window I see the loudest black kid being dragged away. He's big and trying to swing punches. The cops and screws rain blows on him. Behind him they've another black who's getting the same treatment. I see one cop, or screw, fall over, his truncheon drops to the ground. He doesn't get up again. Maybe the others have hit him by mistake, or maybe the black kid has decked him. Either way the black kid will almost certainly be charged with assaulting him.

Inside the van, there's one voice screaming, 'Yeah, smash the black bastards, give 'em some.' It's the cockney. As for me, I'm stunned by the violence, shot through with adrenalin, nerves winding down and in my mind's eye a jumble of images, the credence given to the respectability of blue uniforms.

And then the screw in the short, sharp shock Detention Centre, actually saluting the Visiting Magistrate: 'Good morning, Sir', and the Visiting Magistrate smiling back. The same screw, six foot tall, grey hair, stocky, and the little strip of war decoration colours on his uniform, rushing into the reception saying to me, 'Right you little fucker, they may not have cured you the first time, but we'll see about that now.' And with him punching me on the back of the head, squashing my face into the wall, turning round, holding my bloody nose to slag him off, I'm punched by the other screw in the ear.

Just as well my skin's not black. Welcome to the short, sharp shock.

# 14

# BOB KIRK

I'd been in prison about four years. I was sitting in the workshop taking notes about Shakespeare's *Hamlet* when this bloke came out with some profound comment on the meaning of the play. I was astonished. Here was an educated man, or at least a well-read man. I was pleased as I was having a problem trying to understand what Shakespeare was about, and I thought maybe I could get some insight off this bloke. It turned out his name was Bob. He was doing life for killing his girlfriend and was in his eighth year. It didn't take long to realize that Bob was more interested in drugs than in Shakespeare.

In his more lucid moments I'd go to his cell and converse about different writers. Inevitably the conversation would steer to astral projection, yoga and such like matters. And also it didn't take long to realize that Bob was more interested in escapism into things not of the real world.

Our conversation took on a bizarre turn when Bob rushed into my cell one morning claiming to have left his body in an astral projection experience. I must admit his sincerity and enthusiasm took me along on the journey of credibility. I caught myself actually believing his story. His claim was that sniffing glue somehow liberated his inner soul, allowing his spirit to wander at will. After a few conversations on this subject I found myself uneasily envious of Bob's stories of leaving his body and flying about here and there. I'd usually end up saying: 'Yeah, but you're still in prison. Your physical body is still doing a life sentence.'

I was always sworn to secrecy. It was our secret. Often I'd go back to my cell and think: 'The guy's nuts. What am I doing talking to a nut?' If nothing else, it made a change from the boring routine of prison. And there was a certain fascination and bizarreness that attracted me.

One day Bob asked my advice about his transfer to Kingston. Kingston is exclusively a lifers' prison that some call the cabbage patch. Should he go, and if so, how much longer did I think he'd have to do? I advised him to go, and reminded him that as he was a 'domestic' lifer and had already done eight odd years, he'd soon be out.

The next day when he didn't show up for a game of chess, I went to his cell and found him still asleep with a polythene bag stuck to his face. He'd been sniffing Evostik for a night-cap. The thought of suicide had never entered my head, but it had entered Bob's.

His transfer came and I shook his hand, wished him all the best, wondered if I'd ever see him again in the prison circuit.

About a year went by before I read in a newspaper that Bob had killed himself by cutting his wrists. It was another year before I found out what had finally pushed him over the edge. It turned out that he had been slung out of Kingston for sniffing glue and transferred to another prison. In his second week there, the prison doctor had called him up and asked how much longer he thought he'd do. Bob thought he'd only do another year or so. The doctor said he'd have to do many more years. And that apparently did Bob's head no good at all. That night he killed himself.

# 15

# PRIME

So this is the bloke I've recently been reading about in all the papers — a spy sentenced to thirty-eight years, thirty-five for selling encoded information to the Reds, and three years to run consecutively for allegedly molesting children. This is the man of whom, when an MP mentioned a possible exchange at some future date, Thatcher jumped up and in her dictatorial tone said *No! Let him rot. No deal.*

As a traitor, a spy more in the KGB mould than that of the patriotic James Bond, Prime could hardly proclaim innocence of the sex offences, even if he was. The sex offences could have been a blackmail tactic arranged by the KGB, or they could have been a fit-up, an exercise by the Dirty Tricks Dept to blacken Prime or the KGB, or he could have been selling out for years for idealistic and political reasons. Whatever happened, the whole thing stinks. Prime was supposed to have been sidetracking secrets for years and at the same time running around the country molesting children. The Reds could hardly welcome him with open arms.

Prime's location within the prison system will depend on his co-operation with the security services. If he's a good chap and tells them all they need to know, then they'll strike a deal and he'll be allowed to serve his time on the wing, on normal location, but in a maximum security prison. He'll probably always be a Cat.A prisoner, even after his usefulness diminishes with the passage of time.

The procedure for dealing with spies has tightened up since the days of George Blake, who was trapped by his KGB controller, who had turned defector and told the security services all about Blake's involvement with the Russians. They've learned from the mistakes they made with Blake. He started his forty-two years on D Wing Wormwood Scrubs. He rubbed shoulders with common criminals. He had the opportunity, which he took, to explain his political views, his ideals and philosophy to politically aware prisoners. He was an unsung folk-hero, liked and admired inside and outside.

Blake escaped with help from fellow criminals, and took his many secrets to Moscow. In 1966 the three Gothic windows at the north end of D Wing were without outside bars. The 18″ x 6″ panes of glass were held in place by a cast-iron framework. The authorities had overlooked the fact that, although cast iron is a hard metal to saw through, it's brittle and if hit hard enough will snap. Blake went through the window; behind a blanket draped over the twos railings he departed, dropped onto the north end porch, jumped and ran for the wall and the rope he was thrown, and vanished. The police were puzzled by a bunch of carnations left on the pavement with the rope. It turned out that Blake's helper had used the flowers as smother for a walkie-talkie; anyone seeing him waiting in the getaway car with a bunch of flowers would assume he was a visitor to Hammersmith Hospital.

1965 saw the escape of Ronald Biggs, one of the Great Train Robbers. Sentenced to thirty years, he went over the wall at Wandsworth. As a direct result of these escapes and the embarrassment they caused the Government, the Mountbatten Commission was set up, the result of which was the inner security fence, camera surveillance, dog patrols, radios, and segregation of political prisoners.

I'm working as the library orderly, the skivvy. Prime comes down from the hospital with two screws as escort. He wants to choose some books and collect his newspapers and magazines. He's ordered *The Sunday Telegraph*, *The Sunday Times*, the *Observer* and — strangely — the *Sunday Mirror*. The magazines are *The Illustrated London News*, *Men Only* and *Playboy*.

I talk to him at the counter. I talk quietly, so the screws who have joined the library screw can't hear. 'Ah, so you're Prime. Why are you in the hospital? Is something wrong with you?'

'Nothing wrong, not medically anyway.'

He's not looking at me, the lack of eye contact part of his reticence. I fill out the library ticket: Name . . . Location . . . I write *N?* for nonce with a question mark, my own little game, just to see who takes what books. The rapists search out sex books, the child molesters books like *Caravan 86* or *Family Photography*.

'How many books are we allowed?'

I notice the *we*. Like he's one of the chaps now.

'You're allowed six. Six officially, but as long as you don't run off with them to Parkhurst or Russia, and drop me in the shit....' I leave it there. He sucks his gaunt cheeks in, nodding his head. He's tall and thin, his wavy hair grey, head bowed. He has the air of a thinker, like he's already spent years in prison, and lives in his head. I feel the usual awkwardness. Like everyone's first visit to this library, he doesn't know what the procedure is.

'Go ahead.' I wave to the shelves. 'Find your books.'

A quick eye contact — the first. The cheeks are sucked in again. 'Buckshee paperbacks are here, on this shelf. You can take as many as you like. Fiction is by authors' names, alphabetically, you'll see the letters. War and stuff like that on the far shelf. Religion, sociology, psychology and parapsychology along this side.'

The three screws are in the office. Cons are either locked on the wings or out on exercise. We're locked in here, the passageways deserted. As usual, the screws are talking about work — the merits or demerits of x shift, the word *work* being suspect since the cons do most of their work. I fill out 'Prime' and 'Hosp' on each of the book-card holders, six to start with. I wonder which will wear out first, him or the cards.

Opposite the control-room, workmen had dug rose bushes up and laid paving slabs. Prime's exercise area. Two sides are brick walls, the other two are honeycombed concrete and thick unbreakable glass, a box twenty feet high for Prime to walk around on his own.

It's taken him twenty minutes to select six books: Sidney Sheldon's *Rage of Angels*, Plato's *The Republic*, *The Oxford Book of English Verse*, *Voices in My Ear* by Doris Stokes, *Advanced Mathematics*, and *Treachery is Their Trade* by Chapman Pincher.

Date-stamping the books, I say, 'Do you think they'll ever swop you?'

'I really don't know. I'm still going through debriefing.'

Pretending ignorance, I say, 'What does that mean, debriefing?'

'They come up once or twice a week and ask an awful lot of questions.'

I've one eye on the screws, who've seen us talking. The library screw brings out his papers and magazines, the hostility so obvious in his tone. 'Here you are, Prime. Have his books been stamped?'

I nod.

'All right then.' The tone conveys finality: the shop's closed. To the hospital screws he says, 'See you later chaps.' He unlocks the door and stares at Prime whose arms are full of paper. Prime walks ahead of the screws, his arms full of uncoded words.

# 16

# THE VIOLENCE

'Wakefield. The locals call it Murder Mansion.'

He's in his early twenties, an undergraduate newly enrolled in prison's school of crime and hard men. His qualifications are tattooed on his skin. On his right hand a single letter on each finger spells HATE; on his left hand the letters ACAB, for *all coppers are bastards*.

His affected walk is rope-like, as though he is holding an orange under each armpit. This was acquired at Borstal along with the long scar on his face that he's proud of. Both arms are covered with various tattoos, some done painfully in Borstal, the others in the backstreet tattooist's. The tattoo on his left wrist is smudged by a suicide scar. His face is bony as though the skin has been stretched over a skeleton's skull. He has spent seven years in various institutions and is now serving a six-year sentence for assault and robbery of an old man.

At 7.20 a.m. one day, dark clouds crashed together causing a downpour over the prison. Inside the prison buildings most prisoners had started their daily routine of slopping out, making their beds, washing, shaving. The screws, sleepy, bored, no more vigilant than at any other time of the day, took little notice of men going from cell to recess with chamber-pots, bowls of hot water.

From a cell a naked man staggered out. Blood from serious head wounds ran in rivulets down his body and dripped, leaving a dotted trail. He staggered all the way down the landing, past prisoners who looked with morbid curiosity and fear; none of them went to help him. Somewhere along the blooded trail the medical staff were alerted. When they reached the injured man the blood was already being mopped, some smudged as bloody footprints.

At the end of the landing the prisoner had collapsed. Blood continued to seep from his skull. On his left hand blood was congealing over the letters A and B.

* * *

A guy who was on remand for attacking women in the street with a razor, made a matchstick-sized spike of wood in his cell. When he was unlocked, he jabbed it into the eye of the first bloke who happened to walk towards him. He had carefully carved a barb in the spike.

* * *

A six-foot tall Cat. A prisoner arrived at a prison punishment block. He had been ghosted from Long Lartin after taking a screw hostage. He had held the screw captive with a knife to his throat for several hours in a cell.

The prisoner quietly finished his punishment time and was allocated to one of the wings. Within a couple of hours he was returned to the block saying he didn't want to be on the wing, in the prison. Hidden in his underpants was a piece of electrical wire.

He repeatedly pressed the buzzer in his cell until the door was unlocked by the smallest block screw. He grabbed the screw, pulled him into the cell, and tried to garrotte him with the wire. The screw managed to get his hands under the wire and shout for help. The wire cut into his hands as he swung about the cell. His ordeal lasted only seconds. The prisoner was overpowered with reinforcements from the wings. He was dragged into the strip cell.

The prisoner was charged with attempted murder. At his trial he said that he tried to kill the screw *because they wouldn't let him have a cat in his cell.* He was sentenced to an additional five years on top of his life sentence.

* * *

Another had already killed a man with his fists, got a seven for manslaughter and did every day of the seven, the story was. This time the facts, the newspaper facts, were in the *Doncaster Post.* Drinking in a Doncaster pub he followed a man out of the back door. The man was crossing the courtyard going to the toilet, when he was punched to death. His mate, following his footsteps, was also punched, but although he didn't meet quite the same fate, he suffered irreparable brain damage which left him paralysed.

He was sentenced to life for the man he killed and twelve years for attempted murder.

In prison he was quiet, polite, kept to himself. Working in the kit store, another prisoner who knew full well what he was in for, insisted on fighting him. The argument was silly, childish, over an extra towel. Verbally pushed, he said, 'OK, let's have it.' In seconds he had punched the guy to a pulp.

* * *

On D Wing at the Scrubs, a lifer who was just starting his sentence stabbed a black prisoner in the neck with a broken bottle, for no apparent reason. Another inmate, ex of the SAS and Magistrates' Bench, went to his aid and stemmed the flow of blood until the medical screws took over. His action was automatic. For years he had been taught to keep the wounded alive, though, paradoxically, the killer instinct had also been drilled into him. Possibly, in equal amounts, he knew how to kill and how to keep alive the wounded better than anyone else on D Wing. His action in helping the man was also a humane gesture; it didn't require thought. It was impulsive. Unfortunately for him, many other prisoners on the wing didn't see it that way, or didn't want to. Many, because they are cynical and bitter, saw ulterior motives; to them it was a grovelling exercise, an opportunity to gain a merit point in the parole stakes, or they thought he was using his SAS training in first-aid to show off. Others thought he should have done nothing. He should have minded his own business, as they did. 'He should have let the black bastard bleed to death.'

Prison being what it is, his gesture will likely follow him throughout his sentence. In many cons' eyes it will be seen as a negative act. In his prison file it will be recorded favourably, but suggesting perhaps a naiveté to the ways of prison.

* * *

Two prisoners at Parkhurst decided to hang a nonce, an old man who was doing time for molesting children. One of them brought a half-bat in from exercise. The idea was to knock him out first and then string him up to the bars in his cell.

Pacing up and down the landing, psyching themselves up, watching his cell, his movements, they went in. One had a plaited rope, made from the stitched edging of sheets, the other the half-bat which he smashed down on the old man's head without a word being spoken. The old man, the nonce, staggered from the blow and started to shout. He was hit several more times in panic. But still he shouted. His other assailant managed to get the now bloodied rope over his head; he was manically trying to tighten the rope to shut him up when the old man defecated.

Realizing the plan had come unstuck, with the blood splashed on them and the shouting and the old man's stink, they left his cell. They left him a bloodied, stinking mess.

At the end of their trial for attempted murder one was committed to Broadmoor, declared insane and psychopathic. The other was given a life sentence.

The one sent to Broadmoor was released two years later, declared sane again, fit to return to the human race. Back in society he teamed up with a 19-year old girl, an ex-psychiatric patient. In Chester they broke into an 87-year old woman's house where they smashed the woman over the head and killed her.

Both were found guilty of murder and sentenced to life imprisonment.

* * *

PP9 batteries are put in socks. Tubular steel bed legs can be screwed off. Stanley knives, marquetry knives, disposable razor blades pushed into White Windsor soap and thrown at screws or cons, glass wrapped one end with a rag for a handle, table legs two foot long, some with nails to make holes. Knives in the kitchen, one of which, a butcher's boning knife in the hand of a man, a nonce doing life and twenty-five years, a man with nothing to lose, a man with black tunnel vision, was photographed and finger-printed after being used to kill a prisoner at Parkhurst.

* * *

Some are time-bombs, ticking away waiting to go off. Some pump iron, keep in shape, keep the bomb primed, in good condition.

Some you can tell from the eyes like glass beads, there's a warning there. Others are composites like *Wanted* posters: hands grubby with ingrained dirt and fingerprint ink, nails bitten to the quick, tattoos everywhere, dots, letters, snakes, butterflies, hate, love, death, honour, girls' names, *In memory of*, *Mother*, - - - -cut here - - - - across the throat, across the wrist.

Hands that have punched faces, men, women, children, broken into homes, stolen cars and raped and assaulted and molested and murdered. Hands, sensitive, gentle, that have typed words, caressed and cared for women, children, stroked the family pets, worked hard for family, house and home. They are washed time and time again with clean sweet-smelling soap, yet still the guilt remains.

Fingerprints match evidence, match charge sheets, match courts and the meat waggon, the sweat-box on the way to prison, to shame, humiliation and degradation.

Our hands bring us here.

# 17

# GINGER BEERS

There was Penny — aka Michael Mole — who transformed his gender from male to female. Or at least it looked that way in the prison mugshots taken when he came into prison and left it. At one time he was in the British Army, stationed in Hong Kong. With his Army issue rifle he shot one of his fingers off. Thereafter he was discharged, considered unfit to be a soldier. In some sort of domestic dispute he killed a member of his family and was sentenced to life imprisonment. As he had already started treatment with hormone injections before his imprisonment, he was allowed to continue his treatment during his sentence.

In prison he was known to the staff and prisoners alike as Penny. Considered a woman, a female unfortunate enough to be born male, he was referred to in the female gender. People applied the words 'her' and 'she' to him. New prisoners confused him for one of the welfare staff. Although he always wore bib-and-brace overalls and a prison shirt, there was no mistaking a pair of breasts sticking out. He wore his hair long and used make-up, giving the outward appearance of a woman.

His effect on some prisoners was like that of a dog on heat in the Battersea Dogs' Home. The sneaky and perverted would hang around his cell or watch his cell from other landings. Some made him presents of soft toys in pathetic attempts to gain sexual favours. Some screws also sniffed around his cell. Once an SO screw staggered out of his cell, so pissed he had to lean on the wall and inch his way along to the centre. Rumour had it that he left minus his wallet.

Penny served nine years before leaving prison and having a sex change operation. Before his discharge, a woman welfare worker took him shopping to buy women's clothes.

Most homosexuals tend to play down their sexuality in prison. As outside, homosexuals are stereotyped as being effeminate and weak. In prison a show of weakness is dangerous. Weaknesses are picked at and exploited. But the effeminate type who is attracted to prison is usually tough and violent. One who was pestered for sexual favours reacted by stabbing the pest dead with a wood chisel.

Doubtless there are men who have the capacity for such behaviour somewhere in their personalities, and who in long years of sexual starvation indulge in it when in a normal environment they would have continued a heterosexual lifestyle. There are men who adopt homosexuality as soon as they are imprisoned; once outside again they revert to heterosexuality.

In sexist ignorance, prisoners, like people outside, assume that homosexuality is rampant in women's prisons, and that the female screws are all lesbians and that their only motive for doing the work is sexual. This assumption is never applied to male screws.

# 18
# THE ESCAPE

It's summer 1984. I'm in the middle of the eleventh year of a life sentence. This is the first time in my sentence I've come so close to the outside world. I work on the inside gardens. Seven days a week I come out, walk around inside the prison, maybe weed a bit here and there. It's always a wind-up, yet I can never resist looking up and over the wall. I torment myself daily. Because the prison is built on a hill, it's possible to see over the wall and the other world beyond. During the day the sounds of an infants' school spill over the wall. In fact, some parts of the other world are quite close.

At night I sit on the wide window-ledge in my cell and watch traffic snaking away up the main London road. Looking over the wall at people who live outside it seems to me they are oblivious of the prison. I never see them look up. It's as though the prison doesn't exist and we are in here *out of sight, out of mind*.

Freedom's so near yet it could be a million miles away.

Today, I'm to go to hospital. I'm having a barium meal. I suppose it's to be expected. After hunger strikes, stress, and years of prison slop, my stomach is complaining.

The screw takes me into reception. The reception screws wear blue hospital-orderly jackets, I don't know why. One says, 'Do you want to wear your own clothes?' I think he's taking the piss. The incredulity must show in my face. He says, 'You can wear your own clothes, if you want. Seriously.'

My clothes have been squashed into a box and although they were laundered I haven't worn them or seen them for ten and a half years. It's such a nice feeling having the social part of my personality back on again. I sit down in the waiting-room, drink a cup of coffee and feel a sense of disorientation. I've never been more aware of the clothes I'm wearing. It feels so strange.

I hear the taxi pull up. I'm jolted back to reality when the screw takes the handcuffs out of a bag. I vividly remember wearing these clothes in another reception, another prison, going by another taxi to court, to be sentenced to life. It all seems so long ago. And nothing seems to have changed.

So I'm cuffed to the screw, sitting in the back sandwiched between the two screws. I can't understand why I'm allowed to wear my own clothes. I'm half hoping that they've made a mistake and instead of going to the hospital we're going somewhere else and I can escape.

We arrive at the hospital. The taxi driver pulls up at the back door. Getting out of the taxi, I realize it's the first time I've put my foot on the ground outside for years. The feeling is hard to comprehend. I'm still doing life, I'm still a prisoner, yet here I am, in my own clothes standing on the ground in a world I've only seen over walls or through windows of mobile prisons for so long.

One screw goes off to let someone know we're here. The screw I'm cuffed to unlocks the cuffs. I'm stood in a passageway outside the X-ray room, with the two screws next to me. It's a great feeling being away from the prison, away from bars, walls, and barbed wire. I'm X-rayed. I change back into my clothes. The cuffs are put back on. The taxi appears and too quickly we're on our way back to the prison. Looking out the taxi window I try to see as much as possible; attractive women I look at for as long as possible. My heart sinks as we drive through the prison gate and it closes behind us, blocking off the light.

Reflecting on this experience, alone and lonely in my cell, I decide to escape.

I've been looking at the means for a long while and didn't realize it.

I'm working alongside the YP wing. I'm pulling wild couch grass from a bank below a privet hedge. I rake the bank and throw stones, a toothbrush, bent nails, into a wheelbarrow. On the other side I'm planting flowers.

I'm planting flowers when the skip lorry comes in.

Pat is here again taking the piss. 'Wot's this, a fackin' LSD trip?'

'Leave it out, Pat. You're only jealous anyway.'

'Look at them flowers. You've got all sorts mixed up together. What are you up to? I know you're up to no good. Don't give me the bollocks you gave the Guvnor.'

Pat's a nice guy. I warm to his humour. Like most cockney villains his pattern of speech is often in machine-gun bursts. He has the cunning of a fox.

'All right Pat, I'll tell ya what I'm doing. I've found an old sewage tunnel that leads under the wall. It's partially blocked off this end [I make out I'm checking around that no one's listening] and when you're not nosing around I'm unblocking it this end. D'ya fancy making one?'

'Yeah, you're up to summing that's for sure. I've been looking at the top field. If I was starting my bird fings would be different. That's bollocks about the tunnel.'

'Well, I'll send you a postcard then. Goodday.'

'Come round an' I'll show ya how to do the tomatoes. The geezer showed me how it's done.'

Pat's one of the few guys I wouldn't be worried about, if he knew what I was planning.

My heart pounds. I wheel the barrow full of sods and rocks. I can't afford to fail. It's 13 August. I'm not superstitious. It's a beautiful, sunny day. I'm wearing nick jeans, a light-biscuit coloured pullover and trainers. I've timed the lorry's collection several times. I think I know what I'm doing. I walk round to the skips. But the lads on the painters' VCT are all sitting by the open windows, having their tea-break. I exchange small-talk while emptying the barrow. This means I've got to go back and fill the barrow again. I give it ten minutes. More sods and rocks. This time there's only one guy by the window. I'm really keyed up. As I bung the rocks into the skip I catch a quick look at the geezer. He's new in the nick, I don't know him. I think *fuckit, I'm taking the chance.* I step into the barrow and jump into the skip. As I look up, the guy spots me and his mouth drops open in surprise. I put my fingers to my lips in the *keep it dark* sign. He nods, mouthing *all right* with the thumbs-up. I can only hope he keeps it to himself, at least till I'm well away.

The skip is half full with various smelly rubbish: dustbin-liner bags, potato peel, rotting food, piss-sodden mattresses. I move things about to make a hollow and wriggle into it. Flies and wasps buzz about. Outside sounds are telescoped. I'm listening intently for the lorry; it should be here any minute. In fifteen minutes the midday count will be done.

Ten years and five months I've waited for this moment. Now it's here and the thought makes my heart pound. I'm so keyed-up (a nice expression) I feel like I'm buzzing with the flies.

At last the sound of a lorry. Slowly it nears, with it the screw's walkie-talkie. *Sierra 2 to Control escorting skip lorry over.* I wriggle further into the rubbish. It's now ten to eleven. In ten minutes I'll be a body count not there to be counted. The words 'penal dustbin' come into my head. I'm just hoping that all this goes according to plan and the screw or the driver doesn't look into the skip.

The lorry stops, the driver gets out of the cab. A few words are exchanged. Two wooden boards are placed on the back and my fate is sealed. It's dark. The lorry backs up to the skip. There's a clanging of chains. The cab door slams shut and I'm airborne. The skip bumps on to the back.

*Sierra 2 to Control escorting skip lorry to main gate over.* The lorry pulls out of the compound heading for the gate at walking speed. I think, *This is it, I'm on my way.* The skip sways slightly and the vibration from the engine makes a droning noise echoed and amplified inside the skip. It's taking so long, I light a match to check the time. It's five to eleven.

At the gate the driver gets out, there's a murmur of voices and he's back in the cab and the engine starts up again. I hear the main door being opened. *Jesus, at last, I've done it. I've finally done it.* The lorry picks up speed, then stops. The engine revs, changes gear, and I'm on my way. I'm outside. I'm in the outside world again. In the world of freedom.

Fifteen minutes later the lorry turns off the road and stops. The driver gets out and takes the two boards and throws them on the ground, gets back into the cab and drives off. I stand up and take a bearing. Magic, we're going along a dirt-track road to the council dump. I make my way to the edge of the skip and jump.

I'm in the Sussex countryside. To my left a small wood. To the right, farm fields and beautiful Sussex Downs. I go through the trees. In the distance I can see a motorway, beside it a village. I've got to get to a telephone so I make for the village. I've ten pence, tobacco, matches and cigarette papers. Not much of a survival kit.

It's now eleven twenty. In the next few minutes the screws will be a digit short. They'll be counting and recounting. The prisoners will be hustled into their cells. The screw's eye will appear at the judas. My cell will be the focus of attention. Screws will unlock the door, look in again and again. But I'll not be there. I'm here, here in freedom street. Here running in a straight line, across this beautiful field. *I've beaten you. I've robbed you of a body.*

I stop just short of the village to get my breath back. I'm approaching a farm. I walk through the farmyard. Next to the farm is a church. I see two blokes and a woman lopping branches off some trees. I say to the bloke, 'Excuse me, is there a phone in this village?' He replies in a bumpkin accent: 'Sorry, no, this place too small. Yu'll ha' to go two mile.'

Next to the church are two cottages, and what do I see but phone wires going to them. An old woman answers the door. 'Excuse me, can I use your phone? My car's broken down on the motorway and the phones are out of action.' She's just a little bit suspicious, but says OK. I produce the ten pence.

Now I keep my fingers crossed that the guy is in. The phone rings and rings. 'Hello,' a sleepy voice answers. 'Hello, who's that?'

'It's me. I've broken down. You said you'd pick me up.' I'm hoping he recognizes my voice. I can't give too much away. I can't mention names. He says, 'I'm with ya . . . Christ, I didn't think you'd do it . . . Look, where are you?' I ask the woman, and tell him.

'Hang on there.'

I thank the woman, hoping she has bought this breakdown crap and she doesn't phone the police.

Going through the village is a lane that comes off the motorway. The cottages are on one side, the farm and the church on the other. That's the sum total of this place. I hope my mate can find it. It's nearly twelve. Now all the local police will have my description. The cons back at the prison will be shouting out of their windows. This lunch-time they won't be bored. There'll be a flurry of excitement in the prison. Some cons will wish me luck. One, I know, will have a secret smile.

I wait at the bole of a tree partially hidden by a bush. Every car that passes causes my heart to quicken. I don't know what car my mate's got. Every few minutes I check the time. It's twelve thirty. If anything has gone wrong I've decided to hide in the church grounds and then, say about four or five in the morning, walk along the motorway in the fields until I find a service-station and accost someone for a lift to London.

I don't doubt that my mate will get here. My only worry is that the police will come snooping before he arrives. I haven't known this guy long. He's a Scot, about 29, and has been about, as they say. He's a hustler as far as I know. I got to know him in prison. He's been out only three weeks. I've had so many let me down over the years, so many promises. Prison promises, I call them; blokes say they'll do this and that when they leave, but very few have the strength of character to follow through. They've meant well, but once outside, it's a different story.

A car brakes hard. The back door opens quickly. I'm in and we accelerate. My mate hands me a pair of dark glasses and a leather jacket. He says, 'Sorry we're late. We hadn't enough petrol. And we couldn't find the frigging place. There's choppers over the nick. Oh, this is my missus, Maggie.' His wife is driving, very skilfully, I might add. No panic, no head turning. I say hello and compliment her on her driving.

We drive through villages, little seaside places. I don't know where I am. The three of us are on edge. We stop behind traffic. There's a bridge being lowered. Maggie says, 'Don't look behind but there's a cop car.' I move my head and catch sight of a police van in the rear-view mirror. He's on the radio. I move slightly to my left. Maggie's eyes catch mine in the mirror. They're wider than they should be. My mate says, 'Don't let's get paranoid. It could be anything. See what happens when we move off.'

For five minutes we're stuck there, trying to be natural. At last the bridge is down and the traffic ahead starts to move. We sigh with relief. But the worry is still behind us. I look sideways now and then, thinking this would be what a 'normal' person would do, but I'm careful not to show too much profile.

'If it's on top I'll try to make a break. You just say you picked me up hitch-hiking.'

We've gone about three miles and the cop car is still behind us. Suddenly it turns left. I look around and see one of those detached-house police stations. My mate, Mac, surprises me in his coolness. This is the real test. This is putting all the talk and bravado into practice. He's risking a two-year jail sentence, his wife might even get the same, yet there's no nail-biting.

'Stop here. We need cigarettes.' We stop outside a newsagent's.

Mac gets out and quickly walks into the shop. Maggie lights a cigarette and offers me one. I say, 'You're risking a sentence for me. I hope you think I'm worth it?'

'Mac thinks you are. He's told me about you. That's good enough for me.'

I reach over and open the door for him. He's brought two icecreams, and an ice lolly for Maggie.

Coming into Brighton, Maggie slows down to about thirty. We're now more relaxed. I begin to actually take notice of the houses, streets and people we pass. It seems strange without bars and handcuffs. Maggie and Mac are talking about people I don't know, about a situation I don't know. I only take in the way they're talking. It's intimate, the way two people who are in love and know each other well talk. I become aware that I'm alone with my thoughts and realize it's a habit I'll have to get out of.

My mate X said, 'You can stay here. We've a girl staying, but she's gone home for the weekend. The bedroom is on the right.'

The bedroom was cold. The whole large house was cold. I switched on the light. The bed was neatly made. On a table an assortment of makeup, perfume and a box of Tampax. No pack of contraceptive pills. She'd probably taken them with her, in her handbag. I looked around for a photograph of her. In the wardrobe, clothes neatly stacked, shoes at the bottom, handbags, most of them empty, in one or two, bus tickets, crumpled receipts. Nothing of interest, and no photograph.

I wanted to see what this girl looked like. In the dressing-table drawers bras, knickers, pullovers, slip — but no photograph. No secret diary. No secret vibrator. I was disappointed. Not much at all to indicate who this girl was, what she looked like. Maybe I'd meet her. I hoped so.

A few days later we were driving off when his girlfriend said, 'Look, there's Alison.' She was standing on the other side of the street. She had just got off the bus and hadn't seen us. My mate blipped the car horn. She came over. 'We're going to have tea. Do you want to come with us?'

She opened the back door and sat next to me. 'This is a mate, Dave. Dave, this is the girl who's staying with us, Alison.'

I said hello and wondered if this girl was going to come into my life. She's got great legs, I thought, but I could see sadness in her eyes. There'd been some heartache. But I hated the deceit. I was a lifer on the run, an escapee wanted by the police, by the screws who'd lost a body, by the Home Office Lifers' Department where my lifer's shadow lay across a mountain of paperwork. I was swimming in a sea of lies. What did I do? she asked. Straight off pat, I said, 'Oh, my work . . . I'm a central heating salesman.' To raised eyebrows.

Sometimes I got confused. More than once I woke up thinking I was still in prison. And regardless of what state I went to bed in, I still woke up early. I had my hair dyed a trendy two-tone blond. That night I went to bed pissed. Looking in the mirror the next morning I got a terrible shock. There was this stranger staring back at me. It was hard to keep the marbles together. It was a lonely existence, in some ways worse than prison. Everywhere I went, the shadow would follow me. I began to imagine faceless people in offices with my files on their desks, waiting for my return.

Stepping into a pub for the first time in over ten years, I panicked when the barmaid came up to me. I ordered a half of bitter when I wanted a pint. When she said 'Which?' I said, stuttering, 'Any, any.' When she said forty- something pence I heard fourteen pence and like a miser, counted them out. She corrected me, looking at me as if I had green skin when my face was turning a shade of red. I glanced around the pub and thought in my prison paranoia everyone was talking about me. I sat down in an alcove in a corner, my nerves at breaking point. I was sure my gaffe and my out-of-fashion clothes marked me as someone fresh out of prison, and therefore suspect, to be avoided. My self-esteem, my ego and my personality, suddenly disintegrated.

A year or two ago, I think it was, I heard it for the first time — a desolate wailing, two-tone and American. At the time I assumed it to be an ambulance siren. Gathering my wits in the pub, wondering what to do next, where to go, I was shocked out of my thoughts by the same wailing. Being a hot and sunny day, the pub door was wedged open. A few feet away from me I caught sight of a flashing blue light and a police car reflected in the glass door. I remember thinking, 'Oh no, no, for fucksake, no, I haven't tasted freedom. Don't come for me. Please God, I'll never sin again if you just give me this one chance to enjoy freedom.' Yet I was rooted to the spot, the left of my mind saying *Don't do anything stupid*, the right side saying *Get out through the other door, now, before it's too late and you're nicked*. I breathed deeply, paralysed with paranoia. Neither side won. Fear and recklessness kept me rooted to the spot.

The cop car, answering some call of emergency, wailed away in the traffic. Around the corner in the pub, guys were playing space-invader machines. The strange electronic noises seemed absurd in a pub setting. I looked down at the now empty half-pint glass. Forty odd pence for a mouthful of beer, bloody daylight robbery I thought. Before my imprisonment a pint was about twenty-five pence. A good night would cost no more than a tenner. I hadn't much money but I couldn't face going out on the street without a drink or two. Anyhow it was all a mad dash to enjoy the fruits of freedom while I had the chance.

I lasted six weeks. I was nicked for depriving Her Majesty's Government of a passport. At Horseferry Road Magistrates' Court the cop came up to the cell: 'Well, David Wait. It's so good to meet the real you at long last.'

Mr Green, the duty solicitor, looked puzzled. So did I. 'Are you talking to me? Mr Green, what's he talking about?'

'Come on, the game's up. Look.'

The cop held up a sheet of paper, on the top. 'WANTED — ESCAPED FROM PRISON.' It was a photograph of me. It was me all right. I just shrugged my shoulders at Mr Green. Poor Mr Green.

I was immediately moved round to the other side. They positioned two coppers outside the cell door and left the flap down.

The court inspector came up to the door: 'The charge has been dropped *sine die*.'

What does this mean?

'It means it won't be proceeded with. It's left on the file.'

I'd read about characters in books whose throats went dry. I never believed it, and thought it was the author's imagination. I was so dry I had to ask for water. I couldn't swallow. I felt emotionally sick.

I left Horseferry Road Magistrates' Court handcuffed to one of the two coppers who'd arrested me. We drove along in a police transit van. Looking out at the Thames, the morning cold but sunny, I was gutted. One of them said, 'Do you want to see your photograph?' He showed me a photo on a page of the *Police Gazette*. It looked nothing like me. 'Now you know why we didn't know who you were. Looks nothing like you, does it?' I could hardly answer him. I noticed a sticker on his briefcase — Polizi. It looked vaguely Dutch. He'd probably been to Amsterdam on a drugs bust.

I thought, this is how lifer recalls must feel when they're returned to prison, after a taste of freedom. Yet only those of us unlucky enough to have been through it know the experience. Looking out at freedom is such a personal gut feeling that I don't think it could ever be conveyed to those that haven't been through it.

Entering the reception, two screws from the prison I escaped from were standing there gawping at me. 'Well, look who's here. All right, Wait? Glad to see you back,' said one. I spent six days walking around in circles, in my yellow escape patches that contrasted with the weather, as gloomy as the prison. For some reason I kept thinking of a canary in a coalmine.

I put down to see the doctor. When I walked in he was writing. Without looking up, he said, 'Yes, what is it?' I said I was depressed and could he prescribe something. He said, 'Depressed, ay. See the welfare. Put down for the welfare. They're good people. You need to talk it through. And the next.' Not once did he look up.

The welfare woman looked like a cross between Barbara Woodhouse and Marjorie Proops. But she was a good old sort. She talked to me like I was a schoolkid and she the teacher. Once when I spoke to her on the ground floor, all the guys started to bark behind her back and even in my depression I had a job not to laugh. Daily she would say to me, 'You'll just have to do it, even if it's another five years. You can't throw it all away now. Come on, pick yourself up and do it. You know you can do it.'

I gained a lot of strength from her.

Christmas Eve we went over to the lifers' rec to watch a film called *Midnight Express*. Half-way through the film the projector and the lights went off. After ten minutes or so we were herded back to the wing. On the wing the electricity was also off. We were locked in our cells in the darkness. After a while we were unlocked, but only ten at a time, for tea. The screws had oil-lamps which cast an eerie yellow glow. After we collected our tea we were given no time to wander about but were locked up again. We were told that if the electricity didn't come back in time we would be unlocked only to put our meal trays out, and then we would be banged up for the night.

At about eight o'clock the guys started to bang on their cell doors. Soon it sounded like everyone was banging. The noise was frightening and continued for ages. Eventually the banging stopped, although we stayed in darkness. I tried to listen to the radio; LBC were interviewing people at Christmas Eve parties. I couldn't help it, but I tortured myself even more listening to free people enjoying themselves.

At twelve o'clock Big Ben rang out Christmas Day. There was a huge cheer followed by banging on cell doors and window bars. I lay in bed, miserable, freezing cold and hoping that the noise, the prisoners shouting, would soon die down and I could get to sleep.

Christmas Day the lights were back on. I was lucky enough to get access to a phone. I accosted an SO on Christmas morning and much to my surprise he said, 'No problem. Take your time. It's Christmas, isn't it?' Ordinarily I looked on Christmas as just another day, and I'd try not to think of people outside. That day, though, I had a particular woman on my mind.

Being on the E list, in patches, I had to stay on the twos, in a Cat. A cell.

The rule says that escapees have to have a cell above, below and either side of the cell they're allocated to, to prevent them tunnelling out.

One of my neighbours had only been out of prison twelve days after a twelve year sentence and was starting another twelve. I guess twelve must be his unlucky number. He was a likeable guy nicknamed *The Bear* because of his size. When he was captured someone took his photograph. He was sprawled out on the ground, police pointing guns at his head, and him with two bandoliers of shotgun cartridges across his chest. I couldn't get over how unaffected he appeared by the new twelve year sentence. It didn't seem to bother him at all.

Another guy, Con, still had bullets in his head from the old gangster days. He was doing a seven for blagging. Con would drive us mad singing his head off all day long. Once when I was walking with him on exercise he pointed to the wall, to a tree on the other side. 'Ere, see that tree? When I was first in this nick you could just see that tree. It came as high as the top of the wall. Now look at it.' The tree was thirty foot higher than the wall. I left Con to walk the rest of the circles on his own, and went back to my cell. The image of the tree growing through all those years, while life and seasons came and went all around it, kept repeating in my mind.

# 19

# SPECIAL SEARCH

The cell door unlocks quickly and is flung open. Two screws rush into the cell. They're dressed in brown overalls. One has a two-way radio strapped to his belt. He says, 'Don't move. This is a special search. We're looking for escape equipment. We've been told you have escape equipment in this cell.' The other one says, 'Right, strip off. Shoes first.'

I proceed to strip. Shoes, socks, jeans. They search each item thoroughly. I drop my underpants and give them a quick shake. He says, 'No. Underpants off.' I don't argue. I put the underpants back on. He says, 'T-shirt off and turn around.'

It's obvious they've been informed I have escape equipment and it's obvious they're optimistic of finding it. When I'm dressed again, one says, 'Do you have anything in your cell that you shouldn't have?'

'Would you expect me to tell you if I had?' He ignores my reply.

'You start here, I'll work backwards.'

The cell furniture consists of a locker, wooden school-type chair, a bed and a chamber-pot. I've oil paints, brushes, etc, on the floor, along with a few books.

'There a bucket of hooch here.' He puts the lid back on the bucket, takes it off the heating pipe. He pulls the blankets and sheets off the bed, throws them on the floor. Then he turns the mattress over, checks it closely, folds it this way and that.

My letters are gone through next. He checks each page closely. I know he's looking for key numbers. The shape of keys can be coded in numbers, the numbers represent measurements.

The other one opens the cupboard door, looks through spare kit, underpants, socks, pullovers. I'd forgotten. He says, 'What's this then?' It's a container full of yeast. It's a special wine yeast, and looks like a mixture of salt and pepper. He smells it. 'Is this yeast?'

'I don't know. I've never seen it before.'

He puts it in his pocket. The other starts checking the floor tiles.

'How does the back come off this radio?'

'It screws off. There's two screws in the back.'

He takes the back off, then tries to take the guts out. Fortunately there's a certain way it comes out. I say, 'That's right, pull it to bits!'

'You take it out, then.'

I make the same movements as him. 'Well, it won't come out.'

He takes over, pulls a bit more, gives up, then tries to put his finger under the guts. He decides to leave it. Inwardly I sigh with relief.

I've hidden something else in there, in the guts.

He takes a final look around the cell. 'You finished?'

'I think so. What about the windows?'

'I've done them.'

One picks up the bucket. They leave the cell and slam the door.

# 20

# ALBANY BLOCK

We talk through the flat bars and a few inches beyond a wire mesh. Our words bounce back from the shiny sheets of metal that cover the security fence four feet away.

There's a new guy in the next cell. He's on the book, doing three lifes. He's brought with him an air of hopelessness. It's several days before I see him on exercise. But during that time I get a face in my mind of what he looks like. I expected an ugly face, a dullard, someone to be avoided but pitied. I'm totally wrong.

He's a small, slight guy, about 22. Not handsome, but not ugly. The accent is broad Yorkshire. The vocabulary is limited. Every short burst of speech is punctuated at the end with 'Know wat I mean?' And yet not a question, not even an affirmation that you're listening to him, as though his talk is to soothe himself. I find listening to him very irritating,and I think it would be all too easy to dislike him. But although I find his story repulsive, I'm morbidly fascinated. His story comes out muddled at first: a bit from the middle, then how he got into the mess, which turned out to be not the beginning but somewhere along the way. When I managed to get a word in, and asked him to tell me what the actual start was, he clammed up.

Eventually it comes out: he was in Risley Remand Centre, in the hospital, when he met a Scots guy who was finishing an eight. The Jock inveigled him into a homosexual relationship. The Jock, whose name we don't know, I'll call Reptile. He promised the guy, who I'll call John, a job. John, being easily led and immature, said OK, although afterwards he realized he never liked Reptile in the first place. Reptile was a good deal older than John and well versed in crime and violence.

So they met again on the outside. John didn't say, but the guess was that the homosexual relationship continued. It didn't take John long to realize the offer of a job, at least a non-criminal job, was a lie. Reptile didn't have a business. He was, like John, a petty criminal.

Somewhere along the line two other young guys came into the picture. Like John, they were easily led and followed petty criminals. So they came under Reptile's spell, breaking into houses and shops with the Fagan Reptile waiting in the pub with his hand out.

One night when they'd robbed a fair sum of money, Reptile took them on a pub crawl. In a pub Reptile chatted up another young guy and took them all for a drive to the moorlands. Before they left the pub, Reptile told them that the new guy was a grass and had informed on them to the police about breaking into a shop. He mentioned giving the new guy a kicking.

Arriving at a desolate spot on the moor, Reptile ordered them out. Reptile dragged the new guy out of the car and kicked him a few times. He then ordered the others to kick him, which they did out of fear of Reptile. Then he ordered them to strip the guy. Once stripped, Reptile buggered the guy and forced the others to do the same. John says that Reptile then ordered him to strangle the guy, threatening to kill him if he didn't.

The young guy, after being badly beaten and raped, was strangled with a shoe-lace. They hid his lifeless body in some undergrowth and drove away. John says that Reptile threatened to kill them or a member of their families if any of them went to the police.

A few nights later, they did the same thing to another young guy, another guy who hadn't grassed them to the police or anyone else. It was about this stage in the story that I remembered having read the grubby details in the newspaper. The third guy, the third victim, sussed what was going on and made a run for it. He got away and went to the police.

So John got three lifes, as did the other two. Reptile got life with a recommended minimum of twenty-five years. All were put on the Cat.A list, considered dangerous if they were to escape.

So this was my new cell neighbour — John from Yorkshire, frightened to go on the wing in case he bumped into someone who was a relative of the deceased. Or his nightmare would come true and he'd bump into the Reptile.

After John's story my anger at being ghosted from the Scrubs has subsided. I came here on a Wednesday, I was expecting a visit the following Saturday. Now I've had a letter from a girlfriend to say she came up to the Scrubs and waited ages only to be told I wasn't there. I'm pissed off no end.

And I can't expect friends to travel to the Isle of Wight. The journey would be hard to do in a day. But I know the score. I know I have to rough it in the block for a while. I'll have to readjust to the block rhythm. After all, I've had plenty of experience.

Coming into this block I've been strip-searched, my property's been checked over, with the inevitable items not allowed, by six reception screws. Now the block screws have their rummage. Watercolour paints, paint-brushes, oil paints and some books because I've more than the limit of four, all are not allowed in this block, the screw says.

Albany. Albania. Alcatraz. It sounds like a mixture of those words and images. A prison on an island, the most secure in the country, and the most troubled. I had imagined the screws would be dogs and they are, at least the block ones are. I can see that already.

The tallest, Midlands accent, spotty, dirt-ingrained skin, is saying quickly, 'Give us trouble and we'll give you trouble, all right, Sunshine?' as he turns over my cardboard box, only looking at me on the 'all right, Sunshine?' Immediately

I get the impression he's the loudest and most dominant one. I know from experience the idea is to dominate me from the start, show me where authority and force is before I forget my place in the order of things.

I make no reply, knowing that my non-answer will be taken as assent, but with the possibility of a threat lingering.

Finishing the jumble sale, he says, 'Right, strip-search' and walks towards a cell where two other screws are waiting outside. I notice the spring-loaded lock in the block position with the door wide open. I walk in and quickly turn around, just in case. I strip and the three of them examine each item of clothing; each time they search a piece I put it back on.

The block SO comes over. Fat and fifty with a fag hanging from his lips, he says languidly, 'Wot religion and diet?', in his hand my cell card.

'No religion, vegan diet.'

Without looking up, he writes the details on the card. A long piece of ash falls from his fag onto the cell floor. The strip-search is finished. Just before the spotty one slams the door, I say, 'When do I get my prop?'

'When we've finished searching it.'

BANG.

I'm alone with my thoughts, as though the door banged my living-in-my-head thoughts into action. First thing is to search the cell, make sure there's nothing hidden away I could get nicked for when the cell's searched.

Although I haven't eaten, I'm not hungry. In fact I'm more than queasy. Coming over on the ferry the sea was choppy and the lorries were swaying about in front of our mobile prison. And like the other cons I was inwardly worried, what with being handcuffed to a chain and the only screw with the keys in the front of the bus, cut off from us, and with the sea so rough.

It's getting dark. The cell light-switch is outside. I decide to make the bed. The mattress is on a wooden step, set five inches off the smooth floor, the wood encased in concrete. I'm glad I can't see the piss stains on the mattress. My head is splitting with the tension and travelling.

I've just lain down when the light is switched on and the door unlocked. Spotty and his pal carry my cardboard boxes into the cell. Spotty says, 'Here you are then.' His tone conveys a cynical smugness. I know they've fucked something up deliberately. When they've gone I check my gear. Everything has been thrown into the boxes, letters are scattered about, watercolour paper has been creased. I can't be bothered to go through all of it. I don't want to feel wound up, not on top of this headache. I notice the pattern from the screw's boot in the fag ash on the floor, I quickly blow it away.

Days slowly drag by. I get into the routine, the block rhythm. Only two trips to the recess at slop out, one bath a week. Kit change is the bare minimum. After I've washed my hair in the bowl of water at night, I wash the pair of socks I've taken off and dry them on the heating pipe.

I get back into reading books, novels mostly.

I've written to the chief of the Lifers' Dept. The letter's been stopped by the block SO. When I ask him why, he says, 'Because you're not allowed to write to that person.' I argue the point. He says dismissively, 'See the Guvnor then'. I see the AG responsible for the block who tries to tell me that the SO didn't really stop the letter, but was only referring it to higher authority, and that after reading the letter *he* is stopping it. I then ask to see the No. 1 Governor, the Regional Director and a member of the BOV. The following day the SO tells me, begrudgingly, that the letter has in fact been sent off.

It's all too stupid. I'm writing to the Chief of P2 asking him why I've been sent to Albany and asking if I can be sent back to the Scrubs, to our writing workshop, to all I left behind there. Yet in 1984 I escaped from the Chief's prison when the P2 chief was the Governor there. But I know I have to write to him before I write to the MP. Otherwise they'll say I haven't internalized the complaint using proper channels, which would be reason enough to stop the MP's letter, and I know from experience my only hope lies with the MP.

Three, sometimes four times a day I come out of the cell for slop out. The last one before bang-up is about seven p.m. Then I balance the bowl of dirty water on top of the chamber-pot. What I see when I look to the right is the SO's office, a wood and glass box. Next to that is the adjudication room where the punishment is dished out, kangaroo fashion. Next along is the serving hatch and the corrider leading up to F Wing, the nonces' wing. Straight in front there's a passageway, on the left a row of cells, on the right the recess, then the clothing store and the bathroom. Past that a bundle of clothes lies outside one of the strong-boxes, one of two cells for 'troublesome' prisoners. This is a cell with neither window nor cardboard block furniture, a cell with two doors where the occupants are forced to leave all their clothes outside and wear a space-suit, as it's called, an untearable pyjama suit of shiny material, usually blood-stained.

All the cells are full, *chock-a-block*, as someone says. A lot of the guys want out of this prison; one or two say, 'On the wing, down here, there's no difference, it's all a block.' From what they've been placed on report for, I get a good impression of the pettiness of the wing: *spending too long in the recess; slamming a door; not wearing a T-shirt in the recess; not being on the landing when required to be*. And they all lose remission.

Four times a day, the nonces from F Wing walk past, going and coming from work. The guys in the first and last cells on our side can see them; in the middle we can only see their feet. This is our entertainment. We coat them off rotten. As usual I'm creased up laughing. Some guy at the end has a great line in verbal: 'You shitty bastards, you horrible ugly reptiles, swamp monsters. Going down to the swamps are you? You fucking animals.'

They pick up gravel and throw it over the fence at our cells. Some try a bit of verbal back: 'Yeah, an' we'll do your kids when we get out.' This provokes a barrage of abuse: 'Go on you monsters, you ugly toad-faced bastards, you lumps of fucking dogshit, gercha!'

At night when there are no nonces and we're feeling bored, we'll coat the dog handlers: 'Get your prick out of that dog's arsehole,' someone shouts out, and another guy: 'He's a dog-lover. That's not a dog, that's his wife.' 'Same thing, innit?' There's one who gives us some back: 'Do your bird, you fucking scum. Can't do your porridge, you cunts can't.' He's our favourite target. By now they must dread walking past our side.

The exercise yard is divided up into small sections. Large thermalite blocks, topped like all the walls with barbed wire, separate me from the next guy walking or running in tight little circles. There's a camera for each section, trained on the door that leads into the exercise area, another on the door leading through the high wall to God knows where. Down one side the security fence, on the other side two screws with pocket radios. A prison within a prison within a prison, *ad infinitum*. Coming through reception the van went through six 17′ gates, all topped with razor wire.

D has come down from the wing. 'Hassle from the wing screws,' he says. He's been put on GOAD. That night we all have a smoke: someone on exercise found a piece of puff that a screw dropped from his pocket. By hook and crook we've managed to distribute the puff with enough matches, papers and tobacco, (in block lingo: cabbages, sardines and salmon) for us to have a good night. The best radio, the biggest, is put up to the window and turned up full volume.

More time slowly comes and goes. The only thing that marks the time here is the change in food. I know it's Sunday by the cornflakes for breakfast. Block always increases the appetite, even libido, having something to do with sensory deprivation, no doubt. I have a crappy paperback that I know I won't read. I chose it because there's a picture of a woman on the cover. Pathetic really.

D is having trouble. It's evening slop out. I hear a commotion coming from down the passage by the recess. Raised voices, several talking. Putting my ear to the door I hear the big screw saying, 'You've been told the routine down here, you don't wash clothes in the recess. Now get back to your cell. NOW!'

D gives a string of verbal. 'What's the matter with you lot? I only want to rinse my trousers for a visit.' His voice comes closer as he nears his cell. 'You're a load of cunts. Nothing but bullies.' Another screw says, 'Get in your cell.'

And then: I've done fourteen weeks. I'm going back to the Scrubs. All my property is once again searched, the reception process in reverse. Strip-searched again, the screw confiscates a safety-pin I've been using to split matches. When I protest he says, 'You could poke an officer's eye out with that.' Yet I'm allowed to keep the biro in my pocket.

I'm so pleased to leave this dump, Britain's Alcatraz.

# 21

# THE HIVE

Our van turns off the Westway into Du Cane Road. To our left we see new blocks of flats, on the right, a school sportsground. This road is always busy with traffic, people standing at the bus stop, schoolkids raucous in their freedom, or nurses walking to or from Hammersmith Hospital, passing on our right.

Then we're turning into the Scrubs' driveway. The van stops momentarily while the patrol screw raises the pole and talks into his radio. The van stops again outside the wooden door. To our right a dog handler is approaching. Looking left and up I see the security camera swivel onto us. The driver blips the horn twice. The huge door slides across. We drive forward and stop in front of a barred gate. The door behind slides back again. We're suddenly silent as the engine is switched off and the street sounds of freedom are cut from us.

Looking to my left I see a window like a bank-teller's. The toughened glass has many cracks and from behind it a screw looks at us without expression. At the bottom of the glass I see a stainless steel dish; this is where the screws pass their keys over before leaving the prison, and collect them when they come on duty. I also see a room busy with screws. On a table two TV screens show unmoving pictures of a concrete wall topped with barbed wire, and an outside view of the door we've just come through. In this short tunnel the walls are bare brick. There's a smell of oil and exhaust fumes reminiscent of a garage. On the right a door, locked from the inside and looking like a cell door with a judas spyhole and clad in metal. Our escorting screws have gone through this door. Somewhere inside they hand over our route forms, swap their numbered brass tallies for their keys, and have our bodies signed over as delivered to the prison.

The screws, our escorts, come out. Travelling in the van they were animated, friendly. Now it's as though the black cloak of prison has settled on us, and we realize there was a clear change in the screws' attitude as soon as we turned into the Scrubs. One is carrying a shoulder-bag containing our travelling files. The SO has a bunch of papers which he's checking. They board the van and the gate slides across. We drive into a fenced-in area. On one side two Portakabins, on the left a fence with corrugated metal sheets bolted to it. On the other side a caged tunnel that leads to the visiting-rooms. I notice we're on camera again.

Ahead a glass-panelled sentry-box. A screw steps out and unlocks the twenty-foot wide gates. We drive through, turn right past the C of E church and stop at another twenty-foot gate. We've travelled perhaps a hundred feet since entering the prison. A screw opens this gate from the inside. We drive into a compound and stop. There's two coaches and a small mini-bus parked empty.

We're next to the screws' mess. Prisoners wearing white jackets and trousers and a T-shirt printed with the word MESS serve them tea and food. Although there's direction in this activity, the air's desultory with an intangible feeling of gloom and despair. We walk past the administration building, a two-storey block, its newness incongruous alongside old Victorian architecture. Alsatian dogs begin to bark. We're in a corner. In front of the wall, an alarmed fence topped with razor wire curtains off fifteen feet of no-man's land. In case weeds should grow in this space, weedkiller is regularly used.

We file off to reception, awkward with our wrists cuffed right wrist across to right wrist. In transit a prisoner must be cuffed to someone, another prisoner or a screw. Entering reception our handcuffs are taken off. We stand in a corrider while the screws process the paperwork. After twenty minutes we're called into the nerve-centre to answer questions: name, date of birth, sentence. This is a small room. The screws busy themselves marking names, courts, dates, on betting-shop boards in chinagraph. The PO screw asking the questions does so while looking at our travelling files. He holds our files close to his chest, each one in turn, checking our answers to the information on them. With a practised eye he also checks the mugshot photograph with the face before him.

Our escort screws are told to lock us up. Our names are called out. We file out into the corrider again. We're locked in a large cell. We've been processed like a commodity, like sacks of potatoes or sheep. The large cell floor is scattered with dog-ends and matchsticks. Yellow paint peels off the walls. The high ceiling has long gone nicotine brown. Muffled sounds seep through the door, the slam of gates and the jangling of keys, the sound that is ubiquitous within the prison. We're fed barely warm food dished out on plastic plates, and tepid tea, called diesel in the lingo, that forms a cold dishwater scum on the top. Amazingly they manage to make it taste the same in every prison.

We're unlocked and called out to check our property, taken from us as soon as we entered the building. In the room I've been called into, I see groups of carrier bags and cardboard boxes. They're all named and numbered. The screw asks me to sign several times on my property card. No explanations are given and I don't ask for any. His unspoken attitude tells me he'd be only too pleased to confiscate many items I've brought with me.

Another screw has entered the room with a prisoner. The prisoner gives me a nervous nod. The screw with him says, 'Williams here wants his address-book. He's off B Wing.' The other screw pulls open a drawer, takes out a large brown envelope and shakes the book onto the table. 'Is this the book?'

Williams stammers a 'yes'. The screw flicks through the pages. I don't think he's once looked at Williams.

'You can't have it.' The tone's final, the sentence barked out with menace. 'It's got a map, an underground map. They're not allowed.' He's put the book back into the envelope and slammed it in the drawer. 'See the Governor if you're not satisfied.' The silence is deafening in its tension. I look at Williams' face. He looks totally bewildered and frightened. The other screw, Williams' escort, looks uncomfortable.

The screw's attitude is pathetic, but there's an element of melodrama and mystery to it all. Williams' little black address-book could be all or nothing. It could contain an address or a phone number, his one link with the outside world, maybe a contact to get bail, a key to unlock the mess of imprisonment and a chance to breathe clean air again. If he can stutter his way through a governor's application he might be lucky.

The screw staples my property cards together, then looks up as though he's just noticed me. His face and tone show boredom, indifference and annoyance, all mixed together. 'Yes?'

'My property. Can I have it?'

'Over there.' He points vaguely, dismissively. 'Tell the next one to come in.'

Outside, in the corridors that lead to locked doors, we stand about, watch screws come and go, sometimes escorting a prisoner or two. When we've all had our property sorted, we'll be locked in again. The wait will be for the doctor to see us. Until he's seen us we can't go on the wing.

At this end the floor slopes down to a locked wooden door and gate. I see one of the prison cats slowly walk up the slope. It seems indifferent to prison and everyone in it. We make *pss pss* noises to no effect. The old moggie is just momentarily distracted. With a slight hesitant step he continues his lugubrious walk, passes us and goes into the reception orderlies' tea-room. This is the cat I once saw dashing along with a starling in its mouth, the bird still flapping its wings and screeching for the last time.

We're locked in a large room. In a corner there's a toilet and showers. Around the walls a bench-seating arrangement has been bolted to the floor, and above this steel sheeting screwed to the walls. Like most things in prison its fixed with one-way screws that have to be drilled out. The floor is covered with grey linoleum. There are three formica-topped tables.

Other prisoners are sprawled along the bench. There is the prison smell of sweaty socks, boiled cabbage, pigswill and musty brickwork. Everyone looks bored, tired and dirty. Conversation is sporadic and mainly monosyllabic: 'Got a light?' 'Wot nick y'from?' One bloke says, 'Fuck this for a lark.' The tone is self-conscious and not meant to provoke a response. We have been waiting for three hours since our property was checked. We arrived at three o'clock. The five hours have worn us down with boredom so oppressive we both look and feel totally worn out.

Eventually we're called in to see the doctor. I walk into an examination room that looks like it was once a cell. The screw says: 'Name and number to the doctor.'

'21963. Wait.'

The doctor looks at me and says: 'Any problems?'

'No.'

And that's it. What was once an examination for venereal disease, body lice, or physical deformities, is now a formality. The system has become too big and overcrowded to care what its incoming clients are like. We're told to gather our belongings and follow the screw. We walk down the passageway, out through the barred gate, and cross the gap between D Wing, the lifers' wing, and the reception block. Then up a few steps, worn down by the passage of feet since the nineteenth century. The screw unlocks a barred gate, then a wooden door at the end of D Wing. On each side is another barred gate that leads by spiral stone steps up to some kind of turret. At the bottom of the steps I see sacks of cement in the half-light, and other stuff that looks like rubbish. The smell is very musty. There's dirt and dust everywhere.

We go through another gate and onto the wing. This end of the wing contains the fishbowls — partitioned wood and glass interview rooms where teachers and probation officers and suchlike see prisoners. Everywhere here space is at a premium. We go down the left-hand side past cells that have been converted into offices for the AGs, the Wing Chief, the censors and the screws' tea-room. The passageways either side are about three feet wide, like the stairs and most of the landings. There's a strange, eerie silence, and then sound echoes from the top landing cells. One of the prisoners is shouting and banging his door. We walk past one of the four ground-floor recesses, where the constant smell of urine blends into the pigswill smell from the next two cells that have been converted into a wash-up room for the meal trays and swill bins. I am led up to the third landing. As I walk along behind the screw I can hear distant sounds from each cell door: radios mostly, one a tape player blaring out 'Dire Straits' — the irony is not lost on me.

When we reach the cell, the screw puts my cell card into the card holder which is on the door. He unlocks the door and asks me if I want to get water. First I check the piss bucket. It's filthy and stinks and is half full of urine. I take it along with the water jug to the recess. In the recess the hot-water tap is running. I leave it running and hope it stays that way all night. I'm not that bothered by the bad smells: living with them every day, year in, year out, I'm now used to them.

As soon as I step back into the cell, the screw slams the door shut. I've a pillow-case stuffed with two dirty-grey sheets, plastic comb, stick of shaving soap, plastic knife, fork and spoon, and a pint-sized tea mug. There's a thin foam pillow and two rough woollen blankets on the mattress. The cell smells of urine, grease and dirt.

This is D Wing, the hub, the grumbling hive. I'm home.

# THE HUB: D WING

# 22
# THE BIRDMAN

He is a red band, trusted to move about outside the wing without escort and to work unsupervised, and because he knows birds and his work is to look after them, he is most often to be found in the bird house, the aviary by the west door of D Wing, the lifers' home. Cage birds, prerogative of long-term prisoners, are housed here, prisoners from the egg, bred to be the cell mates of the long distance men, one of whom is this man, stooping among the perches and nesting-boxes. He is their keeper, their orderly, assigned a plum job in the underworld. As a red band he gets about outside hours when other men are normally banged up, and he has two large aviaries and an inner sanctum and the company of the birds to himself. Over noon lock-up he is often there, a grey face at the glass looking out from the grey pools of his eyes, the figure of a man filling out his shadow among the other shadows. A quiet man, softly spoken, he's found his task in prison and clearly relishes it, and the interest and independence and privacy it allows him, living in a wider cage than most, with the birds whose needs and ways he understands.

These birds are prison for the use of, budgies mostly, since that's what a man may keep one of in his cell, in a cage. The door shut, he lets the bird out into the larger cage of the cell they share, a meditation on the relativity of freedom. The bird is a companion, a focus for interest and study, something to share. There is an education class inmates can go to on Cage Birds, there is a large section of the library devoted to their care. For some it is their only relationship with another creature, and the birds move with them to other prisons, and may come out with them at the end. They buy them from the prison from their private cash, for about ten pounds a bird. All this represents commitment: ten quid takes a long time saving out of £2 per week wages; the bird has to be looked after, fed, birdseed and bells bought. For an inmate, such an acquisition may be a major step; for the prison it is some sort of assurance, perhaps a turning point, of the man's future good behaviour, and such an assurance has to be earned in the first place. If he goes down the block he will lose the bird. The bird represents the fact the man has settled down to prison, that he is *doing his bird*.

In the aviary the birds breed and feed and fly about their perches, a great nest of songs inside wire mesh. Though not available as pets, there are other birds in here: red-beaked finches, small and ever busy, pink and yellow canaries whose melodies against the wire perform ironic counterpoint to the clumsy orchestrations of prison life, and grey and yellow cockatiels screeching at the other birds. And rabbits, chewing on the sprouting millet.

It is a cliché. Men in prison adopt birds, and, themselves in a cage, cage others. A man is allowed only one bird, a budgie, and there's to be no mating. Up on the threes there's a sign on the board that says *Any inmate found with another inmate's budgie in his cell will have both budgies confiscated and both be put on report.* It's odd to think grown men have passed such a rule and troubled to letter a sign to say so, or that there might be such a rule that could be broken, but in such a place as this, tension forms around the slightest and pettiest incident; advantage can be taken over any weakness; attachment, even to a bird in a cage, can be picked at. A man showed me a note he'd found on his bed, along with a feather from his missing budgie. It had been nicked. The note was a ransom. They wanted an ounce of tobacco left in the recess at the start of association, or the budgie came back dead. Another man's bird was found dead, pinned through the neck to the notice-board. 'There's a killer on the wing,' men said. Not every prisoner loves the birds.

Over such matters grown men weep. Most prisoners are fascinated by birds, by images of freedom and departure and flight, passengers and migrants over huge distances. Many write about them in poems and songs: the sparrows, pigeons and crows of the prison yard who eat the bread slices skimmed out of cell windows. And there are hawks, preying on the lesser birds. The symbolism holds. From time to time there are great disputes, when the crows gang up to drive off the hawks, and the sparrows hide in amongst the razor wire where the sparrowhawks can't manoeuvre. In kinship men feed the wild birds with scraps, with margarine, with food they cannot eat. They write poems in which they soar over the wall and fly to warmer foreign places. They envy birds, whose lives in reality are endless reconnaissance and hunting. As are their own.

Some pigeons have moved into the wing, and live among the high timbers of the roofbeams, and strut about, and occasionally amongst them there are sparrows and escaped budgies. Up on the fours there's bits of carpeting and bedsheets to shield men below from droppings. Men find it odd that birds shelter in such a place, and envy their ability to leave at any time.

On the four landings of the wing, unlocked men briefly hang about, walk back and forth, or lean over the railings, their hands tucked behind them, looking all about themselves, never still for long, always on the move, peering down the long barn of the wing, rocking back and forth and restless, as if perched, themselves like birds. Jailbirds.

Suddenly the Birdman's gone. He vanished, down to XYZ, some said. He'd shown me the cockatiels he'd bred, and in the aviary I'd been following their progress from eggs to chicks, when suddenly they were all dead. Killed, he said, by the other birds. Then he was gone. The story was, he'd got into a fight with one of the heavies, a South London villain with connections everywhere. In the fight he'd bitten off the man's ear, and for his own protection been moved out rapidly, ghosted in the early morning.

Everyone here is on the way somewhere else. Another man is orderly on the aviary now. Indifferent, the birds strut and preen their feathers, moving up and down their perches, and at noon when the prison falls sleepily still, the canaries seek whatever corner of the sunlight falls their way and sing.

# 23
# ON THE WING

The wing: huge and noisy when men are out of their cells, queuing for meals, making aps, moving about. It is a vast long barn on four storeys of iron landings, cells regularly spaced high into the roof area. At either end double iron doors, and the main doors at the middle by the movements desk, the centre of control, and all this space broken up by metal stairways and crossways on which sit glass boxed offices for the landing officers, their outlines always visible against the light. Along the landings rising into the roof-beams, the cell doorways, regularly spaced, like the cells of a honeycomb. At the far end, two strip cells, windowless and without furniture. Older men and new inmates under close watch are billeted on the ones. Above them, dark mysteries on the landings and in the recesses: the twos, the threes (known as married quarters), the remote fours. On the ground floor — the ones — canteen, tea-room, offices for staff, Welfare, Probation, Education, the recesses, a chapel cell decorated with posters of coy animals and trees in blossom, and at the south end a series of glass-sided interview rooms, the fishbowls. With the men on the wing the place fills with noise: boots, voices, orders, keys, locks, doors, gates, chains, kitchen pans, the dogs barking in the compound, the rasp of the tannoy like a disease. Suddenly at noon, at bang-up time, an eerie calm settles, a silence punctuated by birdsong and telephones.

D Wing, the lifers' wing, paranoia central. Here some 250 long-sentence prisoners live their cloistered lives, for years together. Most are lifers, the bulk of them for murder and crimes of great violence, about half of them for rape and worse. In single occupancy they each live in cells 8 feet by 12, minimally furnished, poorly ventilated by one small window, hot in summer and cold in winter and subject to the seasons as determined by the boiler-room. Some say the walls close in. Some know exactly how many bricks there are in each of their four walls. There are a few short-sentence men up on the fours, for unknown reasons, but most men here are serious business.

Across from the east side of the wing, the nurses' hostel of Hammersmith Hospital provides regular entertainment, regarded by many men as a wind-up. A new man on the wing explained how when he'd first come here the tapping on the heating pipe would wake him. Then he worked out what the signal was: standing on the pipe and looking through his window he saw a nurse, naked, posing before her window. A wind-up. Most men believe the nurses are told the wing is full of nonces, to engender their contempt. Lower down, the rest of the view is less inviting: wall, fence, wire. From the other side there's nothing to see but C Wing, and the distant scrubs, and far away to the north-east the two-dimensional outline of high-rise central London and the Telecom tower.

The place is full of eyes, watching, like the mosaic vision of the bee. And ears listening, and talk. Two centuries ago, when Jeremy Bentham was commissioned by the Government to design its prison at the Millbank, he came up with what he called his Panopticon, a great birdcage affair where the solitary miscreants were under constant observation. Bentham's design was quietly put aside, but Du Cane's prison, built a century later, is only a more solid version; surveillance and observation under confinement is its business still, but unlike Bentham's proposal, the prisoners are not visited by the public for conversations on their crimes. D Wing, built as a women's prison, where the cells are slightly smaller (women, for the Victorians, presumably requiring less space in which to repent), was intended for the rule of silence and solitude. For a time prisoners here were hooded. On some cell walls the socket where the crank was is still visible.

At afternoon unlock men appear and disappear to work or education, others stay in on the wing. The officers disperse, the PO goes into his office, a sign that life is normal. Work resumes: the painting of the pipework, the refurbishing of cells, the pushing of brooms, the paperwork. Men make their journeys to the tea-urn, some, bolder than others, hang about. Officers and civilians go about their business — teachers, nuns, priests, the man from AA, welfare, probation. Down by the fishbowls a man sets up his barber's chair, and cuts another man's hair. In the passageway, Ginner's trying to do some business with the Guvnor, knocking at the office door knowing that he's in there but getting no answer. He waits, he turns and lopes off, his mad red hair flaring behind him, loudly muttering 'overfucking worked, aren't they', over and over. In the fishbowl I'm listening to Jimmy with his guitar singing a song he's written, wondering why is Jimmy allowed a guitar, when Frank isn't, and why is Frank allowed a melodeon instead, from which he conjures his strange, sad music of prison? Jimmy doesn't know. He has an idea for a film: scenes of ordinary life, of domesticity, of love, each broken by the slam of a cell door and the word *life*, repeated and repeated: *life*, *life*, *life*.

Here you never know the truth and rarely come to the bottom of anything. In maximum security the condition is inarguable: as little information as possible is given out. There are official and unofficial versions, and there is silence and indifference, matters of record and matters not, and variations in between, and in these parts fact and fiction are yin and yang of each other. 'Everything is written in in pencil,' Ross remarks. 'Nothing's permanent. It is the empire of the chinagraph.' Crowded and confined as prison is, its constituent units more or less sealed off from each other, it's not a place where information's abundant. It is a rumour factory of many tongues, where very little can be soon worked up into a story, and D Wing is its own particular dimension of the purgatorio.

It's said to be relaxed, though there are days when the tension is abrasive and sulphorous, taut as cheesewire. By comparison with the other wings, with remand and the local, this place is indeed relaxed. Control is something short of rigid, men slightly more often out of their cells, moving about the wing. At exercise and mealtimes the wing down on the ones is a crowded, noisy place, a busy thoroughfare in hell. On this wing there are marginally more privileges and the rules may be ever so slightly toned down, sometimes overlooked, for the sake of a smooth running ship and in the interests of man-management. There's humour hereabouts, barbed though it usually is, between inmates and betimes between guards and prisoners. 'I'll take the cock out of your walk,' a screw says sarcastically. It's half a joke, though at the man's expense, and he's expected to share in it. Sometimes it takes the edge off situations and eases the otherwise unbearable, the grease of difficult communications. It's usually a cruel humour: 'My mother died.'/'Oh, was it an accident?' In here the difference is that for all inmates this is, whether they accept it or not, and very few of them do and none of them like it, home. For some lifers this can be a better gaff: such terms are relative. For London villains it's only down the road for visits, far better than distant Parkhurst or remote Dartmoor, and given time and determination and a sentence to serve, it can be just about bearable; better, some say, than more modern prisons, where they feel like the ratchets on the clock wheels. Compared with Parkhurst, one man said, the wing was easier. In Parkhurst, he explained, the first thing is to get a blade and a wedge for your door.

All the same, it's a heavy sort of place that provokes a sharp intake of breath on entering, abandoning all hope, where the wise and even the stupid are ever watchful. Into the destructive element plunge yourself. If in doubt, blend into the wall. A dangerous place, there are few guidelines other than those of common-sense. Information isn't easily got. Such notices as there are, amount to the bare essentials of church, education, ground-rules, mail and laundry deadlines, the prices in the canteen. The official prison mode is secretive by second nature, security its warrant, and prisoners are not provided with, and find it difficult to get, copies of the rules that bind them. Everything is assumed to be a secret, and some things are, and prison authorities have traditionally shielded their activities and their regulations from both inmates and the press and public at large. Inside, there are no assemblies or general announcements, and no such thing as a newsletter; meals are eaten alone in cells; the tannoy gives out only orders. Work parties, classes, gym groups, are all kept small. Word gets around, and gossip is an urgent currency, but often what's said to be true depends on speaker and context, and most communication depends upon a willing suspension of disbelief. The grapevines and the gossip mills are all the unreliable sources of information, unattributable and unfootnoted. Research is a difficult and often risky endeavour. All questions must be thought out beforehand and phrased right. There are few explanations where there are any. An order is its own explanation. In such a place speculation and paranoia are commonplace.

'A somewhat cellular existence,' Ross terms it. For a time during the April

1986 prison riots around the country, tension was high, though few lifers would have welcomed trouble, and there was none here. To calm everyone down, a ration of Mars Bars and ten cigarettes was doled out from the Governor's fund. The tension dissipated, blending into the larger tension of the world around. For a time after Chernobyl and the Libyan bombings it was hard to know which to worry about most, the inside or the out. The prison's security status was amber to red, but so was all of Europe's.

So there is only the web made of a few baldly stated facts and overstated rumours, and bits of disinformation. Most remain quiet, and say nothing. Many are sunk into suspicious silence. Some speak with largactyl thickened tongues. Some babble and are mad. Prisoners themselves, always on the defensive, give out little, and much of that misleading, whether in self-delusion or by intent. What's said is often double meant, backwards, upside-down talk, couched in asides and much under the breath, serious matter expressed as a joke, and *vice versa*. Questions come as statements, statements as questions. By nature and by necessity inmates conceal, distract, dissimulate, whether they're criminal or not, their codes the underworld's, and always there's the injunction against grassing. In this environment talking and grassing can be one and the same. Therefore, so much of what's said is harmless, useless fan-fan, merely passing the time of day, and must be sifted for content. A man may talk of one thing but be working at another, speaking in a subjunctive ulterior-motive mood. Invariably, there are several subtexts.

For all that, most are direct and to the point; there isn't time for messing about. Most say only the minimum. Where any information, however mundane, can be used to their disadvantage, whether by officers or by other cons, they don't give out any. And there's disinformation, the fox weaving in and out of his own trail. The fact is men like to talk, and some are garrulous. Often, devoid of context or a perspective of the outside — of whatever the 'real' world might be to them — they speak from unidentifiable and indeterminate positions. In so much rigidity there's much ambivalence. Where two or three are gathered together they speak of themselves but not much to each other: conversations come down to simultaneous monologues, where each man tells his tale but doesn't listen in his turn, though they vie with each other. They are each other's cynics, best and worst critics, and doubt everything from the beginning. Where men are mates there's some trust. Over the years relationships and attitudes build up; they share a history that blends into the unknown history of the wing, they share jokes and unspoken references and prison talk, but in reality most of these men are strangers to each other, and most are solitaries from every sort of background and experience. Some are illiterate and some have Ph.Ds. But for their long sentences and being dressed in blue, most have little in common with each other. Therefore they check each other out carefully; some know each other from other nicks, from other nickings, but the overall condition that the host of them share is that each man is alone here, 15 hours out of every 24, plunged intermittently into the crowd of each other. Only the weekends vary the routine, and then more often they are banged up longer, each with himself and what happens in his head. Christmas, the annual tick in the year's clock, passes in near total bang-up. In the summer, when officers take vacations, shorter rosters mean yet more bang-up, and there's always under-manning to put the bite on exercise or education or association. The routine is unremitting, week by week and year after year, and most lose track of time. Only the seasons come and go. Prisoners here are suspended in time, lonely together, brought face to face every day with themselves and encouraged to consider the errors of their ways, whether they do so or not; the opportunities for self-deception are as ever many, and the lie repeated over and over begins to have the ring of truth about it.

Whether or not this regime provokes regret, change of attitude or character, or merely breaks the violent into wary submission, the most immediate concern of all prisoners is their imprisonment. Our question — whether prison works— doesn't much divert them. Later perhaps. Asked, most say it doesn't, and shrug, themselves their own evidence. For all of them, their chief concern is their relationship with authority, with the institution that so intimately wraps them around. Most bear a deep grudge, and a strong conviction of injustice, justified or not. They lose track of time and the outside, their thoughts forever interrupted. They exaggerate. They underestimate. Often, in time, they lose touch with credibility and reason. In the telling, so many details are left out, taken for granted. Theirs is a dialogue of deaf ears and things unsaid. They tell tales of themselves in which the minutae have been honed from much retelling, aloud or silently to the self, to others pressing their own tales, in which the nub of the narrative may be left out, in which there are additions and deletions. What's not said is often what's significant. Salient facts may be missing, the tale pitched in the best light until it has long left its moorings in reality.

Sundry religious groups meet from time to time — the Catholics, the Muslims, the Quakers. Diets can be kosher or halal or vegan. And there are many languages and cultures, and all classes are represented: the West Indians forming into a posse and hooting two-tone siren music when the alarm bells go off, as they often do, and the duty heavy squad starts running; Slavs and sundry Europeans, Arabs, Armenians, Palestinians, Iranis, a mysterious Greek born in the Russian diaspora after the civil war and with a long record of violence; various Africans, miscellaneous Asians, the Sikhs, four of whom from one family are in for murdering one of the brothers' wives, because she had become Westernised, they said. Chiefly she had objected to her husband's handing over his wages to his mother, and to living in her house. Another Sikh had strangled his sister because she had taken part-time work after school in a supermarket. To him that was the same as being a whore, he'd said in his defence, and that, according to his culture, he had the right to take her life. And there are two lone Vietnamese, arrived here as boat people and now doing umpteen lifes, convicted after a Chinese gambling club in Soho was firebombed and many people burned to death. One of them is in the *Guinness Book of Records* for it. They never understood what was happening to them, a young officer says. They cannot speak much English.

As one of the eight dispersal prisons in England and Wales, the Scrubs takes newly convicted lifers and long-sentence men into the dispersal system from a line south of the Wash and Bristol Channel. This means it also takes in lifers from distant remnants of the vanished empire, from the armed forces and outposts such as the Falklands, one man who came from St Helena. One who came from Jersey was under sentence of death there, where the death penalty exists, but no one wanted to carry out the sentence, so he was sent to D Wing. One man explained that all he'd ever see of England was the road between Heathrow and here, and then back again at the end of it; a Philippino who had gone to work on Diego Garcia, an island in the Pacific under British administration but leased as a US base, he had been convicted there and sent to the Scrubs to do his sentence. Others are graduates of exotic foreign institutions, one a man who had spent time in a Greek prison in Athens, who reported on the imprisoned colonels of the deposed junta living high on the prison hog there. One man explains how, in a French prison, you're just locked up with a cellmate for the duration, with a toilet and an insulating coil to cook your own grub with, and a TV if you can afford to rent one.

Most men I met casually around the wing, hanging about in the Education cell, and falling into talk. Most contact was one-to-one. Alone, men would open up; in each other's company they would clam up, keeping the conversation in neutral. With about eight men interested in 'writing', whatever it meant, we organized a weekly Monday-evening workshop on the wing. It was difficult to get agreement for. Since the D Wing riots in 1979, civilians have been discouraged by the officers from coming into the wing on evening association, but I didn't want to meet a 'class' brought under escort — under the heading 'Education' — over in what is optimistically called 'The College', an old warren of classrooms formerly the administration building, and prior to that, the maternity unit and hospital for the women's prison. On the precedent that the nuns and the man from AA came in the evenings, we were assigned the chapel cell opposite the movements desk during association time. In there, with the door on the spring and unseen officers hovering beyond, we attempted what we could among the prayers and the pretty posters, and drank a lot of diesel. Most evenings the officers showed their disapproval by unlocking late, or forgetting one of the prisoners. More often than not they would arrive wound up, and I learned not to fight it, letting them sound off. Most prisoners live in a permanent state of indignation, and aren't — when they're around each other — visibly repentant. They are concerned with prison. Only with the week's anger off their chests could we get round to anything else, and always prison intruded, via the tannoy, via conversation. Largely, it was their only frame of reference. Therefore I encouraged them to talk, and to turn their talking into storytelling, to notice both the how and what of their talking.

'You've got new teeth,' one man says to another. 'No, I've not,' he replies. 'He's got my teeth,' a third man says. 'No, I've not,' says the second man. 'It's a new mouth.'

Quick. 'All prison talk,' they said. 'No one wants to know.' I begged to differ. It was a matter of convincing them that what they said and the way they said it was important. I, for one, was intrigued.

'Men will only tell you what they want you to hear,' I heard. And there were many such warnings. 'Don't bring anything in. Don't take anything out. Don't do any favours, however small. Don't make any phone-calls. Don't get into it, anything. Stick to your business.' These are the simple rules, and they're easy to keep. And there was always the censor to consider, and what a man might say in a letter. One man, talking about writing to his wife, said, 'Suddenly I realize, every time, that they can hear me. They're always listening.' Amongst others, Billy warned me: 'A man might ask you to take something out, and grass you up on the way through the gate, just for the satisfaction of it, so we'll say goodbye now, shall we?' One civvy told how he'd felt sorry for a man who'd complained his girlfriend didn't visit, so he called the number for him and spoke to her, asking would she please come to see him. It was the woman the man was in prison for raping, extending the leash of his violence, using another as his instrument. Some are evil, and cunning comes in many guises.

But 'paranoia is a sign of good health around here', an officer said, and I agreed. I had brought my own paranoia with me from the outside, and my own chilly fears of muggery and thuggery and rape, burglary and mayhem and murder, were mirrored by the inside, where all were in a crowd of the convicted men themselves the authors of many contemporary nightmares. Sometimes a glimpse across a yard at a work-party threw up the tattooed horror of a young man self-mutilated with crude blue swastikas, five o'clock shadow on his skull, and NF and HATE scratched into the rest of him. Another, encountered under escort in the library wearing yellow E-man stripes, had had the entire left half of his face and all the visible rest of him skilfully tattood with birds and exotic flowers and fruit, a self-labelled schizophrenic. And the air of danger bore its own frisson, from those with ABH and GBH written on their souls and the baby burglars and muggers of the local prison, and God knew who on remand, and, on the life wing, killers, some of recent and notorious headlines, some terrorists or others who would take a hostage if they could, some just plain dangerous, mean, stupid, desperate, insane, or psychopathic. Some, an officer helpfully explained, had the brains of squeegee mops. 'As much grey matter as a custard pie.'

What was difficult to know was where anyone was coming from. One man had invented his own alphabet and code, and wrote in it in secret. Some were balmy, some messianic, inventing systems and religions of their own devising. On the wing, a man burst in on me one afternoon, agitated and upset about something. I hadn't seen him before, and there were no preliminaries as to who he was or who I might be or whether he could trust me. Visibly, he was afraid of something. He wanted a favour. In a hurry. He needed a phone-call, and me to make it for him outside. 'I want my vonga,' he said, meaning his money, his bundle, his fifty notes well wrapped, probably for a gambling debt. For a moment I thought he meant an instrument, like a banjo. Would I call his grandfather? *No, John. No way.* He steamed on. He had a visit coming. He needed something bringing in: money. *No way, John. It'll never happen.* Later, in the records, in the hall of mirrors, I found he was doing life for killing his grandmother in a tearup of a drunken rage. He'd beaten everyone up, including the old man, but she had died of her injuries. He'd wanted me to call her widower.

And there were dreams, in which faces surfaced in the crowded wing to remind me of a promise, always unspecified, dreams in which I let them all out on terrified London, and the long spirals of older dreams began to resolve themselves into the turrets and landings and stairways of the wing. Between the night's dreams and the outside and stark waking moments inside, there seemed little difference: the same thick air of oppression and suppressed fury, the tension of ever potential violence, the same whiff of fear and threat and loathing, the incessant rumours of injustice. Outside, I began to see faces that I thought were inside, and *vice versa*. At the beginning, I had dreamed of the hive. I was trapped inside a great sealed behive, with all the bees, and none of them able to get out, and all of them angry. The hive was a great yellow barn, its walls divided tier upon tier into cells, the octagonally shaped doorways of the honeycomb repeating regularly along the perspectives of the landings, and everywhere the bees and their ready stings. And no honey.

I was caught in the great babel of tongues of the unlocked wing: men queuing for lunch or supper, others about their business, some just hanging out, the grumbling of the great beehive broken by commands. From silence, voices would suddenly break out from everywhere, and in the hubbub words fall out of their sentences, language out of its sockets amongst the range of contexts, tones, accents, meanings, mishearings. Contact times were short and hurried, each man wanting to talk alone, and sometimes several talking at once, ignoring one another's presence.

In all this racket of voices and boots and iron, the blandest remark became significant, worried by irony and busy with meaning. One noon with everyone else locked up with their lunch and only the officers winding down and the kitchen crew banging canteens into the trolley, in the strange sudden hush a man sang:

*I'm nobody's child*
*I'm nobody's child*

and another voice echoed down the wing: 'No fackin' wonder, the fackin' things you've done.' Here and there, sudden rage, the easy eruption of a fight, of protest, or some gone mad in it all: a man sitting on the table by the movements desk with a hymn-book and in full voice singing:

*Christ is my Saviour, Christ is my Song,*
*Walking with Jesus, all the day long.*

No one takes any notice. He's practising for the choir. Or the angry voice of a prisoner arguing with his landing officer somewhere in the high galleries: 'It's not my fucking cell. It's your fucking cell.'

I mishear things, misjudge the context of remarks, fall in with savage conversations, encouraging, as I'm supposed to, the telling of tales, loosened up in so much broken language. On the one hand is a monotony of barked orders; on the other, a range of ambiguous responses, including silence. Hereabouts the public language is macho, tough, often vicious, vaunting, threatening. In moments of privacy, by contrast, there's tenderness, sorrow, shame and regret, love and longing for it. But what's out front is harsh and often horrifying in its bluntness. Fuzzy, telling his own story of how he and his three brothers came to long sentences in the same punchup in which a man died, says 'The claret was everywhere'; Bob, in his safebreaking tale, throws in almost as an aside 'so I hit the first one with an iron bar, but I didn't know he was a copper . . . ' And B, brought reluctantly and at length to speech, tells a tale of horror that for a while shuts everyone else up:

'I've only thought about all this recently. Years ago, when I was a kid. I was involved in a murder. Not this one. In Wales. It was a woman was killed. She was cut up and cooked and put in sandwiches. I ate some of them. Later, I was instrumental in fingering the man that did it. I know it was all baloney. Anyway, I was brainwashed, and I went to prison. I went mad, and didn't remember it for a long time.'

All that saves most of it from breaking into violence, apart from the obvious restraints of officers and the block and violence itself, is a thin sliver of humour running through most transactions. An officer, barking out an order, seems to retain an edge of humour in his voice: 'You. I shan't tell you again. Do you want it in semaphore or shall I give it you in braille? Fucking do it.'

It's difficult at times to penetrate tones, to read them. One afternoon talking with Jim, surrealist, painter, life prisoner, sometime extremely violent man, implacable hater of authority, a tough man with volcanic depths of anger in him always close to the surface, years in and still angry, an officer came up. He butted right in, as they do, and drew his finger across Jim's throat in a deadly eyeball-to-eyeball gesture: 'Don't ever do that again,' he said, of whatever. 'Don't you ever do that again.' He was a short, rotund, fiftyish man, and Jim towered over him, his arms folded, tolerant, eyeballing back, blanching, losing face by backing up. His face tightened as he bit back on it all, and then his eyes dropped. 'Aye' was all he said, with a chagrined sort of laugh, and the faintest of grins crossed both men's faces, as the officer turned away.

Jim's paintings are bold oils: brick walls he paints with scrapings of brick dust mixed with paint, distant mountains, birds made of stone and bricks. What he was telling me was apposite of my own confusions, and fell into the tracks of stories I had heard elsewhere. It was not merely that men often left out the essential information in their stories, nor that the contexts were so various. Sometimes I didn't hear right. A man says, of something, 'Oh, I forget', but in my ear it sounds like 'fuckget, fuckit'. Another man has been reciting Longfellow in my other ear; it was a long poem and he knew all of it, and when I turned onto the wing, there was Jim with a sequel to the dildo story.

A couple of months back, there was a tale of a dildo being found in a cupboard some officers were clearing out on A Wing. What would anyone be doing with a dildo in the all-male universe of a men's prison was the question then, and here again was the dildo, or the image of it. It seems the dildo has become apocryphal. As Jim told it, for a joke, two officers planted the item in a man's cell. As a joke, we were to understand. I thought Jim said the man's name was Yahmani, a PLO terrorist, but Jim in his broad Belfast made it sound like *Yer-man-here*, so it was Everyman. So then they raid him in a mock spin, and pull back his pillow, and there, surprise, surprise, it is: 'What's this then?' And so forth. Under his bed is a bucket. Hooch, for which he's nicked. So far he's not laughing at all, nor is the Guvnor on adjudication, where there's no mention of the dildo.

Then worse. Because the joke undermines his image, some of the hard men challenge Yer-man-here and pull a blade on him. He doesn't want any. He's not laughing, and none of this has anything to do with him. He backs off. 'His arse is gone,' the hard men say, macho honour satisfied. 'Leave him.' But there's a feud in it now, and there's a jug of vinegar to be thrown at someone, and a punch-up where one of the heavies gets clobbered, caught without his blade. This is an ongoing story, but one so far without humour, weaving later into Col's report of the man's hooch bust, and that of the three blacks who originally threatened the man with blades, one was moved, and Yer-man-here, finding the odds more to his liking, then turned on the other two, and clobbered one with the leg of his bed. Yer-man's been moved, and the other one's in the hospital. The dildo's vanished.

And other tales of terror. The tea orderly is down the block, for throwing scalding water over another man, for reasons no one knows. Unbearable reality and the wildest fantasy cohabit. And there are prison dreams. Tel says he woke one morning, shaking. He'd had a nightmare, in which he was in the war, and captured by the Japanese. They were torturing him. With sharpened bamboo sticks they were knocking out his teeth one by one without benefit of anaesthetic.

'Thank God the tannoy went off,' he says. 'I woke up sweating. I thought "Thank Christ for that, I'm here in my bed. I'm safe. I'm only in prison." And then I thought, "Shit: I'm in prison. I'm here for life."'

Ginner's had a dream in which he was out, free. He was with his brother, doing ordinary things in an ordinary world, he said, when suddenly he looked at his watch and said he had to slop out. His brother didn't understand what he meant. Another man talks about a dream of fishing, on a wide shore, as the tide came in over the beach. Outside, it had been a serious hobby. But in his dream the fish hooked him, and were dragging him into the sea and down, and he was caught, unable to resist the pull into oblivion.

Yet another recalls a dream he'd had, a recurring nightmare, in which he'd dreamed ahead many times in his life what happened in the end. In the dream he ran down a narrowing lane, with armed police on either side and someone he was responsible for, and was firing back. 'It all came true,' he says, of what turned out to be a domestic row with his girlfriend in which he'd taken her hostage with a gun in her flat surrounded by armed police.

Just prison dreams. 'I've had the same dream over and over,' Simon says. 'I dream the judge invites me back, and I go before him in his robes and his wig, and he says all this has been a dreadful mistake, and he's very sorry, but I'm free to go now. It won't happen.'

Stan says he's written some stories. He's shy, reluctant, keeps forgetting to bring them down with him, though he eventually does. They're short jokey tales of marriage and domesticity, as he recalls it. He explains, he and his wife were on holiday in a caravan, and went drinking. They ended up back in the tiny caravan in a two-by-eight, and he says to shut her up he sat on her face. He didn't mean to suffocate her. The strange thing about his stories is that half of them are hers, from her point of view, written in a different, feminine, hand. Stan shows them to another man, who asks me what I think. What he thinks is that Stan's up there in his safe talking to her, and listening to what she says. 'He's having the voices', the other man says 'up there in his peter. A lot of us do you know.' And he turns to the invisible man looking over his shoulder and says, 'Never happens to you and me though, does it?'

And most that I never meet, who stay up in their cells and get on with it in silence, old lags or young tearaways, villains from villainous families of criminals. Men who are the third and fourth generations of their families to put in time here. A man explains: some are villains who can't but show off and draw attention, and for whom getting caught and doing a stretch is part of the game, part of the risk. 'Some of them just want to be noticed,' he says, 'so they pull a job and then spread money around till they're nabbed.' And there are men like Tel and Nick, who claim to have been fitted up so as to get them off the streets, not necessarily guilty of the crimes they're convicted of. The anti-logic says some might be in for something else, and their confinement is a bureaucratic nicety encapsulating a public necessity.

And there are some I don't much care to meet: Nicky the Nameless who says, 'Poetry? I've written loads of it. I've got a cell full of it. I'll show you. It's good. It's better than any I've seen.' It's not. It's rehashed school anthology, poorly made and full of ego, and Nick doesn't want to hear my objections, accepts no suggestions, hears no criticism. He's bluff, blunt, brutal in his manner, boastful and without self-doubt, sneering at everyone. He brags about his days around the West End, wheeling and dealing, and in accounting for his life, stops short at the murder he committed, a casual and classic butchery. For him it's dismissed as 'the business'. Drinking, he had met a man, at closing time they had gone to drink more at the other's flat. He claimed the man made a pass at him, and he resisted. At any rate he resisted by fetching the carving knife from the kitchen, stabbing his victim repeatedly, cutting off his genitals and stuffing them in his mouth, carving NF in his back and leaving him with the knife in him. He stole the victim's video and stereo, which, being numbered, were quickly traced to him when he sold them; he was speedily arrested and convicted, almost as if he wanted to be. He's fated, he thinks. It all seems to mean nothing to him. Outwardly he is completely indifferent.

Another claims to have been born with the birthmark of the beast 666 on his arm, burned off by his grandmother. He shows me a scar. Another, a wing whore, complains he's got two broken ribs from a recent encounter. S, who says he regrets nothing, adds that the man he killed he'd kill again. Another proposes to write a book warning the young not to do what he did, along a trail of trouble that eventually ended in a stabbing. I ask him if he thinks the young would read it. Would *he* have read it? He doubts it. And there's Weasel, who cadges off other men though outside he is wealthy, and who is always beavering away at some scheme or other, and whose eyes look everywhere else. No one trusts Weasel, always on the make. He whines continually and they say he can't take his bird when he claims his wife's murder was a simple accident. Billy observes Weasel putting in a canteen order for one packet of Rizla for the week. Jim says Weasel told him he'd pay any amount of money to get out of here. 'You can't even buy your own tobacco,' Jim told him. No one believes him. He'd been so confident of acquittal that he'd been out on bail on the murder charge, and had driven his car to the Old Bailey, so that his first business on coming in was how to get his car out of the parking lot. Outside, his dreadful children are stealing all he has; they had appeared as witnesses against him. My task in life one afternoon is to help him write a letter to them.

Other men drop by casually, on the off-chance of a conversation, welcoming any diversion, or perhaps looking for pen or paper, vague; things go from there. One tall and raw-boned veteran of the system drops by and sits staring across at me, demanding my business. His is simple: to voice his hatred of the system, and of the society that stands behind it. He'd done a life already, and another long term before that, and has recently been brought back in off his licence. His stay might now be permanent. He says he doesn't care any more: 'Because I speak my mind I'm considered aggressive. I speak my mind, that's all. Call me Muzz. It's not my name, and I don't want to know yours either. I really don't give a fuck. I've given up. So let them keep me, and when the time comes the State can bury me. I don't give a shit.'

Some, such as Don, were my mates. Don was wing orderly and I could visit him in his cell on a slow afternoon. It was his home and his office, a comfortable roost, and he was pleased to entertain, as if he were at home, though all he could offer was tea or coffee. He wrote stories for children, and told tales as much about the outside as the in. One week he showed me his case written up in *True Detective*, and argued with the details. He hadn't set fire to the geezer to try and hide the crime; he'd done it to spare his daughter the task of having to identify her husband. It was a family row, in which the son-in-law, a former mercenary and heavy villain, had pulled a sawn-off. Twice he'd fired and twice the gun had jammed. In the struggle Don had wrenched it from him and turned it, amazed to hear the gun go off. He shot him dead, and now he'd do his time for it, but home was where he'd like to be. His cell was covered in pictures of his family, of his house and swimming-pool. I liked Don's East London warmth, his grandfatherly propriety, and recalled the murder from my local paper. Don was resigned and often cheerful. He wrote, kept up his business, studied with the O.U., and acted in the wing drama group: 'Then I can be someone else somewhere else for a while.' He lived in hope of serving out his time to release, and nursed his dicky heart along.

Don explained how prison, for some, is something figured into the accounts. For a villain must accept the risk of being caught, and when in prison his own code obliges him to do his bird as unco-operatively as possible, to get on with it and come out to resume life. For some, he explained, imprisonment can have its usefulness. He told a tale about a man he knew, today a successful businessman, and therefore nameless. Some years ago his friend had developed a chain of shops, financing everything on credit, using credit to build up more. Then deliberately he'd gone bust, sold all his stock at discount, paid off his employees. Secretly, he carried two heavy suitcases of cash by devious routes to the Continent and deposited them. Then he returned, walked into a copshop and said he'd been a very foolish man who'd gone bust and run, and told a convincing tale about being fooled by the love of a woman. They gave him four, and with remission he did two and a half, came out, withdrew the money, and began again in legitimate business. He bought for cash, and in time paid off all his outstanding loans. Don's point was twofold: that if he'd asked the banks for such a loan he'd not have got it in the first place, and that for some prepared to handle it, prison can be made to work.

Within this different world, some more or less adjust. The fact is some are at home here, operating much as they move on the outside, sharks in a dangerous ocean, which is how the Professor describes himself. He's been in many prisons around the world, and is an aristocrat amongst villains, a kyter, an international, a man of many frauds, who regards his eight as largely inconvenient. He is openly contemptuous of most other prisoners. 'Amateurs,' he calls them; he doesn't cut and kill and steal purses. He says he can't see himself as ever doing anything else in life. For him crime is a vocation, a thrill, sometimes a lark. He it was who stole Harold Wilson's obituary and sold it to *Private Eye*. He keeps the bankers on their toes, he claims, describing himself as a necessary virus, stimulating the economy, continually mutating to figure out a way through each technological advance.

For some the routine is easy enough; prison has the same appeal as the Army, and they know where they are in an otherwise uncertain world. They are fed, housed, occupied, their complaints ritualised around the system, in the end their remains are disposed of, and for such men life makes few demands and requires few decisions. For many, the outside is inhabited by landlords, officials, tax gatherers, creditors, debt collectors, nagging wives, nattering children. Inside, they are free of most of this, and to them the outside seems a burdensome place, where debts can be left and promises forgotten. For many, the problems begin when they think about it. As Col describes it, his open palm between his eyes, it's like a wall down the centre of everything, wherever he looks: 'Split vision,' he calls it. If he thinks about the outside, his girlfriend, his family, his mates, he thinks that on the whole he'd rather not be here. He'd rather be on his bike heading south on a warm breeze in April, but it's like he's looking at it all down two sides of a wall. The wall gets in the way of his thinking, whichever way he turns, so that all he sees is the wall, the seamless brickwork of his present tense that separates him from his past, from what he calls his life, and from any future he may have. And if he thinks about being in here, then he's acknowledging the wall. He's looking right at it. Once he asked me, as a favour, to go out and walk right round the outside of the wall, and come back and tell him about it. 'What's happening out there?' he'd ask. Prison constantly reminds the prisoner where he is. Col fights back, notching up small victories, figuring out the paperwork, writing letters, keeping himself fit with basketball and the gym. One day he says he's seen a party of visitors being taken round the prison, mostly young girls. They moved he says 'like mobile flowers'.

Ross speaks of his shrunken world 'extending 100 yards in a westerly direction to work and back, escorted'. Ginner, whose weigh-off slip looks like a supermarket receipt saying two lives, talks of the sea, and his blue eyes mist over. On his arm he carries a sailor's tattoo of a sailing ship and the legend *Homeward Bound*. The dilemma, he says: should he recapture as much of the past as he can in his writing, or should he concentrate on being here, in the midst of a life sentence, and respond only to that? He writes to gather his thoughts, that are scattered here in prison. He finds it difficult to concentrate for long, in the turmoil and constant intrusions of the wing. Yet what to write about: the ever more idyllic past and the ever more imaginary outside, or the hard realities of confinement? The past recedes and the outside becomes more and more unreal. 'And dangerous to think about,' Ross says. But by adjusting his attention to the prison he's in, he fears he'll come to accept it, as his condition, which it is. On either road, unreality and madness beckon.

Some, through study, become proficient in the law, in rhetoric, in sociology. One man applied for books to study chemistry; the Governor turned him down saying he'd no chance of becoming a chemist, to which he whipped back 'But the guy in the next cell studies Westerns, and he's got no chance of becoming a cowboy.' For some, prison is the university of time, a great think-tank of crime and human circumstance, most of it tragic, a vast library of unwritten biographies and stories. Here are the plots of elaborate grabs and swindles, daring and imaginative frauds, tales of detection and discovery, cops and robbers, the ravelling and unravelling of mysteries. Tales are told and lived out here concerning risky and brave adventures involving life and death, the dreams and disasters of love, of marriage, of family, and there are great debates as to freedom, the dreams of it, its loss. Fate they study here in the university of time, and degrees of irony, logic (true and imaginary), practical fascism, resistance, machismo, black humour, paranoia, doubt, fear, the approach roads to insanity. 'There's only three ways to go,' Len says: 'drugs, religion, or madness. And they're all three the same.'

# 24

# THE CARROT SYSTEM

In the background the chatter of keys. We close the cell door to, leaving it on the latch. It's afternoon, and quiet on the wing. In the silences between sounds I can hear us thinking.

'It doesn't get worse, it just goes on being bad,' Scott says, describing prison, meaning his life as a lifer. We're sitting in his cell on the ones, a cramped untidy heap of socks, slippers, books, dropped clothes, brushes and unmade bed. His cell says: Scott hates prison, and he won't make his home in it. The way their cells are, expresses lifers' attitudes to prison; some cells are empty but for a body and minimal furniture, and no personal effects. One or two are bare chapels with a crucifix. Some are cosy, lived in if a little cramped, some are home. Scott's isn't. Just as it is, it expresses how he feels, with untidy eloquence, clean but scruffy.

He goes out and comes back, having found two mugs of diesel. Scott's talking about prison — its daily unremitting repression, its constant insult, in general and in all particulars, to his value in himself as a man. Philosophically, he accepts that he is guilty of murder, and that society requires he be punished, confined and segregated, if only as a deterrent to the rest of us. He thinks much about such matters. He understands the mixed motives of his jailors, divided as they are between advocates of deterrence, punishment, segregation, prevention, and what little he hears of rehabilitation, which he regards as cant. So far as he is concerned, he was already deterred before he committed murder, and a recurrence isn't in his book. His crime sprang out of fury at betrayal, at love's treachery, in a particular circumstance not likely to be repeated. He murdered his wife, and her lover. He regrets it, bitterly. He knows it was wrong. He crossed the breaking point, went out of control, and broke the ultimate commandment. He accepts his punishment, though he jibs at it. That's what he says. On the other hand, the prison is far from convinced yet. It has its own point of view, and takes no account of his. Their business, as he knows, is to observe him, and on their observations determine his future, his parole. Their decisions take as many years as there are. All the same, and long after his release, presumably till he dies, Scott will burn in his own bed of remorse, shame, guilt, love that went bad. He doesn't need, and probably resents, the State's constant reminders of his sins. An intelligent and indeed a moral man, he knows he must be confined for many years, until the heat of his crime dies out of him, or until the powers-that-be are sure he's not likely to kill again.

In that time, over the years of his sentence, he is under constant observation. He is reported on, his behaviour constantly monitored in every aspect and moment of his waking life, and, when asleep, checked frequently through the judas by the night shift. All the reports are steadily updated to build a picture of him. He sees the reasoning of it, but that doesn't mean he has to like it. The picture they are building of him, on which important decisions as to his future will be made, by others but not by him, is a picture he doesn't get to see. He has no control over what goes into it. He cannot affect its outcome. This is precisely what he has lost, and what he rails against: all control over his own destiny. He has forfeited the making of decisions, or any right to order his life or influence others who have power over him. He is caught up in the system, and this is his fate as a lifer. He'll never get used to it. His only options are madness or suicide, or somehow grinning and bearing it.

And he thinks about all of them, from time to time.

Long-sentence men stay here on the Dispersal Unit for the first four years of their sentences, those four years usually stretching into five and six as the slow business of reviews and reports takes its longest time. From the prison's viewpoint, there is no hurry, and such procedures take time, and it's certainty they're aiming for. Eventually, ideally, from here men go to less stringent regimes, dispersed around the system, eventually to open prison, hostel, parole, release. Some fail their time here. Some are sectioned off, mad, for ever. Others are dumped sideways into other prisons, the most troublesome shuffled around the system. The business of this wing is the slow observing of the behaviour of lifers, often men who have committed very violent crimes, over the first quarter of their sentences, and the business comes in the form of reports laboriously compiled. On them each man's next move depends. This is called his 'career'.

Here the staff's duties, then, apart from locking and counting, are making reports in which the minutest idiosyncrasy is noted. Society requires it, though of its nature such a task is endlessly repetitive, petty, bureaucratic, biased, at times whimsical. Prison bureaucracy is necessarily cautious, slow and ponderous and all-powerful, riddled by schisms and interests and rivalries, resigned to administering a hopeless cause society doesn't much care about. Though it presents the singular face of authority, it is in fact many-headed, uniformed and civilian, whose reports from all sides are continuous.

Understandably, prisoners are also suspicious of psychologists, as is Scott. They are also part of the powers that assess him. In prison there are skilled and dedicated specialists, but prison gets to them too. In the end, prison workers, officers or governors or civilians, are touched by cynicism. Idealism, which motivates some, is invariably embattled. In whatever event, for the long-term prisoner the powers-that-be are working for an overview of each man in their charge, compiled from many sources, and all this leading to a summary based on the larger picture: an ultimate decision, somewhere made, as to whether or not a lifer ever comes out of prison. For men like Scott, who cannot stand outside the lives they live, there is no larger picture. There is no objectivity. And whatever reports come back from the black hole Scott's life has become, they are always negative.

I think Scott would be content to be confined in less cramped and abrasive quarters. He's not without his vanity, a certain pride, and keeps himself aloof from villains and nonces and troublemakers. Before all this, his life was expansive, he travelled a great deal, he lived well enough. As a businessman he made good money. He was an engineer, a specialized and highly skilled man, with patents and copyrights in his name, a company he directed, with talent and entrepeneurial skills. In here, his intelligence is starved, his skills uncalled on, and he says it's a shame they can't be made use of. Society, he says, ignores the resources it has in its prisoners, not all of whom are natural sewers of mailbags, and not all of whom are interested in crime. He is a man who would like to be useful, even in his downfall. Perhaps it is his vanity again. In here, where he is merely one of many, his punishment is to be set aside, to be ignored. In here, when he speaks of his former life, other men, officers and inmates, think he is boasting, or telling jackanories, talking about himself again. Envy and jealousy are ready responses here. Scott fits the dictionary definition of the word *prisoner*: *one deprived of freedom of action or expression*. He is locked in here. The fact is that he would accept the sudden poverty of his condition, the absence of much intelligent life and the daily abrasive challenge to his sensibilities, if he could see much purpose in it. He will in any case go on punishing himself each day of the rest of his life for those moments when he lost all control and went over the top. He doesn't have to be made to atone, yet he can think of better circumstances in which to do it. 'On the whole,' he says wryly, 'I'd rather be anywhere else.'

He knows that no one feels sorry for him, nor expects they should, though the big softy in him will always want loving, knowing love won't quickly come his way again. Friendship neither. People steer a wide berth around a murderer. A middle-aged man, he spends a good deal of time thinking of his life beyond his sentence, where with luck and good management he might expect to come out on licence in a few years. He's already done five, and he's bored past bearing, but he's used to it by now, although he'll never start to like it. His struggle is to keep his mind alive. When he comes out he will be older, and prematurely aged by prison. He knows the stress of prison may kill him. He knows he's heart-attack material. And if he makes it, he knows he won't be able to pick up his business, and all the old friendships and relationships that died with his arrest. He'll not simply resume his life where he left off some fifteen years before. He'll still have money, though, other men sneer. He'll have the best of it. His likely prospect is to be a recluse, and that may not be so bad. Whatever happens, his sentence will not end. It is internal. It is self-imposed.

On the wing, Scott doesn't mix much, confines himself largely to men of his own middle-age, domestics like himself, sharing interests in music, thought, books, conversation, sharing aches and grouches, gossip, tea. He is visibly a 'good' prisoner — cynical but practical, making no trouble and out of the way when it comes. All the same, with his intelligence he sees easily through bullshit, and often can't resist pointing it out, picking holes in stern rules often arbitrarily enforced. They think of him as a smart arse, a con merchant. They can't bear it when, as he often is, he's right. Simply, he resents all the messing about, the lengths to which he must go with the simplest request, and the continuing victory of ignorance from the mouths of men set to imprison him. Some of them seem to enjoy taunting sinners. As strategically as he can, he lives a quiet life, reading, painting, writing. His writing is factual matter — historical, technical. He's been an author of reports himself, of proposals and feasibility studies and performance tests. Used to technical writing, he's having difficulty with his imagination. He has a wicked and saving sense of humour. At other times he will turn terribly serious, and say in passing, reflecting from the core of his internal monologue: 'They never considered what it meant when they abolished hanging. They never thought about the alternative.' He confides: there are times when he'd have settled for the rope.

He can't win, and knows it, so he lives without hope, falling back on his memories and his developed sense of irony. Whatever is said of him, it will be bad. In his circumstances, all behaviour is suspect, all actions likely to be interpreted for the worse, all speech — including silence — analysed perjoratively. Prisoners, whose word is taken to be unreliable, are surrounded by hostile witnesses, whose words are gospel.

Like everyone else, Scott is perpetually under review. Because, like all lifers, he is under constant observation and routine reports are frequently made on him, and because in prison there is no such thing as a nil return, the reports are usually negative, and have another story to tell. They sketch another picture of him, and since he doesn't get to read them, he never knows what they say, save for some bits he's gleaned here and there. He says they say he is a violent man. Yes,' he says, 'I was. Once. But that's not my character.' Happen so, Scott, yet to lose control once, and kill, may be judged a crucial aspect of character. In yours, in mine. It's debatable, we say. He says the reports are not. Like the records, they claim objectivity; they're compiled from authority's viewpoints; they may or may not be biased, but they're not debatable. What it says in them has the status of fact, true or not, for on them the decisions are made. The reports say he is very cunning, he's been told. 'No,' he says, 'but I am intelligent.' He explains: in prison there's no such person as an intelligent prisoner; there's only the con-man, the schemers and the dreamers. And then he's heard they say he's an inveterate liar. He throws his hands out. What can he say to that? It's an argument he's not allowed to have, and in any case an argument he can't win. It's all a matter of interpretation. Of viewpoint.

He is a man struggling with his image in the distorting mirror. Everything he believes about himself is turned around. The reports cast doubt on everything he says of himself. All his tales of his travels, of business, of his work, are questionable. It is partly, I suspect, that the makers of reports wish to ascribe nothing good to their subjects: in Scott's case, perhaps they can't believe a man of his intelligence and experience, outwardly successful, would be in here at all, and so they undermine his belief in himself. He must be reduced to the status of a mop. The officers who make reports, monitoring behaviour at work and on the landings, are looking at criminals, murderers, as they are trained to look. The nature of their job, and the lofty heights from which they observe their charges, however close their quarters, angles their vision. By habit they take a sceptical and suspicious view, they are more often cynical and sarcastic. At bottom their proper justification is the question everyone must ask, including Scott: will this man kill again? Can he come out again? It is a vital question.

The fact is that few repeat murder, a fact that constitutes one of the few mildly comforting figures in our crime statistics. But some do, for some are psychopaths, and psychopaths are cunning, and conceal themselves. Some, in prison, kill again, sometimes for no clear reason. And in the interests of eliminating the psychopaths — for the sake of the rest of us — there follows this long and grinding process of diagnostic observation. The psychopath's cunning may outlast it. How would anyone know one? A psychopath is difficult to recognize, even by experts, and for the rest of us, reveals a deranged personality when it's all too late. Therefore, all found guilty of deliberate killing must be closely and lengthily watched for the sake of the difficult-to-detect minority who may kill again, so far as anyone can tell. So far as anyone can tell anything. In prison even those officially considered dangerous — Cat. A's, who are dispersed about the maximum security prisons — are few and far between among the run-of-the-mill of violent offenders. Of some 1500 prisoners in the Scrubs only a handful are classified as Cat. A, and it is chiefly for their sake all the rest must endure maximum security.

Within the system, all matters are of note, and significance given to small signs, to gestures, phrases, facial expressions. If a man weeps it is noted down; if he laughs; if he sneers; if he complains; if he utters a threat; with whom he hangs about; if he's quarrelsome; if he's over friendly; if he's into hooch or protection or dope or homosexuality; if he chooses to remain silent and aloof. Men who have killed in passion are perhaps unlikely to find themselves in passionate circumstance again, when released. But for the possibility that killing may turn into a habit, or that having killed once the personality may be permanently cracked, or prison crack it, there must be this watching, observing, reporting. This *is* prison. Without doubt such monitoring is necessary. Scott understands the 'objective' viewpoint of his mentors, the reasons for it, but he chafes at the daily repetition of it.

I am indebted to Scott for his description of what he calls the carrot system, into which system lifers, coming into prison, are drawn.

Sentenced to life, if there's no minimum recommendation, currently means fifteen years, believed now to be unoffically twenty. Remission is possible, and some life sentences are done in less — in twelve or thirteen, or even ten or nine where a man has managed to keep his nose clean, stay out of trouble, not lose remission for time on the block, show remorse, or otherwise impress his parole board with evidence of understanding, and of change. All this is difficult. Whatever proof of change or regret or maturity he puts forward will be taken on suspicion. It is a long road out, and even then, a lifer's sentence is not over; when released, he is on probation for some years, regulated in all matters as to where he lives, with whom, where he works, whom he meets, whether he marries. His parole officer closely supervises him, and in case of doubt he can be summarily recalled to prison. After release from probation he remains on licence, subject to recall till he dies. In this sense the sentence *is* life, of which the first fifteen years or more are spent in prison. Thereafter he remains under supervision, and must modify his behaviour accordingly. If he gets into a fight or an argument with an employer or his landlord, he can be whipped back inside, without the nod of a judge. Currently this is to be a matter before the European Court. Ours is the only country in Europe where a return to imprisonment can be made on the word of a probation officer, without the say-so of judge or jury.

Faced with such a sentence, the mind buckles, guilty or not. Immediately after sentencing, all lifers (unless they're spies or notorious sex offenders) go straight onto the wing. Usually, convicted murderers are received first into the prison hospital, there to be closely watched and sedated; it is understood they are in shock. Many are immediately suicidal. A few days of this and they begin their time on the wing. They enter the dispersal system, though it will be years before they are dispersed anywhere. Once installed on the wing, on normal location, their business is to get used to it, to adjust to life in long-term prison.

From here, the carrot system takes over. The first move, within twenty-eight days of conviction, is to put in a notice of appeal. Thereafter, a request for appeal follows its course, and this may be denied. Appeal is normally granted only on grounds of fresh evidence or some doubt as to the conduct of the trial or police investigation. For some there's no appeal, but most have some hope of recourse to cling to, and therefore fill their long nights alone reviewing the case, the trial, the sentence. Such hopes keep men going in the early stages. Though they're entitled to their papers and the transcripts of their trial, not all can get them easily. Some briefs provide them. Some prisoners, disappointed with their briefs in the conduct of their defence, have fallen out with them, and find it difficult to get a new lawyer to conduct an appeal and search out the papers. Others find that several hundred pages of transcript cost a lot in xeroxing, and some men have no money outside to pay for it. In any case all this takes time, and many letters back and forth. Business that could be dealt with outside on the telephone, takes weeks and months here. And outside officials dealing with a serving prisoner are cautious, proper, non-committal, at times evasive. Meanwhile, prison becomes familiar, and inmates find others to compare notes with, help them write letters and depositions. Long months fill out with long discussion and silent review. The closest focus, here, between prison on the one hand and the dream of freedom on the other, is on the appeal. Men are distracted by it from the sentence, from its length, from their conviction and their crime. They have entered the carrot system, with its paperwork and study, deadlines to be met, legal visits, requests for hearings, hopes raised and dashed again, the vagaries and customs of the law to be understood, forms of address and supplication to be learned. Most cases, however straightforward the accusation or the crime, turn out to be complex when brought to trial.

Unravelling them occupies a lot of time. There's correspondence, the viewing and reviewing of evidence, the search for new evidence, for witnesses. Maybe a year or two or more goes by before the appeal fails, and even then there may be some glimmer of hope for a retrial. For those very few who are acquitted on appeal, and released, the system has worked out. For those who remain, such an example renews their own mighty efforts. So it's a while before a man settles down to his sentence, knowing he must serve it, and even then there may be straws in the wind he can clutch. In effect the carrot system gets him through the first most difficult part of his sentence. By the time his appeal is finally thrown out, he's some years on his way. Thereafter, for most, the plunge into bleak despair, where some top themselves.

And then, all hope of acquittal gone, the prisoner adjusts his sights to the internal workings of the system. Or not. The carrot he's working for has changed. The system now reveals itself as the underside of the slow bureaucracy of prison at work, as this decides his fate and his prison career. He's invited to look forward to the first review of his case by his parole board, his Local Review Committee, a continuing committee of officers and officials who review his conduct in prison and his future, his 'career' in prison leading (or not) to eventual release. In his board's deliberations there isn't much to hope for, but he hopes nonetheless: there is a date, a fixed point in time before which to anticipate and from which to measure time again. His board will meet again and again, at distant intervals. On their deliberations, and their reports to P2 at the Home Office, depends his next move — his dispersal through the system. As a result of all these reports he'll move on, either progressing through Cat. B to Cat. C to open prison to hostel to release — or he'll not progress. With a bad record he may be moved laterally, to one of the dustbins such as Dartmoor, or, if troublesome, to Parkhurst on the Isle of Wight. He may be given a chance for psychiatric counselling and rehabilitation at Grendon. He may be sectioned off to Rampton. He may never see the light of day again.

The carrot system works to get him through his sentence, and many resent the hopes it represents, for it blunts the edge of prison life a little and delays despair. What a man's most concerned about is his EDR, his expected date of release, and by the time he gets it his sentence will be half-way over, and by then he'll as likely serve his time out quietly, focused on that date, not wanting to do anything to postpone it. Though a recent ruling says that all those sentenced to life must have a date for release set on sentencing, prison goes on spreading time thin on thin bread, with each objective quickly substituted by another further goal, and the carrot jerked away. In 1984 the Home Office attempted to bring in a system they hoped would be fairer and that would reduce the paperwork and report writing, the 'tarrif' system, whereby lifers, once they reached the LRC stage, would be given a release date three years further on. In practice this often does not happen, and men get further knockbacks. Most soon grow deadly cynical. The carrot, they say, of any distraction, whether study, thought, or religion. A con to con a con. Some ignore it all, and do nothing, don't even attend their boards. They are therefore uncooperative, and noted up as such.

One man who refused to do a literacy test and left the paper blank was classified accordingly as illiterate.

Scott, five years on D Wing, got his move to another prison where the regime is lighter, the company of other domestics easier, and where he's found work he's interested in, where he feels useful. But he has been given a ten-year knockback; it means he'll go the whole fifteen. For him, the carrot system has run its course. The game is over. The game goes on.

# 25

# THE PROTAGONIST

He surfaced early in the waking nightmare of the wing, a short, lumpy sort of man, grey as old wood, and two knotholes the two darker patches of his eye sockets. Peter. A fiftyish man, ever on the alert while trying to seem not to be, feigning cool, always anxious, always polite. Prison behaviour is most often formal, as his was. We shook hands. He had written a novel, and would I read it? Would I tell him honestly what I thought and would I critique it, making suggestions as to improvement or development? It was finished, he thought, and represented almost three years' work in prison. Perhaps I might suggest a publisher? He had written a lot, he said, poetry, stories, but the novel he pinned the flag of all his hopes on. Older, with a long sentence before him, he would probably die in prison. For Peter the carrot system was irrelevant; he didn't want to get out, and for him there was no appeal. He'd pleaded guilty. What he did was write.

I took the novel and read it, 400 or so closely typed pages, almost to the end. It was hard going. It took the first person viewpoint in the story of a man in middle age, a successful businessman, whose life had fallen apart. It portrayed his life before and beyond its crisis, and by the end opted, it seemed to me unreasonably, for some sort of happy ending the attitudes and events of the protagonist's life didn't justify. It didn't seem a likely tale. It seemed forced.

Gerald, the protagonist, began life well enough. Well-loved, nurtured, educated, he met, courted, fell in love with, was loved by, and married a young woman. She was handsome, from *the right sort of background*, as was he. Their honeymoon and early marriage was *deliriously happy*. She bore a son. Together, *en famille*, they lived lives of pleasant upper-class luxury.

But not for long. Enter fate's first cruel manifestation. The wife fell from her horse, was crippled for life, and took to her bed as an invalid, a ghost upstairs, a nag, a drag, a shrew, a harridan, incapable physically of sex or psychologically of love. Gerald, good and faithful, abided by his vows as to sickness and health, and plunged into his business. As a result, he became very successful, his life made up of foreign business trips and pleasant interludes between bouts of domestic bitchery that left him bruised and puzzled and exhausted. For consolation there was his continuing love for his son and the pleasures of his growth, his own patience and endurance in the face of tribulation. No one could blame him. No one could blame her. At any rate

Gerald didn't; he was always the gentleman, always decent. When an employee cheated him, he didn't prosecute. He forgave everyone. There was one love affair with a woman Gerald met on rare occasions, always reluctantly, that came to nothing. Gerald, in the first person singular, excused and understood himself very well. He did the right things, and if he did anything wrong, he did it for good reason.

I observed: that for men in prison imagining the outside, and writing about it, rooms are invariably luxurious and well-appointed, chairs remarkable for their comfort, journeys always pleasant, hotels the height of civility, and much of the dialogue inconsequential pleasantry. For men like Peter, the world outside where the unconvicted live is heaven to their nether world, and yet a very dreary sort of place where not much happens, and pleasure is the absence of pain and tragedy sure to strike. Feeding on little, the imagination comes up with unreality, with froth. Gerald and his friends and his son's friends were always meeting at the club, or for dinner at the Ritz or breakfast at the Savoy. The cars they drove were Porsche, Rover, Jag and Jeep, the whisky they drank Chivas Regal, their homes country houses in the home counties, a *pied à terre* in St John's Wood, an apartment on the Riviera. As a businessman Gerald was served by diligent and faithful employees. His business unwaveringly prospered, taking him to exotic and fashionable locations. There was the life he led with a cruel and resentful woman, yet he was blissfully compensated in his lifestyle and in his son, on whom he doted. The world Gerald inhabited was the world his author desired.

These are the dreams of prisoners. Deprived of almost everything, why dream of poverty when they can dream of wealth, of suffering when they can dream of pleasure? Outside, just over the wall, the world is infinitely desirable and infinitely unattainable; it slips away beyond subtlety and distinction. Inside, they can invent what fictions they want, though the rules of fiction as of reality continue to apply.

Then in Peter's novel fate struck again. His son was killed in a plane crash. Gerald was devastated, immersed in long grieving. The son, like the father when young, had been handsome, intelligent, full of promise. Now, like Gerald's marriage, he was dead, his companionship and future all gone at once. Comfortless, Gerald turned from his business, which now went into a decline. Even so, nothing was lost. A young man, an employee, turned out to be both shrewd and honest, and saved the firm. Gradually he replaced the son in Gerald's affections. Grateful, Gerald adopted him. Then Gerald slept with him. Then Gerald fell in love with him. Then they both felt terrible guilt. Then the wife died. Then the tale died, altogether.

We met in the shop where he worked, Peter and I, to talk about his manuscript, amongst the clatter of machines and tea under the all-seeing eye of Joe, the workshop officer. Peter quickly brushed aside my comments — that Gerald and everyone else in the plot were unbelievably too good, and that no one was to blame. He didn't see my point that so much opulence and agreeability seemed unreal, that on the outside all chairs were not a perfect fit, a masterpiece of carpentry and upholstery. I was fielding for realism, I guess. I didn't believe in Gerald. Here was conflict, created by accident, solved by accident, and what had been written as an appeal to innocence turned into a treatise on guilt.

'Too many people wearing white hats,' I said, pointing to Gerry, to his wife, to the son and the adopted son and the host of honest minor characters, factotums and employees. No one to blame for anything, no anger with anyone, and hence no passion. Misery and guilt and outrageous fortune, and yet no anger at fate or death or God or the cosmos.

Peter was offended. I had been impolite.

What Peter wanted to know without hearing 'No' was whether his book was publishable, and where might I suggest, when here was I, reader's and devil's advocate, pointing to flaws, inconsistencies, the need for a rounded character the flaws might make human, the need for a rewrite.

We drifted for a while, I persisting, pointing to pages and examples, Peter resisting and shifting. A lot of his friends on the wing had read the novel and liked it. He sulked, then brightened. He had more writing in his cell. Perhaps I could come and read it there?

'He's not allowed in cells,' Joe said, the makings of a wink in one corner of his eye. 'That's why he doesn't have cell keys.'

'No,' I said, for once grateful for the intrusion, 'I can't do that.'

So what did I suggest? I suggested much thought about Gerry, work on him as a character, the question of his credibility, the need for it, and then extensive redrafting, action and dialogue to explore character, a general all-round therapy. Rewrite. Treat this as a first draft. 'It's harder than you think or want to know, Peter.' Peter had no patience with that. It seemed to me that Gerald, like his author, was probably beyond rewrite or redemption. To illustrate my argument, I suggested we look at the character of the wife. Her role in the book was to be the victim of a riding accident, then a virago, a scapegoat, the source of the deep rivers of guilt that continued to flow till her death, and then some, twenty years later. Other than an irritant and enemy she played no active part. Bedridden, she was entirely passive. 'Women aren't passive, Peter. All she gets to do is be fallen in love with, bear a son, and spend the rest of her life as a cripple, plaguing the hell out of him, and then die.'

And then I put my foot right in it. 'Why not take her out sooner? Why not kill her off earlier? It would make no difference, having initially established her as the fountain of all grief. She could as easily die of pneumonia at 25 as cardiac arrest at 45,' I said.

What I didn't know then was that Peter was in jail for killing his wife, twenty-some years before. The crime had only come to book much later, two decades having passed between crime and sentence. He stared at me, and clammed up. For Peter I had committed the ultimate *faux-pas*.

We didn't talk much more, and when we met again, Peter made cool excuses: he wasn't writing at the moment, he'd been busy but he'd get back to it; he had a full life on the wing, painting, reading, playing bridge, listening to music, talking with his friends, who were many, and who liked his work. So who was I to disagree?

Peter surfaced in my dreams sometimes, grey about the gills, a grey stump in an open landscape, desolate amongst desolation, a figure waiting for Godot, his colourless face staring at me, the two slivers of blue that were his eyes unblinking in their dark hollows, all of him moving like slow water.

'That old queen,' another con said. 'He's happy enough in here with all the boy bums he can use. He's better off in here, the old tart.'

I learned that Peter was living his life in reverse. Sentenced in his mid-fifties, he would probably die a natural death in prison, where he was otherwise safe. He was in prison for the murder of his wife, long ago, a crime he'd got away with till recently, and for which he had no feeling one way or another. On the outside it seems there'd been some pressure on him — too much of it. Outside, Peter had been an active and aggressive homosexual. He'd done a previous seven for kidnap and buggery, for male rape. More years had passed and then some threat out there had driven him to confess to the murder when the opportunity arose and the occasion demanded, so he could go safely into prison, as if for twenty years he'd carried a passport about with him, a yellow card that took him off the pitch when the going got rough. It was as if the old murder were a form of insurance, an indulgence, a licence to prey on others knowing he could one day cash it in.

The marriage, short and stormy and unconsummated, had ended one night in 1960 when she came to see him to discuss their permanent separation. He'd attacked her, killing and dismembering her with an axe, scattering her parts in separate graves. Enquiries had been made, but no one had been accused. Suspected, Peter had been passed over for lack of evidence, of a body. She had simply disappeared.

Then, two decades later, in 1983, in a Cheshire pet bog at Lindow Moss, a peat cutter exposed a woman's skull. Close to where the couple had lived at the time of the wife's disappearance, it was in the right location to have been the head of Peter's missing wife, severed at the neck by something sharp. At that time under pressure, Peter flashed his yellow card. He walked into a police station and put his hands up. Confessed, he was tried and sentenced, and now here he was.

As it happened it wasn't his wife's but a skull of Romano-Celtic origin, radiocarbon dated around 210 AD, and now known as Lindow Woman, the likely victim of a primitive judicial or ritual murder. The area has a history of such findings, where the peat acids of the marshlands have pickled the remains of men and women, still bearing the thongs and wounds of death. Herodotus notes Spring ceremonies among the Germans in which a victim was taken in procession to sacrifice, the counterpart of widespread and ancient Dionysian practices. Perhaps the skull was what remained of one such victim. At any rate, it wasn't Peter's wife, but he'd made his confession, and was convicted on it, without evidence of a corpse.

A year later in the same area, peat cutters turned up almost the whole body of a man some 500 years older than the woman's skull, similarly preserved in the peat acids, Lindow Man. The scientists resurrected him, christening him *Pete Marsh*, examining his entrails for the seeds and husks and pollens of his last meal, his body for the injuries he'd died by. He'd been garrotted, his skull smashed and his throat cut before being kicked into the pool he'd lain in. He was another sacrificial victim, a captive perhaps, and from the condition of his fingers either a prince or one kept for sacrifice.

Preserved, part of him sliced away by the peat-cutting machine, bronzed as though by boot polish in the pressed leaf shape he had fallen in, he lies in an air-conditioned case in the Manchester City Museum, folded, crumpled, restored, the treasure of archeologists.

Peter meet Pete. Pete meet Peter.

In my dreams his body rises without a ripple on the black surface of the pool on some windless night of fog and silence. His throat lies open. On the still black mouth of the water one arm trails away, pointing to his murderer, and the man with his hands up to another crime in another century will do. He has come to accuse, and his original tormentors being long gone, any other killer, however many centuries later, will suffice. Peter will do. The dead don't rest without a marker, they say. Amongst the dead who take no account of time, the murdered dead still drift. These men match up, victim and villain. They form, as Borges has said, 'a secret pattern in time, a drawing in which the lines repeat themselves.'

# 26
# ANGUS IN EXILE

Christmas on the wing, a cheerless occasion, barely mentioned, another week much like any other. If there's no cheer it's that there's little call for it, and such cheer as there might be only highlights the surrounding gloom. Opposite the movements desk they've put up a tree, standing in a bucket and decorated with a few strips of coloured foil. Everyone ignores it. No one hangs a bauble or puts a package under it. Men get cards and send cards, hanging on to what contacts they have on the outside. Some make cards, some recycle old ones, painting on paper, making a verse for the solstice. But the festival is minimal here, and for men inside who know they'll be the least of any celebration, the subject of short rostering and a skeletal staff, there's not a lot to look forward to in being locked up for most of it. One man complains he can't be issued with the card his mother sent him. It's electronic. When opened, a little cell inside plays a cheery Christmas tune. But electronics are suspect, and he can't have it.

Angus appears at my door, with the air of someone familiar, as if we'd known each other for years. It's the first time we've met. What he wants to know is have I any books he can read over the break? Poetry he's after. 'It disna matter.' He seems a wild man, always impatient, as if he'd somewhere to go in a hurry. He's read everything he has up in his peter and all he can get from the library — Wordsworth, Keats, Byron, Shelley, Blake, Coleridge. 'Ye're only allowed six books at a time. I can read six books on a weekend.' As a critic he's up to here with the Romantics. 'Gimme something new,' he says. The books he borrows from me are Neruda, Marquez, Apollinaire. He'll give them a whirl. What he regrets is that Keats died young and didn't write more, that there's no Byron or Shelley he hasn't already read, and that Wordsworth went on far too long. 'Can't stand that Lakey stuff,' he says. 'There's just too much of it.'

A week later and Christmas is over and the tree has gone. Around the wing I ask tentatively how Christmas went. 'It went,' Ross says, instantly discarding the subject. They were banged up for most of it, as expected. What else is there to talk about? They had turkey. 'Tinned turkey,' Joey says. 'On the outside they think we have a hell of a time. They don't say the turkey's from a tin, from Government stores, stuff at the end of its shelf life, just like me. It's the fucking European turkey mountain.'

Angus has vanished, and no one knows where. I have no other name for him. He's gone, ghosted over the solstice, as if he'd never been here, and I write off the books.

Three months go by, and I hear from him. He's over on the 43 Unit, and can I go to see him? He's over among the sex offenders, 'in here among the nonces', as he puts it. He's doing all right. As before, he's as immediately familiar as if we'd talked only yesterday. He's not found my books yet, lost in the fracas when he barricaded himself into his cell for fourteen days, but he plans to. As a result of the blockade he was confined to cell with no privileges. That's different from the block, he explains, where loss of privilege is specified. He's been on the block, too, recently, but the timing of all these events seems vague. Right now he's been on hunger strike for nine days, but they've made him the number one cleaner in the unit, a position of some eminence and trust, apparently. It gives him access to the kettle and the tea, and since as a lifer he has a cell of his own, we can sit there drinking diesel for a while. Diesel doesn't count on his hunger strike.

He has made the place as much like home as he can. He has a dartboard, but no darts. He has a radio and a clock. He's rigged a string weighted with a shampoo bottle on the end across the room to the light-switch so that he can put the light off from his bed. He has books, materials, a board game or two that he's made. On all four walls from floor to ceiling he has decorated his cell with magazine cuttings in a great collage of colour and imagery: pictures of women in sundry stages of dress and undress, images of violence from the news, images of time, and the dominant motif of clocks and clock faces, time threaded through the world, the melting clocks of Salvador Dali.

He asks me for a theme. I give him *windows* to think about. The next time we meet he's found the books, and the hunger strike has already faded into history. He has a couple of poems to show: the window of his cell that gives out only onto prison hadn't inspired him; instead, he's thought about the windows in his head. He's written about violence and dictatorship in Latin America, and the fate of those who simply disappear, reaching over great distances from misery concrete to misery distantly imagined. He's written about his cell as if he were looking into it from outside the high barred window, as if it were his skull and he looking in from outside. It's as if the cell's space were the space his solitary mind occupies, as if each time the door slams shut, his mind enlarges itself to fill the whole of it.

We drink more prison tea, and Angus talks about himself, vague about his crime, which he makes clear was murder, but what the circumstance or who the victim was I never ask, he never says. Like many, he takes for granted that I know the obvious, and the conversation continues for a while with its centre blank. His manner says he knows who he is, and his place in the pecking order, and he openly shows his contempt for lesser breeds, his neighbours the sex offenders. He has the common contempt for nonces: 'lower than life,' he calls them. Some days he says he comes out and just wants to strike out. He is a lifer, and even here enjoys his privilege of a cell to himself. He refers to his crime as 'this business that came up'. As ever, in speaking of murder, there is a fair inventory of elisions. In real life Angus had been a psychiatric nurse, and I surmise from what he tells me that the work had got to him, along with drugs. He speaks of people committed long ago by doctors for no evident reason. Other doctors, he says, other report makers, they go on repeating the prescriptions, rewriting the same reports. Just as in prison. 'Those people never get out.'

From the age of 5 to 15 he'd been in care, and institutionalized. His mother had killed herself when he was 12, 'the result of beatings and a hard life' at the hands of his stepfather, 'her man. He beat us all on a regular basis.' He'd stayed in touch with his younger brother, and lost the rest. Outside, he has a girlfriend and a child, who wait for him. Serving life, he says, 'Oh, I can do it, I've done six so far.' He's tough. He can wait. 'It's a matter of where I do it. Of where I do the waiting.'

Like all of them, he talks as if I know what he's referring to. I don't. I ask. He says his reasons for the barricading and the block, the 43 transfer and the hunger strike are simple, and all the same. He wants a transfer to another prison. He's had trouble on the wing, and can't go back there for fear of his life, of a beating or a cutting, and all his actions are part of his strategy to get a move. And then he tells me what it's all about, and solves the mystery of his disappearance from the wing. It is a salutary tale, and what it says of prison is its worst aspect: that no one can trust anyone else, that no one can reveal the simple facts of themselves without risking someone picking on an advantage. And if there's an advantage, someone will take it. On the wing Angus had talked too much. He admits he talks too much. Here he is telling me about it.

For Angus liked his gear, and had bought from the heavy mob on the wing. No matter, save that, ever talkative, he'd revealed in the euphoria of smoking dope the facts of his life: that outside he had a girlfriend and a child, and where they lived, and that they had recently been burgled. And then the heavies moved in. They wanted him to do them a favour. In anticipation of a spin they asked him to look after a bag for twenty-four hours. He refused. So then they put it to him that they knew where his girl lived, and that her place might be broken into again, and that this time worse might happen. It was the department of veiled threats, oblique hints and dire warnings, and they got to him. Reluctantly he agreed to hold the bag. It contained four ounces of black and a hundred and fifty notes, and he put it behind a loose brick in his cell before going to work one morning, but when he came back from the workshop at noon the brick had been moved and the bag was gone. Angus was irretrievably in the brown stuff. No way to replace it. Nothing to do then but make a ruckus and get transferred at his own request for safety to the 43s.

'But it's no problem,' he says. 'I'll get my transfer yet.' In his mind there is no doubt of it. He'll be a pest till they decide to move him, if only to get rid of him. It takes a year of life on 43, but he gets what he's after in the end. He gets his transfer.

# 27

# JOEY IN QUOTES

'That bastard there, to your right: thirty-some cases of sodomy on young boys. Fucker. Nonce. He came to see me about fucking painting. I told him to sod off out of my cell. They think I know nothing but I tell you I know fuck-all. I brought these to show you. Do you like these? I painted these three little fuckers last night. I found these bits of fucking wood in the fucking shop. I fix all the fucking machines for them, you know. I'm the only fucker round here that can. I rewound the fucking generator. They know fuckall. Anyway, mostly what I do is paint in my cell and just get on with it, though I have written a few stories, mostly about when I was at sea, when I was younger. I was at sea most of my life, till I came into this fucking place. I've got them in my cell if you want to see them. You can read them if you want. Mostly what I do is paint, landscapes and stuff. And ships. I painted these little pictures here. You can have these if you want. And some tiles I found, I've painted little country scenes on them, but they need glazing, and I can't do that in here so I've just varnished them. This other one I found the board in the bin. I think it's an old mirror frame. I'll paint on any fucking thing, but I did get some canvas from the art teacher, so I've stretched and sized that fucker and prepared it right, so if you see anything you want it can go out through the fucking office, you know, legit. Say a fiver. Just drop me it in baccy. And some papers. I'm always running out of fucking papers. You know it's nice to meet another fucking northerner in this fucking place. This is my cell, like a fucking art gallery. Ships. This one with the bridge I did last night, took me three fucking hours to get the fucking trees right, and that water, like there's a bit of a breeze on it. You can't see it from here but it's an island. I've caught many a fucking fish just there. You see, I'm not like these other fuckers that just copy. I mean, they copy me. I just paint places I used to know and places I'd rather fucking be than here. When I was at sea I used to think about painting, you know what I mean? I never did any. But now I'm in here I think well, fuck it. A screw offered me twenty quid for that fucker, and that feller outside that came to visit the other day said it was worth at least a hundred and fucking fifty notes. Not that I'll ever see that. Two fucking quid a week is what I get. It goes into my monies, and I can draw on it for my canteen, a few biscuits, stuff like that. Two pounds fucking twenty I drew last week. That's not two fucking ounces of tobacco, a box of matches and a packet of fucking Rizla. So I get by on the painting. That fucker over there owes me two ounces right now. He had the fucking cheek to ask me for another packet last night. You see these ships? I've painted a lot of these. They like ships in this fucking place, for some fucking reason. At Christmas that feller from the outside, an actor I think he was, he left a tenner on the way out for that painting, and he could have taken it with him if he'd fucking done it proper. The screw came up to my door at lock-up with a tenner in his hand. I couldn't fucking take it, could I, and me with not a fucking brass farthing to get me through to fucking Christmas. So I said, "Give it to the sky pilot to put in my monies". I should be getting fucking used to it by now. You see that fucking paint there? Feller from the outside sent me that in. You can't get that any more. They've stopped fucking making it. I like painting shorelines. These here are all the Mersey, where I come from. It took me for fucking ever to paint that bastard seagull, but I'm fucking like that, you see. I never give up till I get it fucking right. And getting this road right, so it goes off into the distance like that, that took a bit of fucking patience. I'd love to walk down that fucking road, into the sunset. You wouldn't see me coming this fucking way, I can fucking tell you. The other day I had a visit. My visitor gave me a pipe, this fucking pipe, so I stuck it in the top pocket of my overall. On the way out the screw sees it, and I said, "Oh I brought that over with me on the visit." He says, "Oh aye, any more stories you have to tell, Joey?" and I says, "Yes. Once upon a time there were these three bears, Mummy Bear, Daddy Bear and Baby Bear." You have to fucking laugh some fucking times. What I'm in here for is accessory to fucking murder. I got fucking life. I didn't kill no bugger, I know that. As far as I was concerned I was just moving some fucking furniture, and driving the fucking van. One thousand fucking quid was what I was getting paid, whatever the big fuckers were fucking making. They were antiques already pinched. They were fucking hot. It's a fucking safe bet fucking lifting stuff that's already been fucking nicked, but the fucking money was fucking greedy, put a fucking heavy on the job at the last fucking minute, and when we got in there he wanted the combination of the fucking safe. The bloke wouldn't fucking give him it. Miladdo went fucking spare. He went beserk and fucking killed him. Fucking mess. So I was ancillary to fucking murder. In court they said it was torture. Me, a fucking torturer. I wouldn't hurt a fucking fly, me. My brief was fucking useless. Never fucking spoke to me in court. I never knew I could appeal, and no fucker fucking told me I had to give fucking notice in twenty-eight fucking days after sentence. It's taken me four fucking years to get my fucking transcripts. You have to fucking pay for them. That's all fucking right if you're one of these rich twats like little Lord fucking Fauntleroy there, that fucking nonce that killed his fucking missus and kept her head in the fucking refrigerator, Lord fucking Vestey's bastard. He says he had a jury of working-class prats, dragged him down to their own fucking level, he fucking says. I've no fucking money on the outside. I've no fucking money at all but what I can make from these fucking paintings. Know what I mean?'

# 28

# THE BROTHERS BORIS AND KARLOFF

Or so they're soon christened on the wing: two huge skinhead brothers just weighed off together for murder most foul, newly arrived on the wing, wide-eyed in the light of yet another prison. They move with a sluggish stillness, wary, confident in their collective deadweight, their faces mostly blank, though they smile often. If they are afraid of anyone here they don't show it, but then they wouldn't, veterans as they are of urban and institutional survival, streetwise and tough, easy with the aura of terror they project. Both in their early twenties, they have achieved something dreadful, their manners say, and they are not afraid now beyond their dark shared apotheosis of murder and life imprisonment. Neither of them is bright, their big, pink, piggy, baby faces blinking in the neon noonlight, two watching vacancies. They have the look of danger, if not for their bulk then for their stupidity. Here, where anything can happen and most things are misunderstood, they are a new menace. There are rumours of them, but they need no reputations. They are the makings of horror fiction and nightmare, but they are grimly and brutally real. Their crimes are recent and they are as if still fresh from them. To other men their crimes are particularly vicious and elaborately detailed, spoken of *sotto voce* in swift incredulous asides, and they horrify other men themselves prisoners serving life for crimes of great violence.

*They skinned her.*

But they're said to be *all right*, in the sense that left alone they will be. They're harmless. Potentially dangerous but harmless. Too stupid to be a problem is most men's verdict, though they keep their distance. Col, scrapper that he is, regards them with contempt, pointing out that all their movements are defensive. They don't want any bother either. But their stupidity makes them lethal, though there are many reasons men avoid them. They are filthy. Everyone smells here, but these two stink. In every way they are repulsive, and clearly an argument with one would be an argument with both. They stick together, watching out for each other. Presumably, by keeping them together at the beginning of their sentences authority has conceded this; it has them under its regard, yet it must work to separate them.

Boris, slightly older, slightly more intelligent, accepts responsibility, looks out for his brother. He sometimes punches him out, to keep him in line, and has, if not the strength, the edge to remain in charge. Where you see one, you soon see the other, Karloff checking in with Boris, Boris checking on Karloff, just as he always has since they were born to the same vicious brotherhood. Also, Boris is slightly cleaner. There are days when he shines from scrubbing, but generally they are both dirty, their prison pallor overlaid by muck, their nails and fingers deeply grained, and they suffer from boils and sores and pustules. When met they insist on shaking hands, out of some formality they have been taught somewhere. It makes the hand itch for water. They are the gruesome twosome, their accents a soft Welsh lilt as belying them as do their soft, innocent faces. Looked at in the eyes, in Karloff's there's just dumb stupidity — fear and pleading, a cloudiness; Boris's are clear and blue and sharp, full of cunning and cruelty.

Boris taps the side of his face. He wants a cigarette, and one for his brother, and sits in the tubular chair, glancing every few seconds through the door, on the lookout, ever the responsible one. Because of this, he's also in for longer, with a minimum recommendation of twenty where his brother has fifteen. As he sees it, it's his penalty for being stronger, and responsible, part of the burden he must hump through life. He says the extra five bear more relation to this than to the crime, which he is mercifully vague about. What he is clearest about is his responsibility for his brother. Somewhere back in the history of desertions and broken homes this message has been instilled in him, and now what he fears is they'll be split up in different prisons, and he'll not be there for his brother. He knows their separation is inevitable sooner or later. Meanwhile, he's trying to teach his brother all he needs to know to survive. But he's hard work.

'He's in the FBI, see since he was born, that one. I've always had to look out for him, or he gets in trouble.'

'FBI?'

'Fucking Brainless Idiot.'

They're not assigned work in the shops, but kept in the wing as cleaners, with special responsibilities for the garbage cans. They take these duties seriously, and regard the rubbish jealously as their particular concession. Their shaved heads, ball-bearing smooth when they came in, as they must have appeared in court, grow a dark fur. They hang about the movements desk together, and try to talk with officers, which gets them nowhere. They're sent on daft errands to get rid of them for a while, though kept always in sight, and they get out of the wing with the garbage cans and the cart each day. Gradually men shrug them off, keeping their distance, dismissing them as animals, as dog-end men and cadgers, always on the make, untrustworthy, and as first diagnosed: dangerous because stupid. They hang round officers. They scavenge in the garbage, and when they can, they take the garbage cans into their cells overnight and tip them out to sort them.

These two are all the brute unthinking force in the universe, solid engines of want and need and greed. They are used to demanding and getting, and they are used to taking, and they don't like 'No' for an answer. Brutalised, they have become brutes, dull from the beginning and further dulled by rough usage, in care one way or another, still acting out the politics of the playground, angry and confused forever.

And Karloff really is dumb, unable to grasp much or remember much. He has no focus on reality, and can't understand numbers. One day he appears with his arm in a filthy sling, and says he's had an accident with some glass, and has had to have 160 stitches in it. 'Twenty,' Boris says over his shoulder, shaking his head. 'He understands fuckall, you see.' It looks like a botched suicide attempt, and from Boris's expression perhaps it is. Another time, Karloff is talking about his sentence, and says he's got fifty years and his brother seventy-five. He shakes his head. He can't grasp it.

But their demands are simple. All they ask for are cigarettes and picture magazines. They make collages from cut-out pictures in their cells, and I don't ask what they use for glue. Boris draws a bit, but he wants no encouragement. He refuses it. He draws a vintage car, black-leaded body, white wall tyres, quite sharp, and shows it to me proudly, then suddenly he turns against it. 'It's fuckall.' Its existence reminds him too painfully of his own. 'What fucking use is it?' He can just about read and write, and Karloff not at all, so there's nothing in my line of work that interests them. In speech they haven't much to say: they judge their lives uninteresting, and virtually over; they have forgotten most of it already. Their stories, such as they are, are repetitious, tedious, sketchy; from bad beginnings they have progressed to bad ends; there isn't much to listen to. Boris sits in broody silence punctuated by a few words, sighs, shrugs and the same bad news, flicking at an imaginary fly. 'I'm thinking I'll top myself,' Boris says one day, his brother briefly out of earshot. The air about him is utterly without hope. 'Fuck all to live for really.' Boris gives in to despair quite often, comtemplating the years ahead. What keeps him going is his most immediate worry, voiced over again and again, that he'll soon be separated from his brother. 'And then I don't know what he'll do, see.'

For Karloff, some way below the line of understanding what is happening to him, despair's not a big option. By contrast, he is often cheerful, for ever in pursuit of simple needs, angering Boris in his ability to find a joke and a giggle in the most childish tricks, and therefore prone to trouble. Boris shoulders the weight for both of them, and considers his life will always be this well-established routine: prison, and looking after his brother, or worrying over him.

'So I may top myself, see.' He says it matter of factly, as the conclusion of all his thinking. For him it's a viable option. 'But then what about him, see?' I can't think of a counter argument: his life, useless so far, a trail of violence and misery and short, sharp shocks, led him and his brother to the casual and almost playful rape and murder of a saleswoman in a sex shop; her life ended horribly as the object of their brutal play. 'They skinned her,' is all men say of them. For themselves they've not much to say of it: 'I didn't. Daft bastard. He did.' Without doubt the world will be safer for their long absence. For these two to be permanently institutionalized one way or another would be most likely for the best, so far as everyone else is concerned. Remorse is alien to them. For Boris, regret is centred on the years of confinement ahead. 'I wasn't even near the place,' he says, but his voice lacks conviction. 'I didn't kill her. He did,' he says, not meaning that his stupid brother did the murder, but that his stupid brother confessed. 'He admitted it. They had him scared and me scared for him, see. They took us in and kept us separate. The cops told him I'd put my hands up when I hadn't. They told me he owned up but I didn't bite. But he did. He believed them. They tricked him.' His voice whines unconvincingly, as if he were trying to persuade himself of what he says. Nothing registers in his face. It is the shark's dull stare.

Moved in a few months, Boris goes to Grendon, where no doubt someone thinks him reclaimable, leaving Karloff alone on the wing, where without his older brother he begins to blend in. They are allowed the occasional phone-call, and once in a while Boris is brought down on a visit. Their closeness is acknowledged, and Boris writes frequently — short scrawly letters in a childish hand his brother can't read, but when he brings them to me to read out to him he attempts to memorize them, and his eyes shine with little baby tears. Mostly what Boris's letters say is brief, the magnified minutae of prison life, a visit he's had from their sister, and how she looked pretty, and the colour of her dress and shoes. Mostly what they say is that he hopes his brother is looking after himself and staying out of trouble. And in his absence, Karloff's less of a sore thumb, and cleaner, as ever usually to be found hanging out by the barred gate by the movements desk, staring into nothing. If he begins to understand what's happening, and a vaguely guilty look will sometimes cross his face, he has no language to describe or envision it. His estimate of numbers is as wild as ever. One day, his arms covered yet again in bandages, he says he's fallen through a window, and has a hundred and twenty three stitches in one arm alone. The next day, the same bandaged arm in a sling, he says he's broken it. Facts evade him. All he knows is that he's in prison for a long time, and that his brother isn't here.

'My brother,' he says. 'You know, I really miss him.'

# 29
# FEBRUARY REVISITED

Men speak of the bars that persist on the outside, after release, as if imprinted on the retina in a long after-image. They mean the habits of suspiciousness, cynicism, withdrawal, over-gregariousness, the persisting physical and mental reflexes of prison, marking a man off as an ex-con. And they mean the trickier bars to the world outside, where we think we're free, where the bars, Breton said, are on the inside. And they laugh, meaning other bars where men drink to get drunk at the end of several tethers at once, and through which many are recycled back into prison. They're unsure as to the question of freedom.

'You only think you're free,' Cambridge says.

And Amos: 'Outside you get to carry the keys to your own prison, and lock yourself in.' Outside he called the outer prison.

'Release from what?' John says. 'I've tried but there's no way I can get straight. I'll be released but I'll never be out of jail.'

I don't know much about John. Cambridge I know a little of, for he is still famous in his infamy. Around the wing he's known as Janet. He was the hooded rapist who struck and ran and spread terror amongst women in Cambridge. Now he says, shuffling past, leaning on a stick, stiff with arthritis, 'I used to run a lot when I was younger. I was always very active.' He's greying over, his long hair parted in the centre hanging heavily to his shoulders, his face aquiline, the face of a chieftain. When he talks, as he sometimes does most urgently, he is intense, and his brown eyes have a disturbing habit of rolling up into his head.

Amos I also know little of; he's black as the other two are white, but they are three separate men who do not know one another, and all they have in common are their convictions for the same violent crime.

Rape.

Amos is a softly spoken man, small and broad like a barrel, very polite, very black. When I met him he was in his first year of life with a recommended minimum of twenty for multiple rape, still getting the fact of it through his skull, still unadjusted to his circumstances, and visibly afraid. He didn't want trouble. He kept himself apart, joined in on nothing. He moved cautiously, stayed mostly in his cell, knew only one or two others on his landing. He said others on the wing, other blacks, heavies, taunted him, questioning his manhood. He meant the bunch known as Rape Posse, their birds of prey young girls in Southwark. It wasn't simply that he was African or they West Indian, nor the fact his manhood was vulnerable to them. He was quite paranoid in a paranoid environment, and he lived in fear, minute by minute, and coming out onto the wing to keep our weekly meeting was at times visibly an ordeal for him. Some days his eyes rolled around in sheer fright, and he'd have difficulty focusing his vision or his thoughts or his attention for long. The noisy distractions of the wing made him jump, and with each bellow of the tannoy he would pause, listen, then struggle to find the thread of his thoughts again. Most of the time he appeared to be making a conscious effort to stay calm, but he gave off the kind of fear that attracts danger. He was, I came to think, quite mad, and often close to implosion. For all that he was a quiet and thoughtful man, who kept himself to the routines he'd worked out. He had his watch, with umpteen digital reminders on it that he pre-set to the times of radio programmes he wanted to hear. His radio was most of his world. Except when on a downer, he was very clean, his face shaved, shoes polished, hair combed, shirt and blue denims firmly pressed: a uniform. At other times he'd let himself go, abruptly as if a string inside him had snapped, slumped and untidy in the chair. And there were other times again when he was animated and excited. Sometimes he was up, sometimes he was down. Whenever we met, I never knew which end of the rainbow he was coming from.

He said he wrote, wanted to write more. What experience he'd had was mostly journalism, some reviewing, some political articles. Regarded by his own as an intellectual, Amos was a revolutionary, a Colonel he eventually claimed, in the ANC. He showed me letters he'd written that of course he couldn't mail, and others written to him, addressed to that rank. Either he was a complete fantasist, or he *was* a soldier. In prison, he explained, in maximum security, political writing was no longer feasible, what with the censor always there. Therefore he must change his style, his genre. He must learn to write in codes. He must learn the ways of fiction. What he thought he'd do was to write songs and poetry he might offer, from prison, to his revolution and the liberation of his country, to which he was committed as a revolutionary Marxist, in whose works he was fluent. And there was time here, and his mind sought activity, and he was lonely. The only other South African on the wing was white, and he had even less to say to Amos than the other blacks.

And he was imaginative. He loved song and especially theatre, where he had done some acting. When he could relax, where opportunities for it were few and far between, he was an urbane, articulate and educated man of some sophistication, who'd travelled widely, and who loved discourse. I found him interesting. So long as I didn't know what he had done, within the special circumstance under which we met, I enjoyed his company. Thereafter, the case altered.

At first I didn't look in men's records for their form, and all I had to go on was what they told me, conveyed in speech and manner and tone and gesture. In my mind a picture of Amos and his crime, against conviction for which he was appealing, began to form. He didn't say what it was, and I didn't ask, and we stuck to our literary business. But the imagination abhors an empty space, and somewhere, I guess, I formed a notion that his politics had led him to an act of terrorism, and that his shift in viewpoint indicated an attempt to change the world by words rather than by bullets, an issue I could encourage. This was, of course, romantic bullshit. Perhaps this image only built itself in my mind. I wasn't sure then, and can't be now. And yet I built it up from whatever Amos said and implied of himself, and stuck it all together with some liberal superglue of my own. I believed of Amos what I wanted to believe of Amos: that he was a politically motivated man imprisoned in a cause with which I might have sympathy.

We read texts together, we listened separately to plays on the Third and talked about them the following week; we held what in any other circumstances would be tutorials, with all the action of the wing swirling about us. We shared Nazim Hikmet, and Isaak Babel and the poetry of Senghor and Aimé Cesaire. We discussed negritude and alienation, and Camus' *Outsider*, and Soyinka, and read the poetry of imprisoned revolutionaries, writings that Amos hoped to emulate. Our conversations included Whitman, Kafka, Melville, Conrad, and the mighty nineteenth-century Russians, for here was a man who had indeed read *War and Peace*, who knew the literatures of his own continent and of Europe and the northern hemisphere, east and west of it.

Sometimes, between our meetings, always interrupted, always abbreviated, in the cell or the fishbowls, I'd sense that Amos continued our conversations alone. Sometimes he seemed to talk as if he'd already told me things, explained them to me, repeating and referring to discussions that must have taken place in his mind with an imaginary me in the nightly quiet of his cell. I noticed this with other men I'd got to know, though in Amos it was quite pronounced. Prisoners live, if they live at all, sentiently, in their heads, and Amos lived very much in his own mind, behind his door, only feeling safe when it was locked. I admired him for his self-organization, the way he kept himself together in the most difficult and dangerous circumstances and without hope. He had support from his family outside, but in here he was alone.

Slowly my picture of him built itself from what he told me of his life: he was a Zulu, he'd been in a training camp in Tanzania, and taken a degree at Patrice Lumumba University in Moscow; he was a cosmopolitan who'd travelled but had not been to his own country in many years. He regarded himself as an exile, spoke of his country as Azania. Earnest and sincere, he was hyper and intense when he was up; down he was often sulky, brief, unreachable, focused on his own inner torment. Though he was always polite, and punctual about our appointments, there were times he didn't turn up; later he'd say he was just too far down, unable to face the wing's dangers, whether real or imagined or magnified by paranoia, his or mine. Between the swings of mood, our conversations continued, weaving, but with continuities. His moods confused me. And I grew curious. So I dropped the phoney baloney and looked in the record.

Amos was a rapist, six times over that they knew about and on which he'd been convicted. He was a beast. Not a terrorist but a terroriser of young women in student hostels around London University over a period of days in which he'd flipped right over in the summer of 1984, a brutal and perverse man who left in his wake pain and grief and lifelong humiliation. He was what other men call a nonce.

When next we met, I tried to reconcile this urbane man discussing Tutuola and Senghor in the barbarous surroundings of the prison with the dark predatory figure of terror that he also was. This man professed liberty and love for all humanity, and equal justice for all, food for the hungry and peace. Especially, it now seemed to me, we had been discussing responsibility, and what society calls crime that the individual might call an act of liberation. Suddenly I couldn't see him as anything but a vicious criminal, the bully preying on the vulnerable and the weak, without remorse or compassion for his victims, an intellectual intellectually dishonest, and now himself living in terror of the heavies and the nonce-bashers. I saw that I had tricked myself. In the three months or so of our meeting he hadn't written anything, nor shown me anything but letters he couldn't send, in which he signed himself, as ever, Colonel. They were his fantasy life. We'd talked a lot, and much of that now seemed to me so much intelligent wallpaper. Perhaps for his sake, perhaps for mine, somewhere in there between us we had built up an image of him, belied by what he'd never mentioned, the most important fact about himself. And I'd consented, stitching together my narrative from the clues he dropped.

We went on meeting, continuing our business. He remained erudite and convincing, talking of Mao and Marx and the coming era of the people, where all would live at peace, without harming one another. Between himself and his beliefs, between his theories of action and his actions, the shadow fell. Whatever else he was, he was also the beast. Beneath all his outward sophistication he was the lurking shadow in the cave, a thoroughly vicious man.

After what knowledge what forgiveness? We faded out on each other. Now I couldn't respect his intelligence while suspecting its deployment. I'd had a dialogue with Caliban, and then suddenly his appeal came up, and he was off to the Old Bailey. His appeal against sentence acknowledged his crimes, claiming sickness, madness, non-responsibility. He said he knew he needed treatment for what he called *his condition*. He wanted to get better, knew he was dangerous, not fit to be about the world with others. When, close to the end of our acquaintance, he came to speak of this, he seemed quite genuinely like a man who knows he is sick and must go into hospital to be cured. Cured, he reasoned, he would be freed, and freedom was his desire. He wanted, he said, to be committed to a secure hospital such as Park Lane, where his condition would be treated, and from whence he might be released. But I was told he was hopelessly manic-depressive, a man with a condition for which there was no cure; that there is a problem does not imply there is an answer.

Amos won his appeal, and on the wing I heard he'd been moved to the hospital, and had asked to see me, for he would be leaving soon, for Park Lane. He'd got his wish, then. In the hospital wing he was sitting alone in a single cell, with his books and his papers in a cardboard box at his feet. He was happy. Instead of the smartly pressed and laundered blues that he'd worn on the wing like a military uniform, he was dressed in the baggy browns of the unconvicted. His family was bringing in his clothes, and his guitar. He was technically no longer a prisoner and need no longer dress as one. If he had considered himself guilty he no longer did so. He was sick and in need of treatment, the court had that day decided. So far as he was concerned, he was already free, a voluntary patient in a secure centre for the criminally insane, to which the Appeal Court had ordered him. He was merely here awaiting transport. As Amos saw it, he had been found not guilty, which was to say that though he had raped six women, he was not responsible. For them, presumably, the technicalities of his guilt or innocence didn't enter the question.

At Park Lane he looked forward to less restriction, less threat, some comforts, attention given to his illness. He would have his books, his music. He was content, and but for the absence of regret or any mention of his victims, then or previously, I might have been happy for him. In fact, though he might not be officially a prisoner, yet he was not free, and now indeed he was worse off at Her Majesty's Pleasure. Where before, even serving life, he might expect to do twenty years, his sentence now was indefinite, with no EDR. Once labelled mad, the mad have a hard time proving their sanity again. I said all this. His euphoria was unprickable. He shrugged. The outside was prison too, and he spoke with relief, with hope of a cure for what he considered a sickness. He had faith in that.

'Outside, you get to have the key.'

With Cambridge, conversation was a hit and run affair. He didn't write. We had no proper business. Sometimes passing my door he'd speak, rapidly and randomly and unprompted, of the weather, of his aching bones. When not huffing on a stick, he'd bowl along with a spring in his step, swinging his arms in a wide rolling gait, as if trotting in slow motion. Most of the little he said began 'When I was young.' He'd jogged. He'd kept fit. He hadn't drank more than a half of lager at a sitting. He was on tryptizol, he said, supplied from the dispensary, and measured out his intake. It helped him sleep, and calmed him down, but what he did was drop it in the morning and get through the working day like a zombie. Because he'd been an architect, or so he claimed, he ran a small construction drawing-class on the wing. It was rumoured they were designing a tunnel. In these brief exchanges he expressed his hatred of prison and of captivity, but resignedly and without much vigour, without any expressed wish to be free. I formed the opinion he preferred to be inside, and felt safe here, from himself, perhaps.

'Out there you only think you're free.'

Most of our conversation took place one afternoon, all in a rush. He was buzzing, anxious, whether on the runout of his tryptizol or on his own decayed adrenalin. He flew in the door at speed, with an evident bee in his bonnet, asking, 'Are you a writer? I hear you're a writer.'

I confessed.

'Are you writing anything about this place?'

'Maybe,' I said. 'I'm a writer. I write about most things I do.'

'Well, you better not write anything about me. Or you'll get a suit. I'll have my brief come down on you.'

Having said which, knowing I *would* write of him, he delivered a swift outline of his life, and how he came to crime. Born just before the war, he'd been a child of the blackout. He loved his dad but his dad went away to the Army, and he kept running away to find him. He described roaming England dodging onto trains in the dark, in the blackout, trying to get to this or that Army camp, never knowing where his father was. On the trains he got into thieving, which he termed *screwing*. He was caught, sent back, ran off again, caught, sent to juvenile home.

'I declared war on society. I kept running away, and then it was homes. With the blackout and that you could get around. It was good for screwing, and nobody took notice of a kid. That's where it started. I don't blame my parents. I blame them bastards.' And his big brown eyes rolled up into his head, and he said, 'So that's it', and departed.

Momentarily I wondered if I had the wrong man. He'd given me the biography of the apocryphal honest crook, misused and abandoned and therefore turned against the world and gone to the bad. It was the version he wanted to believe of himself, and that he wanted written down. He didn't mention *rape*, or elucidate who *them bastards* were. And that word he'd used for thieving, several times over: *screwing*. He meant *rape*.

As for John, I learned little, and he is but one John among many. Eventually, amongst the little he revealed, he whispered from the side of his mouth that his name wasn't John in any case, and that the name he was in prison under wasn't his. Elsewhere in the world, he was another identity, and that also with a record. He just didn't want to get too much on the one slate. He was doing this one under another name. I asked him if he could separate the sentence from the reason for it. He grinned.

'It's me that did it. It's me that's doing bird for it.'

What else I learned of John I gathered from his long sardonic grin, his drawn-out sigh and slow speech as he'd flop into the chair. On him there were no records, only an empty manila folder, so what I knew of John was only what I knew from him. If I knew anything. I was, by then, living in a willing suspension of disbelief, and understanding thoroughly what Coleridge meant. John's tale was a common one. He'd been in and out of prison many times, considered himself as much victim as villain, and lived with little hope. Outside, when he got there, he would still be in prison, he said, going out again where there was nothing much to hope for, and where without hope he'd no doubt dive into despair again, and down that vicious road lay all else he barely mentioned, but one day listed, incredulously, as if hearing himself say it all together for the first time: TDA, ABH, GBH, a burglary or two, theft, assaults miscellaneous and various, sometimes with a deadly weapon, special school, remand home, Borstal, prison, years in and out, and the drink. In the 36 years of his life he had

had forty-five previous convictions.

'Oh,' he said, completing the list with what he'd held till last, 'and I've a couple of rapes behind me.' He was particularly ashamed of them. He was examining himself, for reasons, motives, cause, concluding that he really had none. As a child his mother and his aunt had used him sexually. He spoke of his first attempts at normal sex; they were disastrous. He knew he'd grown up bent; normal relationships with women had all ended violently. He said he saw he'd used drink to shut them out, violence to shut them up, refused love, and gone for power, hence rape. He was working all this out for himself. What he wanted was to be free, to have a decent relationship with someone, and most of all to have something to hope for.

'You're scraping the barrel,' the shrink had said, apropos of no one. 'You're fishing in the dustbins of mankind. And what are you looking for?' he wanted to know.

'Hope,' I said. 'I'm looking for hope.' Down here at the end of things, down here in the pit where there's no hope and only illusion of it, crazy dreams men fashion in their long silences is where I'm looking, believing if I can find it here it must exist elsewhere.

'Hope,' John says. 'Dope more like. I can tell you a story about hope.

'Years ago, when I was a kid, when I was nine, when I was a bad lad and all my parents could do was send me away, I was in this home. It was my first institution. The staff were nurses but to me they were screws. One day this screw came round. Maybe he was a nurse but to me he was a screw. He yelled at me: "Time to write to your parents. Ask them how they are. Tell them how you are. Get on with it." He put a pen and paper in front of me. I couldn't write, not really, but I tried. I laboured for an hour over the paper with the pencil in my fist, and I wrote:

der Muman Dud
I op yoor olrite
John

'It was all I could manage. I spelled every word wrong. Then the screw came round and looked at what I'd written. "That's no good," he said. "Look at this. Everything's wrong. Look at this word here." And he pointed to the word *hope* that I'd spelled OP, and he began stabbing the word on the paper with his finger, and then he began stabbing the side of my head with the same finger, saying "HOPE HOPE HOPE" over and over again.

That's all I know about hope.'

Amos. Peter Cook. And John who isn't John.

# 30

# LENNY'S PAINTING

A sad face, quickly creased and darkened, whether by long-term regret or day-to-day anxiety, it's hard to tell. Other inmates shake their heads at Lenny and Lenny's paintings. If they say anything they say, 'Lenny's head's gone', and they leave unopened the next question: did his head go in prison or were his fuses blown earlier, and is that why he's here?

Lenny paints. 'It passes the time.' He stands in the doorway to the Education cell, neither in nor out, holding in his hand a jar of water and orange peel. He swirls it gently round. 'It flavours the water. It costs nothing.'

Rueful, Lenny's grin. Chagrin, it decribes. Lenny is in his early twenties, speaking rarely and softly with a permanently puzzled tone. He is polite, careful, respectful, proper. Tall, his body largish, his face a sad moon in the door-frame, with a long, wispy young man's moustache, his hair is tied back in a tail behind his head. He has the look of an old Chinese sage. He seems both ancient and puppyish at the same time. He explains: he doesn't work, by which he means he doesn't have a prison job that would pay him a couple of quid a week, and a jar of orange water costs nothing. Lenny stays in the wing all day, sometimes painting the pipework or brickwork, preferring his relative poverty for the time and freedom it allows him to paint pictures on hardboard sheets in his cell. That way, his time is his own, he reckons. He is free, he says, in here. He refuses to work. He is a prisoner, so let them keep him. He says some of this, some he implies. Much of the little he says is through gestures with occasional gentle emphasis, through the slow movements of his body, through the glass of orange water in his hand. A lot of it is said in his eyes, which are piercing and blue.

In any case he is free, he explains, in here, tapping the side of his head with his free hand, the same gesture indicating madness. 'My name's Pow.' He spells it out, his manner almost dismissive: 'P.O.W. That's what it means, my name: Prisoner of War.' This is what he believes: 'Oh, they can contain my body, my person, but my mind is free. So far they can't make my space less.' He means the 8 feet by 12 feet of his cell on the second landing, where he chooses most often to be, locked or unlocked, and where he paints. It is his space, that the lifer, whether by rule or by tradition, calls home where, private or lonely, he endures the years. And he means the interior space in his skull, between the bones. He means his spirit.

Therefore he works only sometimes, either when he can be made to or when he chooses to, depending on the viewpoint. From the prison's point of view, he's a sore thumb, and idle hands make mischief; the officers, reflecting this view, dismiss him as a lazy bugger. Sometimes he's to be seen doing a little paintwork, or serving on the hotplate, or hurrying about the wing on some business, an easy independent air about him. At other times I've seen him up on the twos, going about his chores with his bowl and his bucket and his mug, always with a worried look, moving with leisurely speed, avoiding others. Since he doesn't work in a shop or do education he has the relative calm of the afternoon wing to take care of his business and avoid the crowd, to wash his hair or take a shower or slop out in peace. And to paint. Whenever I've spotted him up there, he's usually been in the act of dodging back behind his door, through which, briefly and from the ground floor below, I've glimpsed a room full of bright colours, shining in the poor light.

Yesterday, out on the yard where other men took their exercise, walking in orderly fashion anti-clockwise round and around, Lenny, in the middle, had lain a towel to mark the space he moved through in the slow graceful ellipses of tai-chi: a free man if ever I saw one, moving as he wished where others moved as they were bid. No one knows why the direction in the exercise yard is always anti-clockwise, always has been, whether as some custom that once started would be difficult to alter, or whether the result of some notion of healthy exercise propounded back in the dim reaches of the last century, on whose principles much of prison practice rests. Nothing much has changed in here, and no one knows where or when in the long history of imprisonment men set off walking round the yard against the clock, a process now irreversible in the ongoing regime of time.

Lenny was openly challenging at least a century's penal tradition, and the great bureaucratic edifice thrown up by it. This was the exercise hour, and this was his form of exercise, and where else was he to do it, tai-chi in the space of his crowded cell being impossible. Very soon, though, Lenny's movements threatened good order and discipline. His was not a behavioural norm, it contradicted all prevailing theories of man-management, and therefore defied the gods. To the officers, Lenny's discipline was indistinguishable from *martial arts*, and so it was described when Lenny duly appeared in front of the Governor charged with offences against discipline, disobeying an order, refusing to walk in an endless left wheel. He spent three days down the block for it, and when he came back and did it again, a further spell in the cooler. His intention, he said, was to do it yet again. It was his exercise. 'It's also my religion. I have the right to practise my religion.'

On the yard Lenny's antics were seen at first as providing comedy and diversion, but they were in reality something else the officers whose job is watching must watch. They might be looking at him when something else happened on the other side of the yard, as the circle of twos and threes and loners, fast walkers and slow, revolved. It might confuse the dogs. You could see their point of view. And in any case how were they to know he wasn't winding himself up for some mighty twenty-foot kung-fu leap over the wire and the wall and the space between to the world outside? In their time, they'd seen some strange things. Some had been here when George Blake took off, and he meditated and did yoga, it was said. They'd seen Bruce Lee movies. And if Lenny got away with it, who might be next with some exotic discipline? So Lenny was stopped, and what came across on the charge sheet was not the gentle art of tai-chi but *martial arts*. They were threatened. They had enough to do, without Lenny's parabolic distractions. Clearly Lenny had scored a moral victory, but moral victories don't count for a lot of anything on D Wing, where if anywhere on earth virtue must content itself by being its own reward. So Lenny went to the block for a while to meditate time and space. He came back and did it again and went down the block again. Perhaps the block was no big deal for Lenny; he lived in his head anyway.

It was on his third block trip that the door burst open, preceded by a single heavy knock.

'Pow!'

He was a big man, the officer, wide and red in the face, wearing a look of permanent anger and frustration, an air that announced abiding contempt and the fact there was never enough time for all he had to do. He was a screw, this one. He filled the door-frame, and loomed without self-doubt through it.

'Pow!'

His accent was broad, his face swollen and red and unfortunately pimpled, his manner resentful, arrogant. He was a cliché, the slob turned martinet, a gem of his kind.

'Pow!'

Whatever he was talking about, his voice anticipated no contradiction. Or maybe this was some sort of ritual greeting peculiar to prison — a full flinging open of the door followed by the bellowing of 'Pow' three times.

So 'Pow' I said back. 'You mean the inmate Pow?'

'Pow,' he said, more gently. Behind him a couple of inmates were awaiting his command, hanging purposefully about. He explained. It seemed they were turning over Lenny's cell while he was down the block, 'while he's on his holidays', the officer said, grinning, pleased with himself, including me in his conspiracy. He turned, gesturing to the two sheepish inmates behind him who were carrying a large cardboard box, indicating the corner in grunt and point speech. They dumped the heavy box and left, like two extras hired to be the parts of guilty men, consenting in each other's defeat.

The box was filled with plunder from Lenny's cell, his hoard of inks and half-used paint-tubes in all the variations of the rainbow, their oils dried where they spilled. Tubes and tubes of them, most of them part squeezed and oozing, like a box of many coloured snakes, they were his stash of primary colours, built up from badgering the art teacher, inherited from other men who'd gone elsewhere, from whatever trading he could do about the wing. They'd confiscated the lot.

'Pow,' the officer said again, explaining everything and meaning everything, and then elucidating further with a possessive followed by a negative and a new assertion: 'Pow's stuff. Not fucking Pow's. Not any more it's not.' He shook his head. 'This lot belongs to you.'

'Not to me.'

'To you,' he assured me, firmly. He pulled back the open door, tapping two fingers heavily on the sign saying EDUCATION. 'That's you,' he said, sure in his belief that behind every door sat the appropriate occupant.

'And there's something else. Up there.' He pointed upward in the direction of Lenny's cell. 'He's got a load of your books.'

'He hasn't got any of my books.'

'Oh yes, he has. About twenty of them. I'll bring them down. Now.'

'Pow doesn't have any of my books. Not twenty. If he has any books of mine I've lent them to him.'

'He's not allowed that many. Six he can have. Twenty's too many of anything.'

The next week Lenny was back again, quiet, impish, subdued. This time he swallowed his pride and thereafter he no longer practised exotic oriental disciplines on the exercise yard. He drew inward, exploring his inner space, he said, when next he loomed through the door. 'They still can't make my space less.' But he sounded less certain of it. He smiled politely, and stooped to lift the large box of paints confiscated the week before, still in the corner. As he heaved it up he turned and grinned. 'You haven't seen this. You haven't seen me.'

'I haven't seen you, Lenny.'

But I have seen something of Lenny. At his request I brought him a copy of the *I Ching*. He gave me a painting. I gathered yarrow stalks from the scrubs and the railway embankment behind the prison, and cut him fifty brown sticks to throw the hexagrams with. We talked thereafter in ellipses and symbols. He showed me poems, short, imagistic, tiny fragments of reality, fractional phrases, language broken up. I couldn't say much. He wasn't interested in anything but his painting. Any new thought only confused him further. Lenny's mind seemed to be somewhere else, and his speech a tussle to communicate from some distant place. He grew his hair longer and tied it back ever more severely, and with his drooping moustache came more and more to look like Fu-Manchu. One day he told me he'd been called to a meeting that morning, his board, convened to make decisions about his future. At the appointed hour he'd taken the *I Ching* along and asked the Governor to throw the hexagrams. The Guv refused. Lenny had gathered up the book and sticks and left the room, refusing to participate any further in the meeting. If they would not share in how he arrived at his decisions, he said, he would withdraw. He considered the sixty-four ancient Chinese hexagrams of more authority in his life than any decision *they* might make.

We talked, occasionally, usually to no conclusion; like his poems, he made short forays, quick observations, and withdrew, content with the point he'd made. His paintings, which he daubed onto sheets of hardboard straight from the tube and shaped with a plastic knife, rarely with a brush, were blurbs of many-coloured oils in conflict with each other. His painting was a form of assault. Mostly they were just colours, banged on and down. The colours shocked each other. Then, gradually, some form began to emerge. In them what seemed to be faces peered mournfully through what seemed to be bars. With time these seemed to become clearer, though as ever Lenny wasn't looking for narrative, but it seemed to me that in it all someone was looking out from somewhere. One day Lenny said, showing me a new painting: 'I think it's clearing.'

As time went by, the faces became more clearly faces. Images began to form in all the mad coagulations of paint. The painting that he gave me was the clearest I saw: in a landscape of many leaves and trees vague figures appear on what seems to be the bright green bank of a river, a *déjeuner sur l'herbe*. The river flows bluely through the middle ground, the treetops beyond filling the painting's upper half, bright and many coloured on the other side of the river, as if they were filled with autumn, with fruit and leaves. The river issues from the side of a building that might be a barn or a bridge or just a wall: a white wall broken by dark openings, doors or windows. A prison wall.

But Lenny says nothing of it. He likes the colours. He likes the shapes the colours make. Of his paintings he says, 'they're coming clearer'. But there's still a great blank in there, a great confusion, his face forever registering that he doesn't understand *why* he is here, doesn't accept the facts proven in court. These are that some years ago, drunk, stoned, maybe tripping, Lenny killed an old man with a hammer for the change in his pocket. They lived in the same house and had been drinking together. Lenny says the man was his friend, and can't explain why he killed him, or accept that he killed him, doesn't believe he did, denies it without hope or any conviction as if he were bemused at the far end of an argument he long ago lost and can no longer be bothered with.

Maybe Lenny is a prisoner of war. But I don't know which war.

# 31
# CRIMES OF PASSION

A decent man, Ron, though Ron's not his real name. A man with a clear sense of honour, of right and wrong, a man of common-sense. Always smart, his wavy silver hair combed and brushed, Ron has a shine on him. In his late fifties, formerly a business man, intelligent and with a developed interest in the world, in politics and society, and behind him a varied career and a good war record earned in North Africa, Ron was an inmate serving life in D Wing for some years, though he's moved on now. While there, he was one who with difficulty managed to keep himself to himself and the company of one or two mates that he trusted, and he lived as fully as he possibly could under the conditions as he found them. He made no waves, kept his nose clean, and undertook to keep his mind alive through books, the radio, magazines, music, writing and conversation. 'I had a life before I came into prison,' he would say. 'I plan to have a life again when I go out.' In a sense, though this was not his intention, Ron was a model prisoner. He did not defy orders or disrupt routine, he had no forbidden habits or vices; he spent his time as much as possible behind his door.

Ron's tale has no sting in its end, and no twist. It is exemplary, a portrait of an ordinary man who, having committed the most forbidden crime of murder, goes to prison, serves his time there, accepts his fate and makes the most of it. As an example Ron is rare, but he is not untypical. In the class of lifer he is perhaps one pole, his behaviour impeccable in difficult circumstances, and down from him his fellow inmates shade off into lesser breeds of murderer. Murder too has its degrees. Though to kill, to take another life, to breach that most forbidding of commandments is the worst of crimes, once committed it falls into categories of more or less: who? how? how many? how many times? with what intent? with what premeditation or motive? In prison some men look down on others in the particulars of savagery. Some murders are more respectable than others in the scale of prison values. Some are a question of definition. Some are arguable as manslaughter, which may or may not result in life. A victim stabbed once might just be construed as manslaughter, sudden fury; stabbed twice it's definitely murder. Some results seem inexplicable, such as the man who having murdered his wife cut her up and distributed the pieces in plastic bags around London; he got a straight six years. In prison such variables give rise to wonder and envy, strengthening the prevailing belief that justice is uneven, capricious, unequal, often itself unjust. Many murders are the result of a daft spree, a piss-up, a fight at a football game. Many are seen as self defence, some as inevitable, one or two as even-stephens. A great many have to do with love, or love's exits and entrances. Some 20 per cent of murders every year are domestic, and these, with crimes of passion, account for many extreme sins. Ron's murder was one of these, not recognized in English law and always difficult to prove or unprove, because difficult to determine as to degree of premeditation: *crime passionnel*.

Not that Ron looked down on anyone else, or he didn't show it if he did. He chose his company, or made do with his own, speaking ill of no one. He didn't gossip. His story is quite simple, quite straightforward, quite ordinary. Some years before, he'd met a young woman, the woman he had eventually killed. He had begun an affair with her that in time transcended his marriage. At any rate the marriage, of long standing, with teenage children, couldn't take the strain and ended in divorce. The marriage was ended with much bitterness. As the divorce went through, he planned marriage with the young woman, and to protect his business, and acting as a man trusting in love, assigned her a partnership in all his affairs that placed his business beyond the reach of courts and alimony and gave her control. She signed the cheques. He signed his life over to her. Divorced at last, decree absolute in hand, and all the rough business at a marriage's end finally over, he turned to look for her.

It seemed that in the meantime she'd grown less keen on marriage, and there were business difficulties — and another man she'd met. Ron, his business stolen from under him, his life in ruins, got hold of a shotgun, waited in his car outside the pub he knew she and the man were drinking in, and as they came out, shot her in the chest and killed her. Which is one sort of end to a conversation. Their dialogue went no further.

Ron made no effort to conceal his crime. Since he admitted it and pleaded guilty, his trial was swift and uncomplicated, though the police and the prosecution blackened him as a calculating and cold-blooded killer, which he protested he was not. By overloading the prosecution evidence, the police made sure he did not get off with manslaughter, although he offered no excuse and made no plea in mitigation. Ron had reacted in criminal passion to what he could no longer bear, perhaps for a time he *was* mad, but he made no such claim. Love generates such furies. Simply, he'd had enough. His life was wrecked; he obliterated hers; all he wanted to do was get on with his sentence, plan a life beyond it. He felt remorse, and kept it to himself. He didn't want anyone's pity or mercy, and felt there were plenty in the world in need of any spare compassion.

The price, for Ron, was life imprisonment. In his case, life set at the norm of a fifteen-year sentence may see him out, with remission, in a decade. Keeping his head down, which isn't easy, he may do it in ten. If so, it will be because the powers-that-be have judged him fit, a man who murdered once in a particular circumstance, and not a man to kill again.

The system as he saw it was designed so that no one could win. Whichever way he went carried a risk, since reports are made on everything, and everything can be interpreted negatively. Ron pointed out that, given the mundane option of going on evening association, the choice was damning. If he went over to the rec he was *associating with known criminals*. If he stayed in his cell, he was *anti-social*. One comment or the other will appear in his file. 'Buggered if you do, buggered if you don't. You fight the system and it screws you; you go along with the system and it screws you.' Given there was no way to win, Ron saw his life strategically from day to day. There were some things common-sense and decency told him not to do: you didn't grass, you didn't hang around the heavies, you didn't hang around the screws, you didn't hang around.

Only considered among his peers is he better than any other man, yet I suspect Ron may be a better man than many.

After a few years on D Wing, Ron moved to another prison. He got himself a deal, to be the 'friend' of another prisoner in another goal in a maximum security unit, closed to the rest of the prison, on a little desert island in time. The offer came via a man in a raincoat without a name, said only to be from 'head office'. It was offered first to another man with a similarly impeccable background, but he turned it down. For Ron the deal has advantages — he's out of the heavy traffic of the wing and in a cosy little unit. There'll be a kitchen, music, books, a TV. And if he does his job right, or just for trying, presumably he'll make it out in just a few more years.

Other men shrug, envying Ron his opportunity. For most of them there's no moral dilemma in betraying the other man. It's a chance to improve his circumstance, to move closer to the gate, to begin to live his life again. They wish him luck.

And then consider G. Our paths have crossed before, G's and mine, some years ago in a cold south coast seaside town I ran away to, to stare at linoleum and the winter Channel. He was there then, and I dimly recall his face behind the counter of the camera shop he kept by the station. There is a dour passport photograph of me he took at that time. His face, fixed now in the wide perpetual *can I help you?* grin of a man who's kept a store for thirty years, has beamed into mine before. His face beams still, though he is never happy nor expects ever to be again. G killed his wife, in rage, in temper, in absence of control. Writing about it in a thinly disguised fiction whose protagonist is much like himself, G uses the clichés *as if in a dream, as if in a nightmare, in a sort of hypnotic state, as if in slow motion it had happened, he had killed her, he was powerless to stop it, he was a voyeur to this dreadful act.*

*He had killed her.*

Beneath the outer face, the tragedy of G's face, of his life, looks out bravely. He loved her. Still does. He did not plan to kill her. He has years yet to come in which to regret that he killed the wife he loved, who'd gone cold on him. She'll never comfort him again, nor any other. He writes this, and says it on the edge of weeping, though his face still wears its uniform of a smile. 'Did your face let you down?' I ask, and he says, 'Yes. It let me down at my trial. I think the jury thought I was enjoying myself, as if at my own spectacle. I think that's why I got life, and not manslaughter.'

So much for thirty years practising the smile of a shopkeeper, a helpful man, a photographer, retailer, businessman, one who might turn up at weddings with his tripod and black cloth, accept a half of lager and a piece of wedding cake and depart.

As with Ron, there was no argument at the trial, no doubt nor denial nor defence, though G pleaded mitigating circumstances and his defence expected a manslaughter verdict. Both men are ageing, in their fifties. Both were in the Army in the war and saw action. Both write, and are thoughtful men, and consider the ways of love. With so much in common, I want to introduce Ron to G, but Ron's gone, moved on, and G has just started down the long life prison road. This is the only place they'll ever meet.

For most men who come here, as prisoners, this is the end, the death of the spirit, of all hope of love. Many express a longing for love, where they have put themselves beyond love, having murdered the object of their passions. Men such as Ron and G are mixed in at close and crowded and competitive quarters with others, some of whom are mad, some since coming here, some earlier, some psychotic, repetitive killers as if from the sperm, some vicious rapists, some just plain old crooks always after an edge and finding one in whatever circumstances, sharks. The place is utterly dangerous for those who live here, and in their long observance they're sifted, those who might be trusted not to kill again from those who might, as they are moved either towards return to the world, or further from it. The fact remains, for whatever reasons and out of whatever pressures, such men cracked, with terrible consequences, and their victims have no voice.

Such is G's rationale. He cracked under pressure, his business failing as his marriage failed, and the overlapping failures of his life dragging him to breaking point. He had no intent to kill her, though the evidence states he came to talk with her with a chisel in his coat. He'd been working with it, he says, and at the moment of crisis there it was in his pocket, in his hand, in her chest. Spontaneity was difficult to prove, since he was tooled up. He loved her, he says, out loud and in the words he gets on paper. She wouldn't talk. They knew it was all falling apart, but she wouldn't discuss why, and then she was leaving him, and all at once he was losing her, his son, his home, and his business. His second marriage at that. He'd held out against the conglomerates and the drug store chains, in his town by the sea, and felt everything collapsing round him, and lashed out.

Now he winds down his life from inside. What money's left from the winding up of his affairs is in trust for his son, but he fears he will never see his son again. His son will no longer speak to him, and has returned his birthday card scrawled over *I hate you*. His former best friend, a man he cared for 'dearer than my own brother', took all his personal possessions to the town dump, and tipped them in. He misses his word processor. And there'll be no photography in here, G.

# 32
# DEATH ON THE WING

Some days it's too much, too much of everything. The spirit wants to quit, to give in to failure and misery and despair, to accept death, to go down into the dark wailing forever, and be done with this poxy planet, where we seem chiefly employed in making each other miserable.

For many each day is like this: *there is nothing to hope for*. None of the things some of us expect and most of us want or dream of will ever come true, and there's no end to this business of prison. On such days death, always close, presents his arguments. There's the possibility of suicide to consider, if only to end the prospect of years more in prison, and whatever life might come after. And there's the possibility of dying in prison in any case. To die there seems the ultimate defeat.

Conversely there's the school of thought that says to make a decision in his own death, and to bring it about, constitutes an inmate's only choice and ultimately defeats the system. Certainly it confounds justice, as the Hungerford assassin proved. In the University of Green Ginger, there's much heated discussion on this very point: who wins in the end, by suicide?

To die in prison, that's another thing, whether of age or the heart's failing. It's one thing to die in the natural order of events, as all of us do, but to die in prison carries its own stigma. In prison some die in revenge, in long brewed quarrels, or as random victims. In prison, there are psychopaths who kill again, some for all manner of obscure reasons, some for none. From whatever cause, death in captivity has more finality, less grace, more of the sharp tang of shame about it, and forms the ultimate epitaph of the damned. So men fear it, speaking of death with a strange familiarity that doesn't disguise their awe of it and their particular desire not to die inside. To die there is to die in a crowded and closed institution where the intimacies of living are difficult to conceal, and privacy a dangerous delusion. In prison, death is a constant, a horizon note, a thread running through everything. Conversations often turn to it; the attention's never far from it. *Watch out for your back* is the kindest advice here.

Men die here, as in any community, though here for some their ends are abrupt, mysterious, suspicious. A man may die and no one but the coroner be any the wiser. For some there's no relative to enquire, or no one who cares to; they are bodies, as they were in life, to be accompanied to another location. There are dark tales of troublesome prisoners murdered in their cells, their deaths made to look like suicides. No one names anyone. It is an accepted possibility. Whether such things happen, men live with such legends and such fears, repeating stories of faked suicide, neglect leading to collapse, cruel treatment. In another prison, one man said, his cell neighbour would not wash; the screws threw buckets of cold water over him, he said. He caught pneumonia and died. In Wandsworth two men conspired against their cellmate, whom they mistakenly took for a nonce, persuading him to hang himself; he survived, but had a stroke. In the Scrubs another inmate persuaded his crippled cellmate in the 43 Unit to hang himself; he failed and the man recovered. Sentenced for it to another eight, he was said to have brainwashed his victim with black magic. At Grendon, having tried to strangle one man in the toilets, a prisoner in for five for rape attacked his cellmate, barricaded the door, and over the next three days raped, roped, beat and cut him, carved a Union Jack in his back, dragging him around and suspending him from the light fitting. Previously in Shrewsbury in 1984 the same man had taken two others hostage, collecting a sentence of another three. This time he got life.

And there is death the macabre, the probably apocryphal, set at no particular date but in another prison, such as the tale, told by officers, of a man dying in his cell. The same tale, told by inmates, takes a different slant, and isn't told for a laugh. The man had been ringing his bell for attention in the night, but no one had answered it and the man had collapsed and died. Discovered in the morning, he was cold. Before the doctor's arrival he was taken to the kitchens to be warmed over on the hotplate so that his estimated time of death didn't implicate the night watch. The same tale's told of other prisons, and a variant from HMP Lewes has the MO asking why the corpse is warm on one side only, and ordering an enquiry.

In jail, death is constantly spoken of in the lingo of frequent violence, the snarl that lurks as threat and implication in speech. Between man and man vigilance and suspicion; between officers and prisoners eternal hatred and contempt, unto death, overtly or covertly expressed. Death, always closer in prison, stains the language and leaves its bloody footprints on the landings, lingering on the stale air and the apocrypha of the wing. Derek tells how, hearing a commotion one morning before unlock, he put his eye to the spyhole and squinted to see a group of officers manoeuvering a body bag down the stairwell. His neighbour had died in the night, and was being shuffled off. He says as they left the wing he heard a screw shout 'One off, Sir,' and laugh. One off the body count.

But for the suicides, perhaps the greatest awe. Some men say they'd never top themselves, others speak of it as a considered possibility, in some circumstances the only way out, preferable to life imprisonment. Some who attempt it merely make a mess, and there's a suspicion they're not really serious about it. And some succeed, their deaths on the wing becoming part of its myth, altered by rumour and repetition, conditioned by perspective and conviction, whispered, mentioned in despatches, and no doubt deeply considered and feared in the silence and the dark where each man sleeps alone.

From C Wing, where the proximity of the life wing excites the remands' curiosity, came a story of a man who'd laid himself out and killed himself on D Wing, 'just before Christmas', either with pills or with a trick played with a rubber band around the tongue. But on D Wing, where I asked around, no one had heard of such a recent suicide, nor of this one in particular. It hadn't happened. This proved nothing: a man, a newcomer or a man passing through, might have died in his cell and been shipped out in the night unseen, and the matter no more spoken of. But on the wing, crowded and busy as it is, new faces are soon noted and often familiar to someone, and everyone is soon identified. Men here like to know who their neighbours are.

In the story, the man stocked up on sleepers sufficient to the task. Choosing his moment, he took the pills, having laid himself out — washed himself, plugged up all his orifices with cotton batting, tied a bandage round his penis, lying on his back with his hands clasped ready for the morning and his coffin — and died. So they would find him at unlocking, dead and ready for death, his body delivered like a parcel, or a message: *To hell with you. You can't hurt me no more.*

Did he win, or was he defeated? What matters perhaps is how the story is told — with admiration, with bravura, approval, conviction, as I heard it. A companion tale exists about a suicide in Durham women's prison. Whatever origins in the truth or what relation to that notion, clearly the tale fascinated its tellers, young apprentice prisoners on remand. In prison the truth of anything is elusive and illusory, and the discussion of death no exception. Whether it ever happened, or what might be supposed by such a gesture, becomes the subject for intense speculation. But all we have is what the story's telling tells, the trace it leaves. And all we have of the dead is reports of the manner of their passing.

What's true for instance about John G's death? He was found face down naked in the shower one night, dying. The autopsy said a heart attack, which was the least of it. He's dead. Men swear they've heard officers say of it, 'one less mouth to feed', and the truth is that another man calls John's cell home now, eats his ration, does his job, grieves and desires in his slot in the great beehive. Another has moved into his notch in the seamless successions of prison life.

What facts there are include the fact John was diabetic, and this figured in his appeal. Thereafter, speculation. On the wing he was said to have been playing games with his insulin and sugar intake, some said to get attention, some said to get to the hospital. Others said as a diabetic he shouldn't have been on the threes and should have been in the hospital in any case. Whatever the truth, whether from insulin shock or not, he collapsed in the shower. Various estimates are given for how long it took to discover him, how long it took the officers to get to him, how long they tried to revive him. C says they got there as fast as they could, B says they didn't try hard enough, D says he was dead anyhow. Rumour and bias and complaint are working at the story, and the official verdict doesn't say enough: heart failure. The borders between fact and report are as ever elusive. In prison, where every motive is suspect, John had been studying for the O.U., where in particular he was trying to find out more about his disability, as this related to his case. His appeal focused on his claim that at the time of his crime he had been suffering the effects of insulin overdose administered by a hospital. His contention was that as a result when he had killed a man and wounded a woman, his former girlfriend and her new love, he had not been fully responsible for himself. This was his defence, true or false. He had been working at it for his appeal.

Whatever the truth of that, it doesn't matter now. John's dead. In his death some saw miscalculation, hope in that a man who was studying was not thinking of killing himself. He was seeking knowledge and to better his circumstances. He was normal. He was working for his appeal. He was working his way through the carrot system.

But his appeal failed. Perhaps he deprived himself of insulin and ran his heart ragged. Or perhaps he overdid an attempt to get to hospital. Or perhaps, his appeal having gone down and nothing before him but more years of the same, he took himself off, having studied the procedure in a calculated and deliberate suicide.

John's dead, whether or not by his own decision. Col thinks, and J thinks, and Ginner thinks that his insulin withholding went awry, that he didn't mean to go over the top. Dave favours the other opinion, that he learned how to stop his heart, and took death's option. John's epitaph, from Dave, came in the mail:

> *A very nice but mixed up bloke. About 39, from Dublin.*
> *Builder. Own one man business. Divorced. Got involved*
> *with a single woman, scorned by a woman's love. Went on*
> *the bottle, mournful maudlin and bloody Irish angry after*
> *giving so much and then being gypped. Ended up stabbing the*
> *new boyfriend till his life expired, and she lost a mincer.*
> *Tragic. Sadness and pathos all showed in John's eyes. A fine*
> *big man. Intelligent. Good sense of humour. But a conscience*
> *that troubled him too much. Appeal failed. Family and*
> *friends deserted him. Couldn't face all the lonely years.*
> *A voice crying out on D Wing. But no warmth or understanding*
> *or support. Yeah, suicide. And the only consolation*
> *is that John won't have to endure a life sentence.*

Defeated. Beaten. Some reject the option: the system's won. Others shrug; death's common in these parts, epitaphs blunt and brief: *he didn't live the life he wanted but he died it.*

And then the other bloke, a week later. He barricaded himself in, but they broke through and saved him. He had every intention of killing himself, but he failed, and lies now in the hospital, sad, sorry and stitched, healing, beaten and turned down even by death. He cut his wrists and his throat, terribly, and yet failed to die. He had taken a month's saved up stash of painkillers, but they only thickened and clotted his blood, defeating his purpose. He excited no sympathy. He'd failed, and made a mess of it, and the weight of general opinion turned against him. Jack the Nameless opined he'd cheated: he'd built up debts, he'd bought gear on credit he would never pay for, having planned to go out, and Anon said he'd owed about £70 on the wing, and the pressure had turned heavy. Others shook their heads, unable to think things could ever get that bad. Steve complained for his mate, who'd lent him his Stanley blade, so now he didn't have one.

Death on the wing. Perhaps the only thing worse, on the wing, is to fail death.

# SONGS OF INNOCENCE

# 33

# ON INNOCENCE

Prison has no machinery to deal with innocence. Its brief is to take delivery of those convicted and to lock them up until instructed to let them go. The prison's business is to feed, house, clothe, count, lock, and unlock. Its welfare, medical, educational and pastoral provisions are largely minimal, however enduring, and most of prison activity is administration reduced to a science of man-management, moving its denizens around the system, compiling reports.

Any man who in all of this insists he is innocent of the crime gets little shrift. Because he is in prison he is guilty, and the system has no other way to deal with him. He must follow out the appeal system as far as it will take him, and this may be a long process. At the end of it, if his appeal fails, and without new evidence he cannot get an appeal, he is expected to give up the struggle, accept his fate, do his time. Welfare may note he is distressed, and Psychology consider what he says as part of his overall condition, but there is nowhere for him to go with his innocence. Even the priest cannot absolve him from what he claims he hasn't done. And if he insists on the matter, he makes life more difficult than otherwise for himself. By refusing to blend into the mass of the guilty he stands apart, focused on his predicament, unable to participate even in the grim rituals of prison life.

It must be said that such men are few, and that from prison it looks overall as if the law, if an ass and often unfair, is somehow efficient. And yet if most of those it sentences to prison are in reality guilty, there are still those who are significant for their denial, well-founded or otherwise. There are several reasons why some prisoners persist in their claim: loopholes in the evidence or the conduct of the trial or of the original police enquiries. Some may persist out of obtuseness or refusal or a desire for attention; some out of continuing mental disturbance. And some may indeed be innocent. One D Wing man was the subject of a convincing *Rough Justice* investigation in 1987; another, a soldier, drunk at a wedding, who had shot his stepfather, and was originally sent down for life for murder, had his sentence reduced to accidental manslaughter and was released, having served four years. Some are capable of great self deception; some are insane or probably were at the time, and have repressed the event. There are some who insist year by year on their innocence, and theirs is a particular hell. There are some who other inmates think are wrongly convicted, beyond the scale of the general sense of injustice all around. And there are one or two who officers and even governors think are innocent, though theirs is largely a private opinion, founded on observation of the demeanour and attitude of the prisoner.

In the first place, a man still claiming his innocence is one of many inmates, submerged in the crowd. 'Sure, mate, we're all innocent in here.' For some the cry of innocence continues for a while as a dying reflex from accusation and trial, a stance difficult to drop. Panda's survey on the matter turned up very few trumps — men who could put the right hand on the heart and hold up the left and say, eyeball to eyeball, 'I'm innocent'. Panda's Hands-up Club had few members: himself and his mate Tel, whose papers were a foot thick, and whose entire daily activities were dedicated to rattling the cages of administrators to tell them where he stood in the matter. It would take a long parliament to unravel his case. Panda's was straightforward: he hadn't shot the geezer. In a car-park, in the dark, amongst a group of men discussing villainy of whom he was one, a gun was produced and fired and the man fell dead. There were others who might have had reason to do it, but he got nailed for it, and had no defence but denial. In most circumstances it is difficult to prove you didn't do something. He fitted the frame. He was being naughty, and the other man's wife was involved, and there were other funny dealings all around. The French police had thought the Mafia at first, and one day Panda came in electrified. He'd just taken an O.U. French exam in which the taped news-bulletin reported in French, for his translation, the very murder of which he was convicted. That freaked him, and got him thinking about it all again. But there was little he could do. The brief had given up on him, and from where he was, it was difficult to find another who would open up his file. So there he was, innocent or not, with no circumstances in his favour, no means to unprove; someone who, because he was standing in the frame at the time, was now fixed in it. His case illustrated the dangers of putting oneself in a frame, of having secrets and activities to conceal, whether shy of the law or adulterous.

In time most men give up the unequal struggle. Most are wearily resigned. Every day they are reminded of their guilt, and the endless barrage wears down their resistance, as their claims of innocence fade away as they settle to their time. The claim of innocence is inconvenient, and seen as awkwardness, rebellion. It's difficult to maintain, surrounded by everything that says the opposite. Innocence burns itself out.

Others are considered guilty more or less: in many cases the prosecution has overloaded its argument, in some police have taken short cuts, in order to ensure conviction. Some men admit to many crimes, but not the ones they're here for, and can construe their cases to suggest a stitch-up: the police wanted them off the streets, and if they couldn't get them for what they had done they'd fit them in a frame for something they hadn't. Steve, who claimed he'd been fitted-up for ringing cars, protested that his was the clean crime of kyting cheques, and was indignant to be in here as a common thief. Many on murder charges argue down their crime to manslaughter, or self defence, or, like Fuzzy and his brothers, have been jointly accused and convicted of murder in a deadly affray where one hand slew but all were sentenced for it. The shades and technicalities are many, and innocence a much divided territory.

In the place of truth, which is hardly ever absolute, there are several scenarios. Mostly what we know of anything or anyone is only partial, a pattern put together from presented and edited versions, according to many biases and sundry imperfections. Perceptions differ and language distorts, the teller of the tale and the listener add their wavering attentions, the memory malfunctions. What we know we obtain from various competing interpretations. History forms its narratives, and each individual life is its own bundle of stories interweaving others. In practice the police have their scenario: they seek motive, build a profile of their suspect, link cause to effect, build a case. True or false, they seek to prove it. In court the police and prosecution put forward one scenario, a plot, events with characters who are to be proven guilty, and persuading judge and jury is the entire object of the performance, by which they make their livings and advance their careers. The defence likewise stitch the details and the images together into a credible narrative in which the protagonist is innocent, at any rate as charged, or find some flaw in the procedures of the law. The verdict is a victory for one version or another, and thereafter forms the basis of all other judgements. Thereafter the professionals of security, welfare, psychiatry and sociology and penology add their reports, each on a self-assured groundwork of objectivity. But none of this is disinterested nor entirely objective, nor can it be: in the drama of the court the scenarios of guilt and innocence compete, and at the result the media present their versions of events, their angles, and whatever was the truth is further confounded, and public opinion set, and all the great misremembered dramas filed away into history.

# 34
# PEPI

'So what you fink, guv?'

Short, neat, tough, the face and stance of a lightweight boxer, which in real life he sometimes was. A hard man, sharp and wily, direct, easily given to mocking, even himself, he spoke in a straight, broad south-of-the-river cockney street slang. A very light tan half-caste, his skin yellowy and grey with prison, he seemed indeterminately Arab, white, negroid, gipsy, Asiatic. He was an Everyman, all the world contributing to his making, and, as he freely admitted, a villain: the son, brother, nephew and cousin of villains, from communities and neighbourhoods of villains, descendant of villains from generations of villains as far back as anyone recalls. Such history as he had he kept to himself, implying an inheritance in crime and street survival, brawling and boxing and thieving, 'a life bred on poverty' akin to the East End background of the Krays described in John Pearson's *Profession of Violence*.

Beneath the dull matt of prison despair, Pepi often had a shine to him, his humour bitterly ironic, but still alive; still a cheer in him. Like everyone here, Pepi's moods swung through the spectrum; he had his good days and his bad. On a downer, he'd be clenched in scruffy rage at the sheer fact of prison, of being alive if prison was to be his life, sulking, unshaven and unapproachable behind his door. On long benders of despair he'd grow his stubble into almost a beard, and then suddenly he'd bounce back fresh again, shiny and shaved and shampooed and with a gleam in his dark brown eyes and a lift in his loping step, sharp-eyed and bushy-tailed. He'd stay up for a while, using the gym, exercising, showering, being sociable, getting about his business on the wing till the next downer, when he'd slump again, and give up.

We met on a good day. He appeared in the frame of the open door, casual, and as if merely passing the time of day, the wing busy behind him, and he still checking left, right, and aft of himself as if at any moment he might depart: 'I've heard you're a writer. That right? 'Ere, I've got a story for you.' He spoke in short jabs, half grinning, casting his eyes down the wing as if the third person he was speaking in were someone else, and this all a bit of a joke: ''Ere. What you fink, guv? How's this for a story? There's this bloke, in here, he's doing life for a murder he didn't do. What you fink?'

Moving into the room, he closed the door on the wing and leaned back on it, his manner conspiratorial, half kidding. 'Yeah, I know what you fink. We're all innocent here. But this geezer really is. He's stitched up. He's in here for summing he didn't do. He ain't the only one, but he's the one I care about, cause he's me.'

He paused to let it sink in. 'Yes guv, I know, it's me, innit? But I never cut nobody, in my life. I'm here for summing I didn't do. I mean, I know I'm a villain. Leave it around and I'll have it. But I never cut nobody. I never stuck nobody.'

And then, fast and to the point: so what was he to do but push to get his case opened up for an appeal, and how did he get in touch with the TV programme *Rough Justice*, and could I help him write a letter about his case? He didn't want to write anything himself, so he wasn't really supposed to be a customer of mine. Fact was, he couldn't write very well. He couldn't express himself, couldn't do the joined-up too good, but I could show him how? Or better still, since that would take forever and him not much of a learner, why didn't I write the letter, and he'd just leave me with the details?

'Anyway, guv, it would take too long for me to learn it, and I'd still be in here while I was doing it, wouldn't I? I just want out. I don't belong in here.'

He registered my disbelief. He grinned and shrugged. 'Yeah, I know what you fink. We all say that in here. We're all innocent in this fackin' place. But I fackin' am.' And then 'I'll show you,' he said, and left abruptly. Minutes later he was back, dumping down inside a rolled-up magazine a transcript of the thirty or so pages of the judge's summing-up of his trial. 'Read this, guv. Take it with you. Read it when you're ready. See what you fink. I ain't saying no more. I'd like to hear what you fink when you've had your mincers over it. Then you can see for yourself whether I'm a load of bollocks. Truth is I am, guv. We're all a load of bollocks in here. But I never cut nobody. I'm a villain but I never killed nobody.' And he left.

At his trial for murder at the Old Bailey in January 1984, Pepi was found guilty of the killing of a man who died from knife wounds after being attacked in the upstairs pool-room of a club in Soho in the early hours of the morning of 24 January 1983. The victim had been drinking and playing pool in the club when, without any preliminaries, another man came in and knifed him. He had run out and subsequently died on a doorstep two hundred yards away, though whether of the wound he got in the club or of another delivered as he ran was unclear. In all there had been three knife wounds; witnesses spoke only of one inflicted in the badly lit club, and differed in their interpretation of events that had happened in a very short time. There might have been another, unknown, assailant. The defence had raised these questions. The question of the trial, and the question put to the jury, was twofold: whether Pepi was the man who had come in, stabbed the victim and left, and if so, then whether or not he was the murderer.

The case was weak, a matter of half light and viewpoint in the early hours of a darkened pool-room. What the jury would not have known was that Pepi had not long before been released from custody. They had heard that the two men knew each other, and that there was said to be a feud between him and the dead man. The judge directed them to take no notice of this, since it was hearsay. The prosecution had not implied a motive, and since murder can be established without motive, they were not to think of this.

The summing-up was marked *Identification Not Proven*. For some reason the police, after arresting Pepi, had not held an ID parade, so none of the witnesses who appeared in court identified him as the assailant. Because there had been no ID parade, the law now forbade any witness to identify the defendant in court as the man he had seen with the knife in the club. No one could now say, 'This is the man', the judge advised. No one did.

At his trial, Pepi elected to remain silent, a right soon to be abolished in the Criminal Justice Bill, though fundamental to our judicial system. Constitutionally the accused is innocent till proven guilty, and the onus of proof is on the prosecution; it's not for the defendant to prove innocence. 'The charge having been brought by the prosecution, it is for the prosecution to prove it, because there is no duty put upon a defendant to prove his innocence in these courts,' said the judge. Pepi agreed: 'It's up to them. It ain't up to me. I can't prove what I haven't done. So I kept it shut.'

As the judge put it, he was the judge of the law, the jury the judge of the facts, and the question for all of them was 'What is the truth?' From the summary the truth was elusive, and the deliberations of the jury can only be guessed at. In the first place, there weren't many facts. The summing-up pointed to absences of many of the features of a murder trial: there was no forensic evidence, no murder weapon, no fingerprints; on arrest, Pepi had said hardly anything and did not sign a confession, entering a denial and a plea of not guilty through his lawyer. There had been no ID parade, and the observations of the several witnesses did not quite agree, there was no evidence but police statements, and in the end a split jury and some problems with exhibits available to them in the jury-room. All they had was Pepi and the frame and the unpresumed motive buried in a hypothetical underworld dispute, and this they were not to consider. The implication was that the victim had grassed Pepi up for the previous conviction, and he'd got him for it when he came out. But Pepi's only statement was the one he made when charged, that he had not killed the man, together with the police statement that, when arrested, he had said, 'Who grassed me?'

'That's it, guv. All I said was "Who grassed me?" I didn't say, "Who grassed me for the murder?" I didn't say, "Who grassed me up for the murder of this bloke on the 24th January." I told you, I'm a villain. I knew the geezer, and I didn't like him, but that don't mean I did him. There's other fings I might be grassed for and there's other reasons I might be hiding, but I still never cut nobody.'

He conceded that he might be doing time for something else anyway, but not life for murder, and it was down to the cops to get him if they could for what he might have done, but not for what he hadn't. Now he had the mark of Cain on him, and whatever might be waiting in the way of a vendetta that might do for him in prison, or up ahead when he eventually came out. When his EDR came up, would someone be out there waiting for him?

Turning to the witnesses' testimonies, the judge said the jury must consider for themselves what to believe, and summarized their evidence. The first witness, a friend of the dead man's, had gone to the club with him just after midnight, where they played pool. Thereafter, he was vague about time. He described the club as not particularly full, with fifteen to twenty people in the pool-room, those who were not playing standing around the walls. He was about to play a shot when he heard a heavy rumbling, and looking up, saw a man coming in the open door where his friend was standing talking to someone and drinking. He didn't think he was holding anything, though he might have had a cue. He said, 'It seemed to me that the fellow entered and just attacked him.' He saw no reason for it. The other man seemed to throw a punch at the victim's head. 'There was a big scramble like a wrestling fight.' The victim ran out, and he 'was left wondering what had happened'. He heard someone say, 'Did you get him?' and the assailant reply, 'Yes, I got him.' In his statement to the police, not repeated in the Magistrate's initial hearing, he said he heard the man with the knife say, 'Yeah, I got him good this time', and go on to say, 'I would (or should) have got him in the kidneys.' Then he saw blood on the table, and went out to look for his friend, but didn't find him.

The second witness also knew the victim. He'd gone to the club about 1.00 a.m., left, went to a film, and came back about 3.00. He had a drink, went downstairs and up again to the pool-room, and saw the man who was later attacked, and stood watching the pool game. He saw some fighting by the door. He said, 'A fellow came in, a half-caste, and asked to speak to the victim, who went up to him. The half-caste had something in his hand, I think it was a knife, and the blade was going all over as the arm was swinging.' The wounded man ran out, with his assailant after him, who then came back. It had all happened in no more than five seconds. He hadn't seen the man before.

The third witness was the club doorman, who knew Pepi. Although Pepi said he'd been in the club that night but had not stayed, the doorman had not seen him. What he saw was a man coming downstairs with his forehead bleeding on the left side, upwards and forward from the ear around the temple. 'I don't think he spoke. He went out fast.'

The fourth witness was in the pool-room most of that night, sitting and reading. He had some kind of work there making change. He said there was no pre-fight, that several men came through the door, and 'I saw a fist coming down.' The fist was clenched, and going up and down, and he assumed the fist held a knife, but didn't see one, and heard no words. He said it all 'took as quick as it takes to tell'. The two men ran out, and he saw blood on the table.

The fifth witness said, 'I saw one man hit another across the face with a knife. I thought it was a flick-knife, that was a guess. The blade was about 4″. I saw blood, and the man that was hit got a chance to escape and run out. That one, the one who was attacked, didn't have a knife. The one that had the knife cleaned it on a handkerchief and he said to the people he was with, and he was with about three others, "I done him good", and after a while he left. I didn't know the man with the knife; I had never seen him before. I saw some blood on the pool table and on the floor. I can see no reason for the attack.'

The descriptions of the movements of the fist holding the knife don't quite agree. One describes a slashing criss-cross movement, the other a downward stabbing. And in the absence of an identification, all the jury had were the descriptions three of the witnesses gave of the man who came through the door. One said he was short, about 5′8″, with curly hair and stocky, possibly half-caste; another that he was about 5′5‴, half-caste, black hair; the third that he was half-caste, about 5′6″, but then 'taller than the one who was cut, who was 5′8″, so taller than that.' Such a man could have been Pepi, but he could have been anyone answering a general description, and all this in poor light. The judge remarked it was light enough to play pool, but the light in a pool-room would be over the table, casting the rest of the room into shadow. The judge was no pool player, and later was to make unfavourable comparisons between Soho and Mayfair as to the expectations of being knifed in the street. But he said: 'The descriptions do not suffice because they could match so many people.'

In the absence of any other evidence the judge then turned to the police statements, directing the jury to consider their honesty; in the end, the entire case rested on them. The police described how eight days after the murder they had raided Pepi's sister's flat in north London. Their search at first revealed nothing but a pair of men's trainers under the settee and some male clothing, but no sign of the defendant, and only the two women who lived there. On further searching it was noticed that of the screws holding the mirror panel behind the bath one was protruding. They took the panel off and shone a torch into the recess. Naked among the pipes there was Pepi, who came out saying, 'Give us a hand.' He then said, 'Who grassed me?' and then added, 'All right, I'll be no trouble, leave the girls out', and got dressed. Arrested, he made no reply. The police evidence then says he was asked: 'Where are the clothes you wore on the night of the murder?', and he replied he'd thrown them away: 'I've burnt them'. 'Together with the knife?' he was asked. 'Yes,' he was alleged to have said. Where had he burnt them? 'I'm not saying any more until I see a brief.'

Pepi denies he said any but the first and last of this. To have done so, would have been an admission of guilt. In court, having elected for silence, he was unable to break it to deny what he held had not been said, and had he spoken up it would, as ever, have been his word against that of the police. The judge made it clear: if these words were not spoken then the defendant was not guilty. He said the words the police ought to have used should have referred to an *alleged* murder, and the replies (if made) were to be treated at best as 'an inference of an admission. This is the essential conversation which links the defendant with the events in the club.' Pepi, according to the police, had said yet more, mixed in with what he had said in his statement. At the police station later, the police notebooks read, he admitted knowing the victim, said he couldn't remember how he knew him or when was the last time he saw him, and asked for his solicitor to be present. Later still, in the presence of the solicitor, Pepi was questioned again. He said he had been to the club on the night and morning of the murder, that he wasn't sure he had seen the victim, and that 'There was never a confrontation between me and the supposedly dead man'. He might have been in the pool-room but was not sure at what time. Asked for the whereabouts of his clothes, he said he changed his clothes often (a habit he maintained in prison), couldn't remember what he was wearing that night eight days earlier, nor where they were. He made a statement under caution that he had not harmed the victim in any way, and after conferring with his brief, he made the further declaration: 'There's only one more thing I would like to say. I did not kill AB. That concludes my statement.'

This was the prosecution's case, resting entirely on police statements. From the police's point of view, Pepi was not a co-operative suspect; the charge sheet says he refused to give an address. He maintains his innocence: why should he help; how should he know what he was wearing that night if he didn't commit the murder? He moved about a lot. He lived around. His replies, his vagueness and his silence, could all be construed either way. They could fit either a scenario of guilt or one of innocence. Other documents in the case were diagrams and photographs confirming only that the victim was stabbed, and where. Nothing pointed straight to Pepi other than police statements as to what they alleged he'd said. And if the jury accepted the police evidence, as presumably most of them did, then the absence of certainty on the part of the witnesses allowed for the possibility of Pepi being the attacker. Here, in an uncertain area of differing witnesses and doubts and absences — of identification, of time, of clothing to examine, blood to analyse, a murder weapon —the whole case rested on inference and police testimony, and the judge largely excluded the jury from making inferences. That left the question of the validity of the police evidence, among the other doubts, the benefit of none of which was to be Pepi's.

At this point a further question emerged. If the jury found the defendant, Pepi, was not the man who had wielded the knife in the club, then he was not guilty and the case was over. If, on the other hand, they were satisfied he was one and the same, then he was guilty, but not necessarily of murder. Was it proved that the victim had died as a result of a wound suffered in that first attack? The judge invited the jury to consider that, though the victim had got the five-inch wound across the scalp in the club, he had not died of this; the wound he'd died of might have been inflicted there or later, after he had run out, on the stairs or on the street. His body was found at 5.15 a.m. in the street; in all the vagueness about time, the second witness had been able to say only that he had returned to the club about 3.00, and the stabbing had happened after that. It was not known at what time precisely the victim had been attacked in the club, nor at what time precisely he had died, nor whether another wound had been inflicted in between these events. 'We simply do not know,' the judge said several times. 'It was said the victim had been to prison. May he have had enemies? Had he had the misfortune in his wounded state to be struck a second time somewhere else?'

The three wounds inflicted on the victim were described in detail by the pathologist, in order to establish links between the wounds and the weapon(s) used. The first, the one that had killed him, was a stab-wound fifteen millimetres wide at the entry in the chest by the left nipple; it was slightly oblique and had been caused by a single-edged weapon with the cutting edge upwards, and went through the upper lobe of the lung, piercing the heart sac and cutting the base of the pulmonary artery. Its track length was five and a quarter inches; it had been moderately rather than forcefully delivered, and it had caused a great deal of bleeding, most of it internal. Penetrating the low pressure side of the heart, the blood loss would have been slower. The pathologist gave survival of such a wound as five to ten minutes at the most, and said the victim might have been able to run the two hundred yards from the club to where he was found. The fatal wound might have been inflicted in the club, or outside it, or later on the street, by the same man who had cut his face, or by another.

The second stab wound was to the lower rib area on the left side, a horizontal wound sixteen millimetres at entry. Apparently deflected by a rib, this wound did not penetrate the chest cavity and went in and upwards for only one and seven eights of an inch. It had caused bleeding but not serious injury. The third wound was the one to the left side of the head, starting four inches above the left ear and downwards for five and half inches onto the temple, ending at the left eyebrow. This was the wounding described in the club by the witnesses as a slash or a downwards stroke of the knife. None had described an upward or forward stroke, the stab wound to the heart. Though Pepi might have been the one who delivered this cut to the face, it did not follow that he had inflicted the others.

And where was the knife, or knives? In their search of the club the police had turned up a knife hidden on the staircase, and this appeared in court as *Exhibit 12*. Its presence was in contrast to the absence of other evidence, and it seems to have figured in the trial as an image or example, the jury being able to examine it, to be revulsed by it. No blood was found on it, nor was any link established between it and defendant or victim. The pathologist, after consideration of the width and length of Exhibit 12 and consideration of the entry width and depth of the fatal wound, concluded that this knife had not caused it. It might have caused the second wound, he thought, and might have also caused the wound to the head. But it was clean, and forensics found neither dabs nor blood. The knife used in the attack had been wiped clean, but this knife was cleaner than that. This knife was not the murder weapon, and was irrelevant to the charge.

So there was, as the judge said, very little to go on: no forensic evidence, no clothing, no knife, no fingerprints or bloodstains, no fibres on the victim's clothing, no matching fibres from the defendant's clothing, no bloodstains on the defendant. The police had not taken for examination the men's clothes they found in the sister's flat; they said they were denied them by the defendant; he says they took them anyway, and because they bore no evidence, disposed of them and made a point of their absence. As to forensics, such blood samples as the police had found in the club proved only that the victim had been bleeding; other samples were old, of indeterminate origin, or the wrong blood group, or at any rate irrelevant.

The jury retired. They took with them the exhibits, including Exhibit 12, the knife that had nothing to do with the murder. They were to consider what little there was, and whether the defendant was the same man as the assailant, and if so was he also the murderer. They were to strive first for a unanimous verdict. Between Guilty and Not they might consider him an assailant but not the assassin, and find him guilty on the lesser charge of wounding with intent to cause serious bodily injury. After five hours of deliberation they requested a further definition of murder, in this case where one strikes another deliberately and unlawfully resulting in death, and at the time with the intent of killing or causing serious injury. Their discussions can only be inferred from this request and this definition. The jury were unable to reach unanimity, and were directed back to seek a majority verdict. In another hour or so this was brought in: the defendant was found guilty and sentenced to life imprisonment.

'So what you fink, guv?' he says. 'Can you make summing out of it? You're a writer, as a story you can have it. Make summing of it if you can, a story. Make a play, what you like. Only, make fackin' sure it helps me get out of here!'

And here he is, refusing to do his time without protest, maintaining his belief he is innocent. Whether innocent or not, he can't respond in any positive way to prison, since he doesn't believe he should be in it. The prisoner refuses to consent, and the theory of punishment is blown. It's possible that Pepi's right, or half right: that either he wasn't there and didn't cut the man at all, or if he was and did, didn't make the deepest cut. There is a whole lot else he doesn't say, Pepi, but then he's underworld and tight-lipped and a practised prisoner in any case. It's also possible that he *is* guilty, and that by highlighting all the many gaps in the evidence, he's working for a loophole to get out of here. Meanwhile, he's here, and on a shaky case. Though the law has made its mind up about him, the judge's question seems as persistent as ever: '*What is the truth?*'

'So what you fink, guv?'

# 35
# JEREMY BAMBER

There is the press story, and what the world believes, derived from the prosecution's case, itself derived from the police's: that he is guilty beyond reasonable doubt of murder x five. But the police at first did not suspect him. The jury that found him guilty was not unanimous, and divided after nine and a half hours 10/2 on all five counts, so there were two at any rate who doubted the proofs demonstrated in court. He was sentenced to life, five times, for the murders of his entire family: his adoptive parents, his sister Sheila, and her twin sons aged 6, at White House Farm, the family home at Tolleshunt D'Arcy in Essex, in August 1985. Sentencing him, the judge described him as 'evil almost beyond belief', with 'a warped, callous and evil mind concealed behind an outwardly presentable, civilized manner'. And he concluded that he had killed out of greed, 'impatient for more money and possessions', and out of arrogance that resented parental restriction or criticism. He killed for an inheritance most of which would have been his eventually, but which on conviction he forfeited.

Thus reported in the press he was known to the world as a man devoid of all human feeling; in the dock it was said he had shown nothing of his feelings in his face or bearing: he was impassive, 'an alert and attentive observer of the drama which was unfolding before him in the Essex courtroom'; hearing the verdict he showed no reaction. He was confirmed on all sides as ruthless. The headlines yelled, and in the fatter papers his character and history were analysed to show him a cold and calculating killer. It almost seemed on such portrayal that he was born to kill.

As a resident monster of the public imagination, dragged out into the tabloids to rattle at the public from time to time, Jeremy Bamber occupies a strange corner in the human psyche. In March 1988 he was the subject of another such rattle from the *Sunday Sport*, recycling old news. In amongst the bared breasts and ads offering women for sex, loomed the face of Jeremy seen through a prison van window, as he was when arrested. Described as a 'baby-faced killer', the word is, according to the *Sunday Sport*, that he and his girlfriend write erotic letters to each other, and that his cell is plastered with provocative pictures of her, and that his hot gropings of her in the visitors' room are ignored by 'kinky warders'. It must be said that, the question of kinky warders to one side, such public passions would not be tolerated on visits. Though I never saw his cell, men who did don't recall any particularily salacious pictures, and they would have noticed. To my mind if she and he want to write erotic letters to each other, what of it? They'd not be censored. The fragment of a letter reproduced with the account is in his handwriting, but itself says nothing other than he misses her and looks forward to her next visit. But for the press, he's still good copy, and any number of fantasies can be projected around him. In October 1988 the *News of the World* ran virtually the same story, featuring another woman as his girlfriend. The question must be: by whose consent are these press tales published?

He knows that history is written by the winners. Such were his first remarks when we met in the fishbowls some three months into his time. He came in carefully, nervously, his eyes two sharp points, remarking for openers: 'I guess you know a lot more about me than I know about you.'

I didn't, though I knew who he was. His trial was recent and had spanned nineteen days at Chelmsford Crown Court, and was well attended by the press. It was the outcome of the still fresh memory of the massacre from earlier headlines, some fifteen months before. I could scarcely have missed it. I said: 'I know what I've read in the papers.' He shrugged, leaving me the choice: 'If you believe them.' He said, 'At my trial the press had two scenarios. If I'd been acquitted, they'd still have had the front page. I'd have been innocent and falsely accused. They were elbowing each other for my story, and waving chequebooks. As it was, of course, they went with the verdict: "Guilty", and they don't much want my story now. They have the court's and the police story.'

Scenarios. This conversation is about scenarios. Stories, fashioned out of rival interpretations of reality, some more fictional than others. And for Jeremy, all there is to set against the official version of him is his own denial, his tale of himself, which he must constantly support in word and deed and gesture. False or true, it is a difficult posture to maintain. Especially here.

We shook hands. This hand had been raised against his father, and killed all his kin. All in one, he was a patricide, matricide, fratricide, mass-murderer, child killer, nonce and lifer just starting out on a minrec of twenty-five years. He was under close supervision. In part this was perhaps for his own protection. He was not popular on the wing.

At 26, he looked younger, tall and slim, a young man who must have been something of a blade amongst the ladies. He was smart in clean blues, and leaned against the door-frame for a while, relaxing a millimetre, occasionally flicking back a lock of dark hair from his forehead. He seemed boyish almost, self-conscious, perhaps vain. But he looked me straight in the eye, and spoke with confidence. He was alert and sharp and in the busy noise of the wing my first impression was of a man striving to appear relaxed, affecting cool in the most vulnerable of circumstances, but the eyes said something different: fear lived in there, and sometimes flamed up, and all his efforts were to keep that fire damped. He was not yet prison pallored, not yet stooped and though wary, he was not yet wary enough for his own good, and spoke too quickly and too openly. He sat down.

Our business was writing, but what else to write about but his predicament? Whatever he wrote reflected it, and dragged in all else. Whenever we talked, the case hovered in the background: his imprisonment, his claim to be completely misunderstood, to be innocent. Reasonably, not much else interested him for long, though from time to time he tried, and wrote about the world he'd known, and childhood, and his travels. Sometimes I could get him to think back into his life, to recall a before, to call up early memories, and he wrote of a wedding he'd been to as a kid where he'd invented a party trick, dancing with a glass of wine on his head, a trick he'd used again thereafter. The marriage didn't last, his poem drily observed at its end. There were the beginnings of some religious speculation in him, some vaguer thoughts on life that rarely came to anything. Something survived death, he thought, but he felt no presence of his dead family. In all he wrote for me, he was plain and proper, schoolboyish at times. He wrote the usual poems about the ugliness and deprivations of prison. But always and early he would return to his theme, to his preparations for appeal, to his refusal to accept prison. He was innocent he said over and over, and would one day prove it: justice would be done and he would be restored to the world, and the press would have to eat its words. On this he was indignant, his tone edging on outrage. They had assassinated his character. He cared about that, perhaps a little over much. His vanity was engaged, I think. His image in the popular imagination, in the press, is monster, and he doth protest. He says that none of their story is true, and is aware that in all the universe he is the only contradiction to the official version of events. So far as he's concerned the killings at White House Farm represent a tragedy further compounded by his imprisonment for them.

The murders, as described in court, were premeditated, planned, bloody, carried out with cold savagery, and arranged so as to look as if Sheila, the sister, who had a history of mental illness going back six years, had killed them all and last herself. She had been diagnosed as a paranoid schizophrenic. To kill five people, twenty-five shots had been fired at close range from a .22 semi-automatic, mostly into the head of each of the victims. The two boys had been killed in their sleep. From the beginning police investigations pointed to homicide and suicide by the sister; the police surgeon who certified the deaths said hers was *suggestive of having been self-inflicted*. The gun had been so placed as to indicate she had turned it on herself at the last. After two days the investigation of the farmhouse was wrapped up, and at the inquest the police confirmed the post-mortem, that Shelia had died by her own hand, having shot the others. The bodies were released for cremation. It was a tragedy. The press closed down the story.

That's one scenario. Another is that Jeremy planned and carried out the killings, reliant on his sister's mental instability to suggest a suicidal holocaust. In this scenario he was capable of imagining it, of carrying it out, and of faking grief and shock thereafter. Later, falling under suspicion, he must maintain the act through long hours of police questioning, legal counselling, trial and cross-examination in court. And still, here in prison, he maintains that he is innocent.

But there were cracks in the suicide theory. Relatives of the family were suspicious, and their visit to the farmhouse after the police had gone, two days after the murders, revealed what the police had missed. In the cupboard where Mr Bamber had kept his gun collection was the silencer belonging to the .22. It had been damaged, and a speck of red paint on it matched the red paint of the kitchen mantelpiece, where there were recent indentations. There was also a speck of blood in the buffels of the silencer, and a grey hair. The police had missed all these, and subsequently lost the hair before it could be analysed. Though the house had been locked from the inside (the police had had to break in, and believed the house secure when the killings took place), they found access could be gained through a fanlight in the kitchen. As to the coroner's verdict that Shelia had fired the gun, her cousin said *she wouldn't know one end from the other*. The case was altered. They called back the police.

The post-mortem on Sheila revealed a heavy tranquilliser in her system, casting doubt on her physical ability to carry out the killings. She was small, and had not been in good health, and clearly there had been a struggle at the mantelpiece. When found, she was lying next to her mother with two bullets in her head and the gun beside her, the muzzle under her chin. Her ex-husband surmised that, had she killed herself, she would have been beside her children. And for all the bloodshed upstairs and down, her bare feet were bloodless, her manicured nails undamaged from firing twenty-five times and twice reloading, and her nightdress and hands revealed no substantial traces of blood or gun oil. And then forensics on the silencer showed that the drop of blood on it was the same blood group as hers. It was demonstrated that with the silencer fitted, her arms would have not been long enough to reach the trigger and shoot herself. She would have had to remove it. But for her blood to be on the silencer she would have had to shoot herself once in the throat, remove the silencer, wrap it up and put it in the gun cupboard, go upstairs, and shoot herself again.

A month went by, and then Jeremy's girlfriend at the time went to the police and told them he had confessed to her that he had done what he'd called *the perfect murder*. He was taken in and questioned for five days, but the police had no other evidence against him. He was familiar with guns, he admitted, but on a farm that was normal. The evening of the massacre he'd said he'd seen some rabbits, and loaded the gun and gone out with it. He'd found no rabbits, and had come back, but he'd left the gun in the kitchen with the magazine close by, instead of in the gun cupboard, and then gone to his own house. He admitted this was careless, with children in the house, and a schizophrenic sister. He said he'd had a phone-call from his father in the night asking him to come over, saying that Sheila was going crazy, and had the gun. But if she had not done the killings then the call had not taken place as described, and he was lying. He'd bumbled calling the police by looking up the local number instead of dialling 999. He admitted nothing else. In the end it was his girlfriend's evidence that led to the opening up of the inconsistencies in his story. The flaws in his story were the silencer and the telephone call. In the background, for motive, there was his parents' disapproval of his way of life, which was expensive, and demanding. There was the farm and his inheritance, an estate valued at £436,000, and there had been quarrels with his parents. His father, a magistrate, and a former Battle of Britain fighter pilot, was evidently disappointed in his adoptive son. Jeremy had entertained some doubts as to his being disinherited, and when convicted, so he was.

She had been turned against him by the police, he said of the girlfriend, still incredulous that she would betray him. She had reason to be angry with him, he said, but not that angry. In the course of their investigations into him, the police had discovered other women, and told her, he claimed. She was a woman scorned and angry, and had turned him in. But it was all untrue. He lived in hope that some day she'd retract her statement. The police had twisted everything.

That was his story and he was sticking to it. Just as he did through all our meetings in the next few months. We'd talk around the topic, but he would always come back to it. We'd talk around notions of received and perceived reality, the distortions of the media, the problem of ever knowing the truth about anything. As time passed he relaxed, growing slowly more resigned to prison, but never losing his determination to clear himself. Some day. Meanwhile, he wrote and drew cartoons; here there was time, he shrugged. Time for everything and the opportunity for nothing, and as the months went by, less and less inclination. He had a considerable correspondence, he said, with women who had written to him since conviction, some of whom he referred to as his girlfriends. 'My girlfriend,' he would say, meaning one of many. And there were others who wrote, 'friends from outside all of this.' Some wrote, he said, to say they believed him. If his belief in his innocence was developing into a fantasy, he was drawing others in to support it. But on the surface he maintained a calm, and I judged him a young man not much given till now to introspection. He had a sharp, reptilian businessman's brain, considerable self-control, and somewhere still a sense of humour.

Week by week we met in the fishbowls, in the afternoons before men came back from labour or education. Jeremy didn't work. He had prison monies, and friends and money outside; this was another reason for many to despise him. He said *they* were pressuring him to work. He didn't really object, save to acknowledge that doing any sort of work in prison was an acceptance of imprisonment, a surrender in the maintaining of the fabric. He was refusing, on medical grounds; the argument was all about missing bits of paper. Meanwhile, he was holding out, resisting. He was, *they'd* mutter when I called him up at movements, 'a lazy bugger'. They said they couldn't get through to him. His main concerns were his appeal, and his plea of innocence. For the prison the problem was getting him on normal location, to work. For Bamber the problem was being in prison and avoiding danger. There had been threats, he said. Some called him a nonce, and other men I worked with, seeing me with him, would turn away. They'd change direction, come back later. Here on the wing, not in a workshop, I guessed he felt safer, and prison work was boring. And I suspected, silently concurring with *them*, that Jeremy was lazy in any case.

As we talked, he was ever watchful, checking the comings and goings in the passageways either side of the glass box. Ill at ease, he seemed no more so than anyone else in prison, where everyone watches; it was merely that his guardedness was unpractised, new to him, apparent to others. He was a new boy. Talking relaxed him, and frisked up a humour in him that he seemed in danger of losing. He'd bring two chipped blue plastic mugs of sweet, thin prison tea, reporting in: a week of not much, letters, his appeal, the humdrum routines of prison. I'd tell him it wasn't school and if he'd written nothing to show, it didn't matter. Sometimes he wrote about prison, sometimes about the outside. He found either side of the wall difficult to focus on. He was shy about showing his writing, probably because when he did there wasn't much to show: a few simple verses and school-anthology reflections, traditional rhymings that sought, nonetheless, to recall the world he had known, to hang on to it, to remember. His schooling had been traditional and conservative, in a private school in Norfolk; no scholar, he'd left at 17, working on the farm. He'd messed about, cleared off, quarrelled with his father, who'd complained he was lazy, and doubted his fitness to inherit. He'd preferred to be a young man-about-town, a bit of a playboy. For a year and a half he'd travelled abroad, and he spoke long and affectionately of Australia and New Zealand. Sometimes in his poems there were oceans and tropics and long Antipodean distances, exotic birds and rivers and beaches and the eye of the surfer's tube. Inside prison, he was starved of colour, and sought to hang on to it. Otherwise he was conservative and classical; his writing obeyed all the rules of introduction, body, conclusion, and took no chances. He spoke as a farmer, as a manager, as a conserver: we were wrecking the planet, chainsawing down the rain forests, filling the oceans with poison. A hole was opening in the ozone layer over the Antarctic, getting bigger. And he would sometimes wonder what would be left of the world in twenty-five years, when he came out. Perhaps we were not fit to survive. Perhaps, by nature, we were evil.

There had been occasional moments of beauty when he had sometimes, rarely, felt at one with the world. For Jeremy the world was an odd and quirky sort of place, a source of amusement and entertainment that had suddenly dried up and turned serious, where there was little justice, and things were not as they were said to be in the social-studies text-books. I came to understand that he was self-centred, had always been so, an adopted child spoiled in compensation, perhaps. All the same, he was disappointed, bitterly, with the legal system and the police, both of which he felt had served him false. He was angry with the press. For him the world in which he'd believed was now just so much propaganda. Politically he was a Tory, a Thatcherite, a businessman, a yuppy, a believer in unhampered enterprise and the free flow of market forces. He had grown up to believe the press and respect the police, an adherent of the party of law and order, but they had all let him down. He was a disappointed man. As he expressed it, his faith in 'the system' had been broken, and all that he clung to now was his sense of bitter irony. That and his appeal. 'I have to hope,' he said. 'I have to hang on to something. And if the appeal goes down I still have to have something to hope for. Perhaps a miracle.' Mainly, he was numb, his mind scattered in many directions all at once, and reeling at the sheer existence of the wall around him. Questions of guilt or innocence apart for a moment, the rigours of arrest and trial and conviction and prison all added up to shock. He was in shock still. Or he had always been numb.

I saw him through a question mark, and the question nagged. *Did he or didn't he*? were head and tail of the ever flipping coin, the question prison provokes: *What is the truth*? He didn't seem to be strong, more of a weakling, and he whined frequently, but what struck me was the strength of his conviction, and the strength it must have taken to maintain it day by day. At times I was aghast at his self-assurance, his inviolable certainty of innocence. And this on either scenario: if guilty, that he could brazen it out; if innocent, that he could find the strength and resources to continue. If innocent, how tragic the violent loss of kin and fortune and future, yet he was not crushed by it. And if guilty how great the effort to maintain innocence, through suspicion, investigation, arrest, interrogation, remand, trial, sentence, and now the continuing rigours of D Wing and all the years ahead. To do all this a man would have to be very determined; he would have to be a very good actor, or a very clever psychopath, or a very innocent man.

Yet there was an absence in his grief, and there I found Jeremy deficient. His eyes and face never flinched when he spoke of his case. He spoke carefully, outwardly like a man who didn't do it, and, if he were acting, acted the part well. When not checking the immediate environment, he'd look me dead on in the eye. Sometimes he talked with some sorrow and some affection of his dead parents, of the events of his childhood, of family life. Once I saw tears in his eyes when he spoke of them. He'd speak again about the possibilities of survival, of ghosts, and said he hadn't felt the presence of any of his dead — when he thought that if anything survives death they might manifest some concern for him, here in prison for their deaths when he is innocent: that they might look him up or show some sign. And yet I came to think it all a little self-regarding, the focus always on himself, even allowing for circumstance. What I heard included no pity for the dead, for their lives cut off abruptly, for the deaths of the two children. There was vehemence and even passion, but all self-focused. Whatever he really felt he didn't show. Or was he merely shallow? Something was missing in him. There seemed an absence somewhere in his speech, and it wasn't just that few men speak of their victims, or are brought only with great difficulty to do so. When he spoke of them it was of *their* absence in *his* life. And though I thought that what I heard in the undertow was sentiment, not love, this too proves nothing.

Nor, I noted, did his eyes flinch one day when another prisoner passing the fishbowl paused, stared at him through the perspex without expression on his face, and slowly drew a forefinger across his own throat; momentarily, Jeremy was distracted from his speech, but his eyes didn't founder and continued looking into mine as he continued talking, with just the slightest waver in his voice, the threat on his periphery. Asked, he said the gesture was a joke, the man a mate of his. Somehow I didn't think so.

Hard to tell, in prison, what any gesture means. I began drawing the conclusion that he was a shallow young man, and vain, full of plans and intentions that rarely come to anything, and that the pattern was not new. It was intensified by prison, as was his egocentricity. That being the case, I thought, perhaps he's not the man methodically to carry through so terrible a plan. Another man thought he might in fact be innocent: 'He's not that good an actor,' he said. 'He couldn't keep it up.'

Jeremy posits the dilemma of all prisoners: whether to adjust to prison, and so accept it, or to resist assimilation and hang on to his vision of the outside, though it becomes increasingly unreal. Because he doesn't accept guilt, his dilemma is more pronounced. Maintaining his innocence, he can't accept present realities. Refusing to do so, the outer world recedes, and somewhere hereabouts unreality and fantasy take over.

And then we had done all we could in the way of writing, and saw less and less of each other. He moved upstairs, and some days I'd see him up there, greyer, hanging out, rocking on the twos landing rail. He'd grin, and saunter down, but as time went by, he had less and less writing to show, and spoke only of his business. He'd had some trouble with a stiff, a crucial piece of new evidence, he claimed, sent from an unknown source. But it had mysteriously disappeared. He'd mention his girlfriends, and his correspondence. There was continuing press attention on the outside, and attempts to reach him. Someone was interfering with his mail. A girl who wrote to him had lost her job because of it; sworn to secrecy, how did her employers know she wrote to him? All this, it seemed to me, made him the focus of attention, made him feel important. And something else I sensed, that in telling me all this he was deftly weaving me into some web of his own devising. Or he imagined he was. And then he had another strange tale, and whether he'd made it up or whether it really happened was again a question of competing scenarios.

It went like this. On the Wednesday night after lock-up, an officer had come to tell him that his girlfriend had been badly injured in a car smash, and was in a certain hospital's emergency ward, on the danger list. In the morning, unable to phone to confirm or enquire, he took a chance on Welfare and Interflora, despatching flowers from his monies to wish her better. Then on the Friday he was allowed to receive a call from outside: it was the same girl, upset to have been phoned on Wednesday night to say he'd attempted suicide in prison. There'd been no accident, no hospital, no suicide attempt. It was a wind-up. Somewhere between the two of them someone had done double-barrelled mischief on the telephone. But who?

The truth recedes, and with it Jeremy. Another girl, another girlfriend, had been the victim of three break ins, two beatings, and one severed sheep's head dumped on her doorstep, because of her association with him. By whom, and how did anyone know? And there's his hate mail. What he described were dark and secret malevolences moving out there in the night. Or they were all inside his head, and he was weaving me in. 'Someone out there hates me,' he said, 'and wants to cut me off from everything and everyone.'

He drifted off into the crowd. He grew greyer, yellower, more withdrawn, turning into the colour of old newspapers. Prison was beginning to drown him in its silence. With less and less to say for himself, he began fading into the paintwork and the bricks, increasingly absorbed in the time-consuming business of his appeal. In early 1988 an application for leave to appeal was turned down; he is applying again, still insisting on his innocence. He described new and gruesome evidence for the appeal. He hoped to persuade to turn again the turning witness. Still patient, he began to accept there was a long road ahead, whatever happened, and always hoping for a miracle, the dream of miraculous release, the official who would appear and say there'd been a terrible mistake, and walk him to the gate. He had to have something to hope for, he said at the last. The only alternative to hope was death.

'Who knows,' he said. 'Who knows what will happen? Where there was a bad man might turn out to be a rose.'

# 36

# RABB

He is a wee Glaswegian, a new face on the wing, though not new to prison. Small and skinny and thirty, haunted and sparrowish, permanently undernourished, out front he's direct, inwardly canny. Sometimes he laughs, even jokes, and can be talkative and friendly, his pinched face briefly lighting up. It doesn't last long; being cheerful makes him miserable, and goes against his prison grain. Mostly he's taciturn, minds his tongue, checks and rechecks his information, knows he can trust no one, forms relationships always short of friendship, stays tight. Like everyone else he's thin-lipped, changeable and moody and variously on the swing from suspicious to paranoid, often gloomy, sometimes gossipy, all his humour at his own cost. Sometimes depression blackens him into silence, and his eyes flatten out, like stones, and his own words on paper scowl back at him. He seems on the point of giving up as hope fades out in him. In his time he's been on D Wing before, so he knows his way about, and the ropes. In his environment he is a survivor, moving with his own certainty, something of an aristocrat, a man with his own integrity and meaning. He sleeps, reads, stays behind his door much of the time. He thinks a lot, though his own predicament is always at its centre, and he has become articulate in prison. He doesn't work, and has no interest in it; it's boring making brown overalls and doesn't train him for a trade in the great outside. On arrival on the wing he'd spent a few days in the tailors' shop going through the motions, breaking needles, till they sacked him. He gets by or goes without, and scorns their wages. Sometimes he's not around but down the block for some offence; he says he doesn't mind. The wing gets him down and it's peaceful down the block, and they leave him alone for a few days. He can think there.

'And by the bye,' he says, 'I'm innocent.'

He's in his eleventh year of a life sentence, still claiming innocence. He's writing his biography, which is all battle, and largely his version of the narrative of his arrest and conviction. And he writes poems expressing all his longing for beauty, colour, touch. He shows them, pressing for my response, at the same time verballing his tale, an outline biography of misery. Orphaned at 8, he'd gone from orphanage to detention centre, left Glasgow for Manchester, gone back and forth, living a rough and tough and mean existence, mostly on the move. He wants me to read everything at once while he talks at the same time. On the loose pages I can't read his tiny writing; it's neat, tidy, mannered, but minuscule, a self-taught hand. It seems mirror work, as if he were writing in reverse on the inside of a glass bowl. He reads out the poems, but through it all someone is hammering on a pipe along the floor above, and his quiet voice is lost. Insistently traditional, he rhymes and iambs his way through the bitter ironies of prison life, his longing to be free, his want of what he defines from here as normality. He wants sex, he wants a woman, he wants love.

At 19 he was arrested for murder, and has been in prison since. Maintaining innocence, he says the police twisted everything, there was only circumstantial evidence from witnesses, they had him scared and he was frightened and worried for his pregnant girlfriend, so he confessed to get them off his back, thinking he could rescind the confession in court. But at his trial the jury accepted his confession and the police statements, and he was sentenced, and he's been fighting it since. He applied for an appeal, but was turned down for lack of new evidence. He sketches this in while I'm reading his tiny writing, and the hammering above us continues, and Billy comes in to show me something that can't wait, and then Jack, half-way through a haircut, to ask for a pencil. In the poems and from what Rabb says, it's apparent there's been a crisis, some six months back, probably a breakdown; there is a woman, somewhere, whom he's talked to, glimpsed, an unrealizable passion, idyllic and distant and doted over. Given his life, neither the breakdown nor his emotional immaturity are surprising.

His problem is his insistence on his innocence. It is —again — a matter of proving where he wasn't by proving where he was, and he can't, and the years have swallowed up these events. It is a matter of disputing police statements, what he calls 'supposition and manufactured evidence'. Difficult to disprove, and debatably shaky as the grounds of his conviction are, all he really has is his belief in himself as an innocent man languishing in prison, but there are other explanations for that. He sees the psychologists reluctantly, knowing they are observing him, sparing, though perhaps not sparing enough, in what he says to them, and it has been explained to him that prison has no means of dealing with his claim, it has no other function but to confine the guilty; it accepts and acts on the courts' verdicts, and refers him back to the judiciary, which refers him back to prison. Caught in this short circuit, the purposes of prison, retribution and deterrence, frustrate and are frustrated by this man. For the psychologists, there are only three probabilities: either he is guilty and is repressing the memory of his crime, and therefore he cannot atone for it and move towards release; or he is a psychopath, able to mask himself, and doesn't recognize the murder as a crime, and — amenable or not to treatment— highly dangerous; or he is indeed innocent, and wrongly convicted. There are no alternatives to these diagnoses.

'My release depends not on whether I am innocent or guilty, but on my good adjustment to the standards of any particular prison environment.'

It has been suggested he just get on with it — conform, accept his punishment as if he were guilty, go through the motions and get out. He won't do that, and the hypocrisy enrages him. They tell him his insistence blocks his release. They think he may re-offend, he says they've told him, and since re-offend in his case may mean murder, they plan to keep him inside for as long as they can, and his being referred back here for observation must imply the possibility he'll be sectioned. They fear he'll go back to the scene of the crime, and they speculate on his motives. He says he plans to do just that, to clear his name. He needs a witness. He needs an alibi. The years in prison will have been wasted if he cannot clear himself. That's all he wants to do with his life, he says. For him, his innocence is more important than his freedom. When he thinks about it, there's nothing out there: 'I'm so poisoned by anger I'd ruin any relationship with a girl or with any kids we have. All I want to do is prove my innocence.'

He cannot be released until he repents, they say. He recoils at the idea of the murder, expressing pity for a victim he did not kill but bears the blame for; unlike some men, he doesn't say, 'She's dead and my being here won't fetch her back.' He's sorry for her death, but didn't cause it, is the counterpoint of his own remorse. 'But I can't repent for what I didn't do.'

What's striking about him is his insistence, and its consistency. More important to him than being in prison is his desire to clear himself, and that, he says, will go on after prison, though this way it will take longer, and may never end. Wanting freedom, he doesn't want to be freed as a served-out murderer. In eleven years, though he's got used to prison, he's not accepted it. He has adjusted to prison but not to his sentence.

But from here it all looks impossible to unravel; someone would have to go back eleven years to track down witnesses and persuade them to change testimonies or establish him with an alibi; it would take a detective and a lawyer — time and money — to dig out new evidence with which to persuade the Appeal Court or Home Secretary to reopen the case. And in reality he doesn't know where any of those involved are now, and talks as though people didn't move and change and memory fade. It's as if for him that suburb of the world is frozen as he left it, as if with his arrest everything stopped. At that time he was beginning to settle down; he had a girl and a family on the way, and was planning a home. From time to time he wonders what happened to the girl, and speculates he has a child, boy or girl he doesn't know, eleven years old. In the meantime in prison he's tried all channels, but none have worked out. The problem is he signed a confession and now he's stuck with what he signed for: murder, and life for it.

'In here they try to isolate you. So it's difficult. They break up any outside contacts we have.'

He is lost, becoming more lost with every day in prison, falling into its black hole. He knows there's no hope, even when he snatches at it, as at any straw. Like all prisoners the one thing on his mind is prison, but in his case there's one thing more, and that even more obsessive. He is a man vanishing into the limbo of himself, falling into inner space. All his connections, his lifelines, his communications, are falling away, and he knows that soon there will be no air to carry his cry, no one to hear it, no way even his cry can escape the crush of prison gravity.

Cynic. Optimist. *A cynical optimist* he describes himself. A loner and drifter in the prison system, moved from nick to nick as a man who won't fit into any regime, in the last six months he's been in five prisons. He's being shoved around the system. He's here for reports, maybe for a year, back up the snake from Cat. C to Cat. B and maximum security, years into life. From authority's viewpoint, he's not making any progress towards release; having followed his lifer's career through dispersal prison to Cat. C, he might by now be contemplating a move to open prison and his EDR, but he's as far into the interior as he's ever been. He was unable to accept Cat. C prison; he says that, after years of dispersal, he couldn't accept a more relaxed regime, where the screws seemed friendly, but were using the exchange to gather material for their reports. He prefers things tough. That way he knows where he stands. He chooses silence. He won't go back to Cat. C. He won't co-operate. So now he's back on a dispersal wing, on obs, and he may never get out. He'll go to fifteen and beyond, to seventeen where a review must be held, and then perhaps beyond into forever. He may be sectioned, shunted into some siding for the duration, in a hospital for the criminally insane. He knows this is possible. 'Rampton.' He shrugs. 'Broadmoor.' He shrugs again. 'That might not be so bad,' he says. 'You get days out. At least I'll know it's the end of the line. There's nothing more they can do to me there.' I doubt that's true either.

Sentenced on circumstantial evidence and his own confession, he was lifed for the bludgeoning to death of an elderly woman in her flat in a suburb of Manchester in late January 1977. The evidence was sparse, though much blood. There were no fingerprints, no murder weapons found, no hair, fibres, bloodstains or finger parings taken at the scene that matched any of his, nor anything on him that matched him to her and to her brutal death. The police theory was that someone, a young man identified by a witness as resembling Rabb, had walked home with her to carry her shopping, gone in for a cup of tea, been caught dipping in her purse and battered her to death. She had been struck sixteen times with a blunt object about the head and face, and died from these injuries. Blood was everywhere, and on the meter, which had not been broken into. Whoever killed her had panicked, had a go at the meter, and run off, taking the murder weapon with him and leaving behind a purse containing over £200, and change on the table. She was discovered two to three days later, her door still open, the electric fire still on. The police made extensive enquiries, but the trail was cold.

Months after the murder, Rabb was picked up, questioned, picked out of an ID parade by a neighbour who said she'd seen him with the victim on the day of her death carrying her shopping, and spoken to them both: 'When's the wedding?' The victim had said the man was going to decorate her flat. The neighbour said the victim was shy of strangers, and she was surprised by this. Relatives confirmed this; her brother-in-law called regularly and undertook any maintenance. He said she was shy of men, and strangers, wouldn't invite either in, and didn't like anyone meddling in her affairs. Another witness said that

Rabb had arrived at her door that night covered in blood. He said he'd had a fight, but disagreed about the date. There is a large area of disagreement here. In court a bloodstained pair of jeans were produced, found in a house he had stayed in, but it was not his blood and not the victim's. In fact it was menstrual blood, and the exhibit irrelevant. He was pulled in four months after the murder, though he had been living in the area throughout that time, present but not accounted for. He hadn't gone away. He hadn't entirely acted like a guilty man, or at any rate not a murderer, and therein lay his problem. Eleven years later he still can't seem to act guilty.

*Circumstantial evidence*. Questioned, in the end he made a confession. He had been living in the same area as the victim for about two years, at various addresses, and so there were coincidences. For a time he had worked in a factory in the same area the victim worked, and he may have travelled on the same bus to or from work, and on other occasions may have served her cigarettes in the bar of a nearby pub where he had also worked. He and the victim lived in the same neighbourhood, and had inevitably crossed each other's paths.

Brought in, he was a profile for the man the police had been looking for. He was Scots, a loner, and had a record. He was secretive, a drifter, with a history of fecklessness and wandering. As such, under questioning, his answers generated suspicion. There were things he couldn't remember, and things he was vague about, and he couldn't account for the clothing he'd worn at the time of the murder, four months previously. When the police made house-to-house interviews after the murder, he had been in the area and not come forward. He said he'd hung back because he was wanted for non-payment of fines, that the father of the girl he was living with was looking for them, so he stayed low. She was pregnant, and under-age, and her parents were determined to break them up. But he fitted the general description of a scruffy young man in blue about 5′5″ with a Rod Stewart haircut short at the front and long at the back and a Scots accent; he'd lived around in various lodgings and squats in the area, and moved frequently between Manchester and Glasgow. In the identikit picture issued by the police the face is not at all like his, and has a harelip which he doesn't have. But in all the other ways he looked like he might fit.

According to the police, the victim came in from work, went shopping, met and came home with her assailant, who carried her shopping. Their task was to identify the suspect with the man seen with the victim in the afternoon. Their witness described a white male of 25–30, thin build, thin face, who appeared to have something wrong with his upper lip. She described his accent, hair, jacket, and a pair of gloves he was wearing. Later police efforts were to seek to establish that this was Rabb, and to find the whereabouts of these clothes. He'd had his hair cut short since. He didn't know about the gloves, had given them away, had swapped the jacket with a mate. His answers seemed evasive. Under questioning he denied he'd killed the old lady, and frequently broke down. From time to time the police noted that he cried or shook. From the off they accused him of the murder. He denied it. Gradually they pared down his denials, cornering him. Certainly they had him frightened. They questioned him for two days.

Eventually he confessed.

The witness who identified him said first that he resembled the man she'd seen with the victim; of the line-up she said he was the only one that looked like him. But on a previous line-up with another suspect back in March, she'd picked another man, and seemed equally sure. On a second line-up she picked out no one. On the third she picked out Rabb: 'he is the same man but his hair is darker, shorter, and he is a good bit cleaner.' The only other key witness was the woman who said he'd come to her house late at night covered in blood. He denied this. There were other statements, all of which merely confirmed that he was feckless, always on the move, had few clothes, drank, couldn't handle it, and was violent.

The police had only this and his confession. Forensics came up with nothing. The clothing they examined could not be established as having had contact with the deceased. In all the blood nothing was definitive. Blood on the kitchen bench and the dining chairs could have been the victim's, but not the accused's. Blood on the meter could have come from either. Blood on the jeans came from neither. Some blood was cat blood, though there was no cat in the flat. Some samples were insufficient, some tests unsuccessful. The fact is there were bits that fitted, the circumstantials; by concentrating on them the case was proved, and the confession confirmed it. In his confession he'd said she'd caught him dipping, he'd hit her two or three times and run off, dropping the heavy ornament he'd hit her with and a purse down the rubbish chute. Other details he couldn't remember. In his statement he admitted murder, and asked to see his girlfriend; most of his confession is taken up with asking to see her.

He says he did this to get out from under, thinking he could deny it later. He says he was worried about his girlfriend, and just wanted to get it over with, but the jury accepted his confession, denying his denial, and he was speedily found guilty. He applied for an appeal, but no grounds were found sufficient to reopen the case. In the years since, he has maintained his innocence, writing to various organizations asking for help in establishing it, but the problems remain the same — a vagueness about where he was on the night in question in January 1977, some months before he was to be asked such a question, and the confession he claims he only made under duress, and the present whereabouts, a decade later, of crucial witnesses, the difficulty of persuading them to make statements, to be accurate after so long a time. His only hope lies in establishing an alibi, at this decade of a distance, and in getting witness statements revised.

'That's all I care about. I didna kill her. All I want to do now with my life is prove I'm innocent.'

In the meantime he claims some witnesses denied they'd made statements used in Rabb's interrogation; he can't figure out why the second witness said he'd come to her house covered in blood on the night of the murder, and says that happened three months earlier, after a fight. He disputes the evidence still. There is no doubt in his voice when he speaks. In prison it's difficult to maintain a lie in the face of so much convinced opposition, the daily grinding on for years of the harsh engines constantly reminding the prisoner of his guilt; to withstand this requires consistent strength and determination. Some officials, he says, some individuals within the service, have come to believe him. His brief is still interested. But none of them can do anything without new evidence. He's stuck, and the dead weight of the system presses him down. The only suggestion it can make is that he act as if he is guilty in order to get out in due time; acting otherwise, he impedes the very processes that would eventually free him.

'They're saying I have to act guilty when I'm not. That's the system then. That's going along with the system. According to the shrink a man like me claiming innocence this far in is either repressing the memory of his crime because he doesn't want to admit he did it, or he's plain psychotic, or he's innocent. So I said to him: "Which do you think I am then?" '

And on and on, for years, the same focus, the same doubled-up obsession, and clearly he will never get over it, and this alone may keep him in. As ever, no doubt is resolved in his favour, and there are no nil returns. Everyone he comes in contact with must act as if he's guilty: administrators, officers, psychiatrists, welfare, defining him as having another problem to the one he says he has, and treating him accordingly. Guilty or not, he is stuck with it. The State has rolled over him.

# 37

# PAUL HILL

One of the Guildford 4, jailed for pub bombings at Guildford and Woolwich, Paul Hill is one whom the State has not forgotten, not least for the consistency of his denial, along with his co-accused, of the charges on which they were convicted. In fourteen years in prison, much of that time spent in periods of solitary, Paul has maintained his innocence. On the wing he is generally recognized by those who are guilty as one who is not of their number, and there are some officers and some governors who privately doubt his conviction, or the means of its obtaining; these are general doubts, that apply to all ten imprisoned of the Guildford and Birmingham cases. But the officials are largely pragmatists, and as ever the verdict is what counts with them. Guilty or not, there are the routines of prison to be got through, for them and for him, and if his assertion of innocence marks him off from the crowd then he has suffered the more for it, as much as for what he is accused of: bombing pubs; blowing people up.

Small and thin, he walks with some bounce, with a self-confidence I suspect he must will himself to have at times. His eyes are deep-set dark hollows; in pictures that appear from time to time in the press, he is still the youth he was when arrested, an old photograph. Prison has knocked the naiveté out of his face. When he was arrested and first in prison he was, he says, 'totally naive, absolutely green.'

Inside, he does not behave like a prisoner, like a guilty man; in the end, with some men, the plea of innocence seems willed, woven out of debatable records of facts and their interpretations, disputed evidence, circumstantials. Prison imposes its cunning on everyone. But with him there is no guile. He does not so much insist on his innocence or continuously lambast prison (though neither's exempt) as focus his attention on how to be proved one and be out of the other. To his mind, he knows beyond a doubt he and his co-accused are innocent; it's a matter of time and their endurance. His energies are intelligently reserved for his case, but he is aware there is a life beyond all this. Meanwhile, he sees himself as a political football, a hostage caught in the web of the British State. He's not oblivious of everything else, as some men in prison are; he is aware there are co-accused, and others like him, and that after him there will be others falsely accused. His struggle for his own freedom has a context. Endurance is all. At times, he is close to endurance's limits, and knows it. He describes, at times, *clinging by his fingertips, on the edge, on the brink, of sanity.*

But he will not give in. He quotes me Dylan Thomas's lines:

> *Do not go gentle into that good night.*
> *Rage, rage against the dying of the light.*

Because he lives with hope and plans one day to live a normal life, he was married, on 12 February 1988, to Marion Serravalli of New Jersey in the RC chapel at HMP Long Lartin. In the press she describes Paul, whom she met through correspondence and has met only on supervised visits, as a man with traditional Catholic working-class values and aspirations, as *old-fashioned*, a view I concur with. What he would like to do is to live a normal life, to have a family and children, to work and be ordinary. That would not be possible in Ireland, and England he wants to leave forever. So he hopes to live a quiet life in America, 'to let life go past'.

Outside, the cases of the Guildford 4, along with the associated Maguire 7, and the separate, though similar, cases of the Birmingham 6, continue to draw attention. Grant McKee, in a *First Tuesday* documentary on the Guildford case in March 1987, entitled it *A Case That Won't Go Away*. The gaping holes in the prosecution evidence, the conduct of the appeal and the treatment of evidence arising since, were gone into there and in Robert Kee's two-part *First Tuesday* documentary *The Guildford Time Bomb* (July 1986), and in Kee's book *Trial and Error*, which, like Chris Mullin MP's book on the Birmingham case, *Error of Judgement*, raises many awkward questions both as to the conduct of the police and the conduct of the law. To date, 200 MPs have called for further investigation into the Guildford and Woolwich convictions, and Amnesty International has called for a reopening of the Birmingham case on the grounds that the Appeal Court, in turning down the appeal and by giving none of the accused the benefit of the doubt in any of its judgements, has overturned a fundamental principle of British law. Growing support has come from legislators, churchmen, the media, and the judiciary and legal professions, urging the reopening of the cases. Ultimately, they have serious implications in terms of justice, the workings of an unwritten constitution and of the law, and of the British Government's relations with the Irish, and beyond. That the Irish Government feels little confidence in Irish people getting a fair trial in British courts lies behind its long disinclination to ratify the extradition treaty, a European agreement, and this affects extradition arrangements with other states, amongst them the USA. This treaty has now been ratified, but there are many reasons for and a long history of the causes of this suspicion, and together the Guildford, Maguire and Birmingham cases perpetuate it.

Slight of frame, quick, sharp-eyed, Hill talks with confidence in a rapid high-pitched Belfast accent, a little over loud, as if to say why should he murmur? He's tense, as who would not be. He writes songs, poems, reads a lot, thinks, and is impressively articulate. His long hair flips either side of his thin face, and he's continually flicking it back, and blinks a lot. He is continually moving, nervous, twitching. Prison, and the particularly harsh treatment given him, is taking its toll on him, but he is impressive, this man. Apart from the question of the little evidence there is, his bearing denies all — his surroundings, his sentence, guilt. This factor, as Ludovic Kennedy declares of all ten accused in an article on the Guildford and Birmingham cases in *The Observer* (21 December 1986), 'carries no weight with the law but much with me'. And he continues: 'It is that guilty men over a long period of time speak, write and act in a totally different way from innocent men. What the Crown is asking us to believe is that all ten are not only callous murderers but also brilliant actors who for more than twelve years have succeeded in pulling the wool over the eyes of everyone who has spoken to them.'

The Birmingham 6's appeal was turned down in January 1988, though their case and the conduct of the original evidence and the subsequent appeal continue to raise tricky questions, not least in Ireland. The Birmingham decision was the first in a year of heavy knocks to Anglo-Irish relations that seems deliberate and wilful, calculated to anger Irish sensibilities. What the Irish see is the perversity of British justice, a savagely uneven application of the law as it suits British policies: no prosecutions after the Stalker-Sampson report because they would not be in the public interest, together with a statement from the Master of the Rolls, Lord Donaldson, that the activities of the secret services must be above the law for security reasons. The Stalker report into the RUC's alleged shoot-to-kill policy, submitted to the DPP in April 1987, has still not been made public. These decisions must be balanced against the disappointment of the Birmingham result, the continuing Diplock courts in the north and a long series of complaints about them, feet-dragging on the Guildford enquiry, and the release of the only British soldier to be convicted of murder while on duty in Northern Ireland from life imprisonment after serving only three years. No ordinary lifer or common murderer would be so lucky. He was released back to his regiment, the only restriction on his licence that he should not serve again in Northern Ireland. In the case of another soldier, who shot dead an unarmed man, it was decided not to prosecute. Decisions such as these seem cynical, and not everyone shares an absolute faith in British justice. From across the water British justice is seen as a blunt one-sided instrument, relying for the most part on confessions and police evidence, though this in fact is *English* justice, for in Scotland such evidence must be corroborated in court. In Northern Ireland the high ratio of convictions based on confessions was the subject of an Amnesty International report in 1980, and other Amnesty commissions have found evidence of torture and ill-treatment of suspects by police both north and south of the border. As a result, the British Government stands convicted of these offences before the European Court of Human Rights.

In this climate the Guildford and Birmingham convictions drag on. What in fact happened was that in the autumn of 1974 the Provisional IRA began a terror campaign in mainland Britain that lasted till the end of the following year with the capture in the Balcombe Street siege of the active service unit responsible. Among the initial outrages of this campaign, in a long war that mainland Britain does not perceive as a war, in October 1974 bombs went off in two pubs in

Guildford, killing five people, and a month later in a pub in Woolwich, killing two. The pubs, used by off duty soldiers, had been selected as military targets. Later in the same month the Birmingham bombs went off, when two pubs in Birmingham were attacked. 21 people were killed and 160 injured. It was the largest mass murder in Britain at that date, a record since lost. All the bombings were part of the same IRA indiscriminate terror campaign, run by a faction that didn't care about civilian casualties, fighting a war without neutrals. The resulting public panic suited the IRA's purposes just as well, and there was considerable pressure on the police by press and government to make arrests. That time was, Paul recalls, 'a witch-hunt on the Irish community'.

Eight people were charged with the Guildford bombings, of whom four were convicted — Paul Hill, Patrick Armstrong, Gerry Conlon, all originally from Belfast, and Armstrong's English girlfriend, Carole Richardson. Armstrong and Hill were further charged with the Woolwich bombing. After intensive interrogation all four confessed to conspiring with persons unknown to cause explosions. Police arrested about forty people, including Conlon's aunt, Annie Maguire, her family, relations of Hill, and everyone in the squat occupied by Armstrong and Richardson. Several people became the subject of exclusion orders. The bombing charges against Annie Maguire were dropped, but she was charged with possessing explosives. Of the three others charged, two with murder and the other with conspiracy, all were allowed bail and the charges eventually dropped at the request of the DPP. In this, the first hints of a mystery begin to appear. Requesting their discharge, counsel for the DPP said that though there were good reasons for these three defendants to be charged, 'in preparation of the matter for trial other considerations have to apply'.

The case of Annie Maguire and the other members of her family arrested with her developed separately, and affords an example of how the prosecution may choose to divide up case and evidence. Cardinal Hume, who believes that the Guildford 4 and the Maguire 7 are all innocent, thinks there should have been two trials but that all together form one case in which the evidence is sparse, based largely on confessions later repudiated in court. In the Maguire case, where there were no confessions, the prosecution relied on forensic evidence alone. In the Guildford enquiries Conlon is alleged to have confessed that his aunt taught him how to make bombs. She, her husband, her two sons aged 16 and 13, her brother-in-law and her uncle and a visiting friend from Belfast, were all pulled in and subsequently convicted of handling explosives, including those used in the Guildford and Woolwich bombings. The only evidence offered against them was forensic, and disputed, as is the forensic evidence in the Birmingham case. Hand swabs taken after arrest were claimed to prove the Maguires had been handling nitro-glycerine, when there were arguments to the contrary; one of these tests was later shown to give the same results after handling a wide variety of common substances — playing cards, furniture polish, postcards, even cigarette packets. When the results were challenged, the nitro-glycerine traces on the swabs were so minute they could not be retested. The samples had been destroyed before the case came to court.

Annie and Patrick Maguire were sentenced to fourteen years each, their sons to four and five years, Giuseppe Conlon the brother-in-law and Uncle Sean Smith to twelve, and Pat O'Neil, who'd come over for a holiday away from Belfast, to nine. Giuseppe Conlon died in B Wing hospital at Wormwood Scrubs. All the others served out their time, still protesting their innocence, the last of them — Annie — being released from Holloway in late 1985.

The trial of the Guildford 4 took place at the Old Bailey in September 1975. The first person to be arrested under the Prevention of Terrorism Act introduced to counter the IRA terror campaign, Paul Hill was ultimately to be sentenced to the longest term of imprisonment passed in a British court till that date. The prosecution evidence rested wholly on their confessions, which they denounced as forced. Paul's arrest had come first, in Southampton, where he was staying with his girlfriend. At Guildford he was first interrogated by two RUC officers about the kidnap and murder of a former British soldier in Belfast. He says that in the end he made a deal, and wrote out a confession admitting a part in the kidnapping so that his girlfriend would not be charged. Subsequently he was convicted of the Belfast murder by a Diplock court. Then, questioned on the Guildford and Woolwich attacks, he made a series of statements implicating Conlon and others. All the accused produced long lists of accomplices, naming friends, relatives, each other, some of them giving fictitious names, and the discrepancies in their statements were later to be used against them.

In court all denied their confessions. They were all four found guilty. Sentenced by Lord Donaldson (now Master of the Rolls), all received long sentences, two of them indefinite. Carole Richardson, then under 18, was detained at Her Majesty's Pleasure. Patrick Armstrong was given life with a minrec of thirty-five years; Gerry Conlon life with a minrec of thirty years. Paul Hill was sentenced to life with the recommendation, spelt out by the judge, *that he should never be freed*, other than when old or infirm or close to dying.

When arrested, he was 20. He was from the New Barnes Estate, in West Belfast. He describes leaving school at 14, and the hopelessness of trying for jobs and not getting them; as ever, when he said what school he'd been to, he was Catholic. Nothing to do there, he says, and calculates that of the thirty lads in his class at school about half are dead and ten in prison. He says he left to avoid getting into trouble, and had been coming to England since he was 14, to get away. In Belfast he may have been on the fringes of the IRA; there is a missing Armalite and the question of the murdered soldier, and some suspicion that the Provisionals as well as the RUC were after him. Of this, he says it all comes down to an anonymous informant and the larger frame drawn around him — all down, he says, to the same police accusations and statements made under duress. He had a good work record, mostly as a labourer on construction sites. In England he stayed either with relatives or in a Catholic hostel in Quex Road in north London. He had a girlfriend and a steady enough life, and was in work. He'd gone home for Christmas in 1973, and returned to England in August of the following year. He was a school friend of Gerry Conlon. They met up by chance in Southampton that same August. The other two, Armstrong and

Richardson, were in a squat together in Kilburn. Carole, 17, was from Newcastle, and had recently left home for London.

Apart from the confessions, the police evidence was not convincing. According to them, an informant in Belfast gave Paul's name, and claimed a Home Office memorandum had previously warned that he was coming to England to do bombings. Since it was security information, the allegation was not provable. As Alastair Logan, Paul's solicitor, wryly points out: 'Belfast informants are notoriously unreliable', and he asks why, if they were looking for Paul, did they initially come looking for his brother Patrick? The police produced a photofit picture of a girl seen running between the two Guildford pubs who was identified by a Northern Ireland intelligence officer as Paul Hill in a wig. Later, the photofit was identified as a girl killed in the explosion. There were no fingerprints, no identifications, no forensic evidence. All four stories were inconsistent. Descriptions of suspects seen in the bombed pubs described none of the defendants. Witnesses' alibis were not forthcoming; on the night of the first bombings Armstrong was in the squat, but vague; Conlon was in the Quex Road hostel, but the person he was with had since gone to Belfast and could not be persuaded to return; Paul was with his girlfriend and had a witness to say so. She was not called. He says she was not called because the prosecution did not want her to be, as neither were his aunt and uncle, with whom he'd stayed on the night of the second bombing. In addition, Logan points out, Armstrong and Richardson were on drugs and in poor health, and the latter was undergoing withdrawal symptoms; she was so ill the police called in a doctor who said that though she was hysterical and hyperventilating she was fit for interview. Logan believes that at the heart of the matter all four were scapegoats, and that the Surrey police were under pressure to get results, and patched together what they could with whom they had. Discrepancies in the accused's confessions were put down to deliberate IRA obfuscation techniques. It was the time of the witch-hunt, Paul says: 'They needed results. I'm a result. We're the results.'

Carole Richardson's alibi was the strongest, but this too was to be demolished, though in an interesting fashion. She claimed she was with friends at the South Bank Poly on the night of the Guildford explosions, a guest of the band, *Lindisfarne*. At the same time the prosecution alleged she was one of a couple who left the bomb in the first pub at 7.00 p.m. on 5 October, the doorman at the Poly confirmed he had seen her. Two friends said she had met them in a nearby pub between 6.30 and 7.00 p.m., and Ray Laidlaw, the band's drummer, confirmed this. There is a photograph of the two of them in the bar. Later he retracted this statement after one of the two friends who had met her in the pub was himself arrested and held incommunicado. He later claimed the police assaulted him and hinted that his mother, confined to a wheelchair, might die in an accidental fire (*Newcastle Journal*, 1 July 1986). In court this retraction was amplified by demonstrating that it was possible to drive from the *Horse and Groom* in Guildford, where the first bomb went off at 7.50, and be at the South Bank Poly in 45 minutes, 'something that is impossible unless you are in a police car and can break speed limits and cross red lights,' Alastair Logan comments. The police test, in a squad car, made it in 48 minutes. Even so, Carole Richardson could not have been the woman seen in the *Seven Stars*, where at 9.20 the second bomb went off. In her confession she claimed to have planted both. To account for this, the prosecution, led by Sir Michael Havers, had an explanation: she had been lying in her confession, and this together with all the other inconsistencies in the statements of all four, was claimed as evidence of a new interrogation technique developed by the IRA to baffle the police. We now enter the world of mirrors. This explanation being presumably acceptable to the court, all four were found guilty.

Subsequent events have confirmed and prolonged the verdicts. Erroneous or not, questions continue to surface and the accused continue to assert their innocence. In his book *Trial and Error*, Robert Kee shows how the Maguire and Guildford cases dovetail, though in reality all are separately accused, lumped by police and prosecution into linked conspiracies. On the appeal, heard before Lord Roskill, Kee shows how in turning it down, Roskill was concerned most to uphold the findings of Lord Donaldson. As most appellants soon suspect, one judge dislikes overturning the decision of another; there is a professional understanding, it is widely believed. And there is also the larger consideration of confidence in the law to consider. If one case based solely on confession is discredited, many others may surface. If too many appeals are successful, too many prosecutions that convicted them must be faulty; the one stands as a critical measure of the other. Because public confidence must be upheld in the workings of the law and in the investigations of the police that lead to prosecution, clearly what is served here are not the interests of justice but of the law and the State. But the law is not about itself.

In any case, the weight is against the appeal in the first place; if in the original trial the burden of proof lay with the prosecution, who must convince the jury of the facts as they present and interpret them in their scenario, now it is innocence that must be proven. The accused must prove where he was not. Now convicted, he must work from the disadvantages of imprisonment, through all the labyrinths of the system, to come up with new evidence for an appeal. Presenting the original case again will not do, and an appeal is normally allowed only where it is considered that new information has turned up: a foolproof alibi or witness not known or available previously, objections to the police investigation or the conduct of the trial.

With cases as politically explosive as these, the procedures weigh even more, presumably. The remarks of Lord Denning in the Court of Appeal in 1980 when he denied the Birmingham men leave to sue the police are apposite, and awesome in their implication. The Birmingham 6 were originally turned down on their first applications for leave to appeal in 1977; Lord Widgery had found nothing unsafe in their convictions. Still contending that the convictions were based on forced confessions, the six then applied to sue the West Midlands and Lancashire Police for the beatings they claimed to have received under interrogation, but this action was halted by Lord Denning. The police had appealed against it. Lord Denning said that if the six were allowed to bring their action, and should they win, this would mean that the police had indeed beaten and threatened them and had lied in court, perjuring themselves. Therefore the six's confessions were forced and the convictions based on them wrong. That the six would then have to be pardoned or their case referred to appeal or retrial so that their release would be inevitable, was, he said, 'such an appalling vista that every sensible person in the land would say "It cannot be right that these actions should go any further. They should be struck out." '

And they were struck out. The implications of this are quite staggering: the law and the police must be upheld at the cost of justice, and we are all in trouble, every sensible person in the land. It would not be proper, according to Lord Denning, for the police and the law to be scrutinized and found wanting, even though innocent men lie in prison, because this is a requirement of the State. It is — again — a decision not to prosecute made in the public interest, in this case an imaginary concensus of sensible persons. And we begin to see how policies applied in Ulster are coming home.

On the other side of history, these nine Irish men and one English woman (plus the Maguires) are pawns in a political board-game called law and order; individually, meanwhile, they are in prison, a place from which appeal is difficult. Application must be made to the Appeal Court registrar, and the Home Secretary can theoretically refer any case to appeal if he thinks fit. But between the Home Office and the Appeal Court there seems to be some difference of opinion in the matter. The Court of Appeal has itself ruled that it can open any case on any evidence should it consider the interests of justice require it. In recent years successive Home Secretaries have sought to limit the possibility of too many cases being reopened, largely by insisting on new evidence. There have been, however, cases that cried out for retrial on evidence that was not new, and in an attempt to circumvent difficulties arising with the definition of what might constitute *new*, in 1976 Roy Jenkins, then Home Secretary, added the sufficiently woolly *or other consideration of substance*. Since then the adjectival *new* has reattached itself to any consideration in an application for an appeal.

In any case, if leave is given, the Appeal Court consists of three judges and no jury; there are only the judges of the law to consider new evidence that should have been before a lay jury, the judges of the facts, before the verdict. For there to be an appeal, there must be new evidence, yet here the conditions of the trial are altered, and evidence that ought to have been before a whole court is increasingly judged only from the bench. The appeal can either be turned down, or upheld, in which latter case the judges can quash the old verdict or hand the case back for retrial. Whatever their decision, it is made without a lay jury. The Guildford appeal was judged, new evidence and all, by three judges led by Lord Roskill. In the Birmingham appeal the judges consistently accepted prosecution assertions and denied the considerable doubts aired anew in the case; Amnesty's observer points out it was for the prosecution to prove that the six were not ill-treated by the police, and this they failed to do. This matter of a decision made solely by judges has become a common practice in appeal court procedure. Lord Devlin has termed the result of this *only the semblance of a verdict*. In the omission of a jury the Appellate Judges deny or uphold, *seemingly indifferent to whether a jury has heard all the evidence or not, as if . . . they alone should be satisfied of the safety of the conviction . . . that if they have no doubt then neither should a jury*.

The Guildford appeal came up in 1977. As new evidence the defence submitted that, in the trial of the Balcombe Street Siege men earlier that year on bombing charges, three of the accused had admitted to the Guildford and Woolwich bombings, producing evidence of their involvement. Edward Butler said that his first job in the terror campaign was Woolwich, and when asked if he was with Hill and Armstrong he said he'd *never heard of them*. Joseph O'Connell told the police Hill and Armstrong knew nothing about Guildford, and that his active service unit was responsible, and at his trial said from the dock that three of them together with Brendan Dowd were responsible for both Guildford and Woolwich, and that the Guildford 4 were innocent.

Despite this, and the confessions Alastair Logan obtained from them, these men were tried on several charges, but not for Guildford and Woolwich, despite forensic links established between these offences and others they were tried on. A report prepared by Det. Supt. Hucklesby, later head of the anti-terrorist squad, was prepared for the DPP. He found that there was enough evidence to charge Butler with the Woolwich bomb. There were forensic links, and the confessions of the Balcombe Street men were voluntary. Several months went by before the Guildford 4's lawyers learned of these admissions, and an appeal was then got together based on them. At the Balcombe Street trial the DPP, on the advice of the Treasury, left out the Guildford and Woolwich charges, and the forensic links between them and the other charges were suppressed. These charges were not made, and the links were deliberately left out, with the result that the Balcombe Street men refused to plead. Logan was convinced that the prosecution forensic witness had omitted disclosing these links to the court. When challenged, the prosecution said they had been asked to leave these links out by the Anti-Terrorist Squad; challenged on this, the commander of the Squad said the instructions came from the DPP. 'If this is the case,' Logan says, 'this is a conspiracy to pervert the course of justice and is an offence. Yet though articulated in open court and in the press, nothing has been done about it.' Once again, the source of evidence retreats into the shell of the State.

At the Guildford appeal Lord Roskill dismissed the new evidence, citing minor discrepancies, and said he believed the two Balcombe Street men were lying and though they *may* have been responsible for the Guildford and Woolwich bombings, if so, then *with* the Guildford 4, and that the appeal and the new evidence amounted to *a cunning and skilful plot* to get the four acquitted. Once again we see reflections from the mirror world. Once again discrepancies in evidence were put down to clever IRA anti-interrogation techniques. Logan echoes Devlin: 'The Court of Appeal tried the evidence itself, even though it does not have the power to do so.'

Since the appeal's dismissal, the Guildford case continues to surface. Paul Hill's missing witness, never called at the trial, has remained willing and available to testify that on the night of the bombing she saw him in Southampton. Paul sees nothing new in this, and says she has always been available but uncalled. The witness, who had never gone away, had now come forward to support Paul's alibi. Her appearance in the first *First Tuesday* documentary in July 1986 no doubt helped prompt the Home Secretary to order a six-month review of the case, the result of which in January 1987 found no grounds for action in either the Guildford or Maguire cases. The report cited factual errors, innuendo, omissions and distortions, but denied hope of a reopening.

Then, six months later, in August 1987, following the publication of Robert Kee's book, the Grant McKee *First Tuesday* documentary in March, and the representations of an impressively qualified deputation to the Home Secretary, an investigation was ordered to be carried out by the Avon and Somerset police into the original conduct of the investigation by the Surrey police in 1974. With a growing body of considered opinion calling for the case to be opened up, there was new evidence, and would now be an enquiry. Apart from Paul's witness, other new evidence comes from a witness who supports Carole Richardson's testimony that she had been at the South Bank Poly on the night of the Guildford bombing, confirming the earlier part of her testimony discredited at the trial. There is also evidence from two doctors as to her condition when arrested and interrogated, the result of examinations carried out in 1976 for the Home Office by two psychologists specializing in suspects believed to have made false confessions. Their report concludes that at the time of arrest her statement was *very probably unreliable*. Said then to have been a heavy drugs user, she was in a state of high anxiety when arrested, and very probably suggestible and not in a fit condition to be interrogated, and her confession therefore suspect. As Robert Kee points out, the difference in lifestyles between the Guildford accused and the Balcome Street men are striking; the former did not seem at all likely suspects for such an operation. Nor does their subsequent behaviour. Between the Guildford and Woolwich bombings Carole Richardson had complained to the police about an assault, and one of the Maguires had gone to the police only hours before his arrest to enquire about his missing brother.

At any rate the 1987 enquiry was announced soon after the deputation saw the Home Secretary to urge the reopening of the Guildford case. It consisted of Cardinal Hume, former judges Lords Devlin and Scarman, two former Home Secretaries and Ministers for Northern Ireland, Merlyn Rees and Roy Jenkins, and Robert Kee. Their arguments, and a growing body of reasoning opinion, grow more and more persuasive. Not least amongst those who sustain Hill by believing in him are his family. He receives no succour from the IRA, for the simple reason he is not one of their number. Other high-powered support for the Guildford prisoners comes from Lord Gifford, Lord Fitt, the Bishop of Down & Connor and other churchmen, trades union branches, and MPs and Euro-MPs in British and Irish and European parliaments.

The police enquiry's report is still not available; the Home Secretary has announced he will consider it, together with uncalled witness evidence supporting Conlon, over Christmas 1988. Meanwhile Paul waits, he hopes, and lives in hope, confident of his position in all the proceedings, and of their eventual success. Challenged on a newspaper report (*The Guardian*, 15 August 1987) that if his sentence were overturned, he would still face a life sentence for the murder of a British soldier in Belfast before the bombings, he says this too is a false accusation. That allegation comes from the same source, he says wearily, along with everything else: through the police in Guildford from unverifiable sources beyond.

Shortly after I knew him, I read he'd been moved from the Scrubs to Long Lartin; arrangements had been made for his wedding in the Scrubs, but the move voided the arrangements, his fiancée's residence permit ran out, and a new date had to be figured out for Long Lartin. In the press it was given out that he'd been moved because the Birmingham 6 were on the wing for their appeal, and while this may have been so, the fact that two of the six had been there several months while he was on the wing seems not to have mattered until the appeal. This movement caused inconvenience and delay to arrangements for his marriage. Such arbitary treatment is in keeping; he points out that before the Balcombe Street admissions, Brendan Dowd and Joseph O'Connell had been held on normal remand awaiting trial, but when they made their admissions exonerating the Guildford 4 they were removed to an SSB; to him it's obvious they were moved out of contact because they had admitted to the bombings he and the others are in prison for.

In prison he lives strategically and tidily, often on the move from one prison to another, often suddenly, striving to keep his mind alive, aware that prison, and the particular treatment he gets, and the long ramifications of his case, inevitably wear him down. At times, he says, he can't conceive the notion of prison for his natural life. At other times, he says, he wonders how much he can take, and a phrase he uses recurs again and again: 'Words fail me. Words fail. If I was to tell an ordinary person what's happened to me they'd say I was insane.' And he admits to being bitter. 'I've lost the best ten years of my life between 20 and 30, the years that you make your life, you find someone, you settle down, you graft for your house or whatever.' He avoids being over hopeful, knowing too often where he falls when his hopes are dashed. When the Balcombe Street men made their statements his hopes soared, he says. He was exhilarated. 'I've curbed that now. I've put a rein on that. You're in the clouds one week and then crash, you're on the floor.'

Bitter, he remains philosophical. About him he sees men who, after ten or twelve years, have become robots. He describes himself in some ways as the same age he was when he came in, his development arrested by prison. At times he comes close to his limits, he says; 'there are days you can see yourself the silent screaming in the corner.' Not surprisingly, he has had a history of trouble, some 150 adjudications to date on GOAD charges. Guilty or not, he says, he won't plead; he is held against his will. He has spent some 1500 days in solitary, under rule 43B under order 10/74, in solitary for 28 day periods, sometimes renewed for further periods of 28. 10/74, named for the date of its introduction, specifies no charges; it confines him on the block without a reason in the interests of good order and discipline.

They have taken everything away from him, he says, though he has two people in his life that he didn't have when he came in: his daughter who was born while he was awaiting trial, and his fiancée. Otherwise they have taken everything. He describes writing letters with burnt matches, of finding spit in his food or water, and beatings. In the end, though, he says, there's no more they can do to him. 'If after thirteen years they can't refine how they get to me, I've no respect.' He recalls being put on a block, and going into the strong-box and stripping off; it mystified the screws: 'You're supposed to be dragged in there kicking and screaming. I walked in.'

'Three things they can do to me: starve me, beat me up, leave me naked. I was born naked, and many times I was hungry, and my father made sure I got beat. They've shown me everything they have, so there's nothing else they can do to me. I've no fear of anything, only of the unknown.'

Solitary he describes as an envelope, a closing in and around. His days in solitary, added end to end, make up almost four years of the fourteen he has served. As he describes them, block days are utterly tedious, and calculated to break him down; sometimes he must wear an E-man suit though he's never made an escape attempt; exercise is solitary, all visits behind glass, and a red light is always on in the cell. The day's inflexible routine is –

| | |
|---|---|
| 6.30 a.m. | Box of clothes in. |
| 7.00 a.m. | Slop out, one trip, with po and water jug together. Mirror and razor in. Breakfast. |
| 7.30 a.m. | Slop out, mirror and razor out, bed out. |
| 12.00 | Dinner. |
| 1.45 p.m. | Slop out, one trip. |
| 2.30 p.m. | 1 hour exercise, solitary, weather permitting. |
| 5.00 p.m. | Supper. |
| 6.30 p.m. | Slop out, one trip. Bed in, pyjamas, clothes box out. |

All that, as he says, is part of the scheme of things. He keeps as fit as he can, and his mind working. He waits. He goes to church a bit, though he says he is not deeply religious. His appraisal of British justice is searing. So far as he's concerned, he is a simple man, a Socialist, a Nationalist, a Republican, beliefs that are not yet illegal, and that do not make him a bomber. And he sees himself in the context of complex political manoeuvrings, a pawn in a game, *a hostage*.

Since the raising of their case to more prominence he says his treatment has in some ways improved, and that the Irish Government and embassy's interest has helped. But he is still in prison. 'If I'm in the best prison in the country with a colour television set in my cell it's irrelevant to me because I can't be free in my head.'

Their conviction, he says, served three purposes. It appeased the public and the press, not by apprehending the actual bombers, who went on for a further year in their terror campaign, but by producing scapegoats. It gave the police credit, and restored confidence in authority. And most important: 'It was a warning to the Irish community in this country not to get involved in any part of the war in Northern Ireland. The PTA was designed to do this. They know we're innocent,' he says. 'That's not the point. It was a warning: this is what we can do to you even when you're not involved.'

'My mind is free,' he says, 'but the minds of my keepers are in chains.'

And he says:

'My name is Paul Michael Hill. I'm serving life for murder at Guildford and Woolwich, charges I've consistently denied. As my case is being reviewed I don't care to enter into either the circumstances of my arrest or circumstances under which confessions were taken from us in Guildford police station. I do so simply because I think it would be dangerous to talk about them at this stage. At a later date, should the review prove unfruitful, I shall enter into those matters. I intend to discuss, if possible, my treatment since my conviction while in prison.

'In thirteen years in prison I have been moved a total of, I believe, 44–45 times. I've been moved between prisons as follows:– Winchester, Brixton, Belfast, Wandsworth, Bristol, Albany, Bristol, Hull, Durham, Hull, Leicester, Leeds, Long Lartin, Gartree, Wandsworth, Gartree, Exeter, Winchester, Wakefield, Albany, Wandsworth, Winchester, Parkhurst, Canterbury, Parkhurst, Wormwood Scrubs, Albany, Canterbury, Albany, Winchester, Albany, Parkhurst, Manchester, Wormwood Scrubs, Manchester, Wormwood Scrubs, Manchester, Gartree, Liverpool, Gartree, Lincoln, Hull, Wormwood Scrubs, and Long Lartin.

'I've spent a total of around 1500 days in solitary confinement, the vast majority of which has been for good order and discipline, which basically in itself is not any offence. When I say it's not an offence it's not one which is punishable by the prison discipline system. I'm just removed from a prison, no warning given whatsoever, and moved hundreds of miles to another prison, sometimes on the day of a visit. The vast bulk of my solitary confinement has been for no reason whatsover, though I have spent periods in solitary confinement for actual offences against discipline. I have sometimes been removed from prisons on my way to gymnasium, on my way to exercise, on my way to labour, which meant that I've had nothing at all with me: I've had no radio, writing materials, a pen, tobacco, books, nothing whatsoever. So when I'm taken to another prison I'm in solitary confinement and I basically have nothing apart from what I stand up in. And the bed's removed and all that I have for 23 hours a day is a po, a basin, a cup, a plastic knife, fork and spoon, a soup bowl, and a water jug. Total silence. Obviously I'm in a punishment block, and almost all the time I'm lodged in the strong-box, which is a cell with double doors, a low bed which is a large raised platform about 6″ off the ground which is concrete, upon which my mattress is placed. My mattress is removed in the morning about 7 o'clock and given back to me at night at 8 o'clock. So apart from the yard that I have exercise in, I sit in the corner all day or I pace the cell. When one's held in solitary confinement in a local prison they say that we're under the authority of the Board of Visitors in that prison. Now I've been visited by the BOV in some of these prisons, and I've asked the BOV that came up to my cell door why I was in solitary confinement, why I had been removed from my last prison, how long I was likely to be in solitary confinement, and the response I've had every single time is they turn to the prison officer who's there and they ask the prison officer what am I doing there. The prison officer says I'm here on good order and discipline, and they say to me they know nothing about it, which is totally absurd, seeing they are the watchdog committee as it were, responsible for my well-being in that prison.

'I've been assaulted on several occasions in prison, three times pretty severely. I was assaulted in Hull prison, in the aftermath of the Hull disturbance in 1976, when I was forced to run a gauntlet of prison officers from my cell while collecting my breakfast, and I was beaten back along the same gauntlet. On being removed to another prison I was beaten down a flight of stairs and placed in a cell. I was removed to yet another prison, where I had a period of constraint, where I was lodged in the strong-box, naked, with a body belt. A body belt consists of a broad leather belt round the waist about 4″ broad with handcuffs either side, and a padlock on the front. This was kept on for a considerable period, several days, during which my food was just pushed into my cell and I had to lie sideways on the floor and eat off a dish. This wasn't removed even when I went to the toilet, which made my toilet physically impossible.

'I was also assaulted in the aftermath of disturbances at another prison in 1983, during disturbances that I had no involvement in whatsoever. I was removed by a MUFTI squad to the reception area where I was taken in a van to a nearby prison, and in the van, going the short distance to that prison, a towel was placed around my neck from behind, and I was forced into a corner in the back of the van. It was difficult to breathe and I was punched and kicked in the back of the van. I was brought into the prison where they stopped between the gates and the hospital. I was driven to the hospital, where I was bundled along a landing, which is the same landing where people are housed whilst they are waiting transfer to Broadmoor or Park Lane. I was lodged in a strip cell, I was threatened, I was stripped, I was again put in constraint. I was threatened by medical officers who had a needle which they said they would use on me.

'The next morning at half past six I was removed to a prison in the north of England, where I spent a considerable period in solitary confinement, a period totalling I believe ten or eleven months. This was broken up with several stints in Wormwood Scrubs, where I had come for the mutiny charge which had been given me for the disturbances in 1983. The mutiny charge was in fact overturned and was thrown out by the High Court. During my stay in the northern prison my mail was collected by the censor, and after 20 or 30 letters it would be enclosed in an envelope and sent back to the sender bearing the legend *not known at this address*.

'I have great difficulty attempting to describe what solitary confinement means to the person it affects. Its effect on me has basically been to make me totally hyperactive. I suffer from nervous energy, and after long bouts in solitary confinement I find it increasingly hard to engage in conversation. I know what the person's saying but it just goes in one ear and out the other ear. I listen to a conversation for about ten or fifteen minutes and I suddenly realize I haven't understood a thing the person has said. Solitary confinement to me has completely raped my memory in as much as I find it hard to recall instances, and I find it hard to put names to people I should know.

'Solitary confinement itself, i.e. being locked in a cell, if that was the only thing, that would perhaps be bearable, but it's made even all the more difficult by the people holding me there. I've gone on exercise in some prisons and I've returned to my cell that night and I've attempted to write a letter and I've found the refill of my pen missing, which basically means I can't write a letter until I get my canteen the following week and I'm able to purchase a pen. I've spent periods of between a month, two months, three months, where I haven't even entered into conversation with anyone apart from asking for my weekly letter or a VO.

'I view solitary confinement as an attempt to destroy me mentally and psychologically, so if ever the time comes when we're exonerated and we are released, we will not be in a condition, a lucid condition, that we'll be able to tell things as they were, and explain exactly what happened to us. I'm a Category A prisoner, which is the highest categorization, which is one where your escape is dangerous to the police, the security of the State and the general public at large. I've been informed in the last month that my visiting conditions are, to put it bluntly, to become more brutal. I've been informed that I must send a sterile set of clothing to the visits 24 hours before I have a visit. I must then go to the visiting area. I enter one room where I'm stripped in sight of two prison officers. I leave that room naked, I enter the other room, where I put on the sterile set of clothing which has been sent from the day before. I then proceed along the corridor, which is thirty yards, with the two prison officers, and then I'm stood on a box about 8″ off the ground, a wooden platform where I'm rubbed down — I'm searched again physically, which is totally absurd in view of the fact that I've just been strip searched. I then enter a visiting-room about 6′ by 5′ wide which is basically a table, two chairs one side, two chairs the opposite side. There's a partition travelling the length of the room under the table, and there's a board — a swing-door — at the side. I'm told that I can embrace my visitors before the visit and after the visit. For the previous thirteen years my mother has sat beside me, and I've sat beside my girlfriend, and I've been able to engage in family discussion whenever possible. A prison officer is within four or five feet and can observe the whole visit. Now I've been told that a prison officer has to be in the room, one on my side of the partition, one on my visitor's side of the partition, which makes family conversation or anything personal completely impossible. I have a daughter who was born whilst I was on remand who because of the circumstances is pretty fraught. She's only seen me in a succession of prison visiting areas. I haven't been able to have one personal word with my daughter in thirteen years.

'As I was saying, I'm treated as if I were a high risk prisoner, in total contrast to other inmates that are on this wing. One inmate in particular has murdered five members of his family, cold-bloodedly, including two children. All of these people he shot in the back of the head systematically and without feeling or emotion purely for financial gain. That inmate is serving a recommended sentence of twenty-five years. He has his visits in a normal visiting-room, and therefore is seen as no threat to anyone. There are many men on this wing, many Category A prisoners, who are serving recommended sentences, who are serving the most vile sentences for rape, for the killing of children, for a collection of sex offences. None of these prisoners receives the same visits as I do; they can conduct their visits in a normal visiting-room, and they can conduct a normal, meaningful conversation with their family, something which is virtually impossible for me. This has been the source of great pain to me, simply because I'm here for nothing in the first place, and I see people who are blatantly guilty being treated more humanely than I've ever been treated or am ever likely to be treated.

'There's a popular myth doing the rounds that since the publicity with regard to our case and because of the involvement of many eminent people who are now saying that we are totally innocent, that our treatment in prison is becoming more humane. This is not the case at all. If anything, my treatment has intensified for the worst. It's purely political in as much as the only people who receive these visits are Irish, along this wing, and because those innocent people who were convicted for the Birmingham bombings are now at the Appeal Court, they have been told that they are being removed from the High Risk visits, obviously as a result of their case going back to the Appeal Court. That simply epitomises the political nature of the visits.

'I'm highly critical of the Irish Government's involvement as regards my treatment in prison, and when I see the moves being made on behalf of other people — i.e. British hostages, American hostages, French hostages in the Lebanon, British mercenaries in Angola, drug smugglers in Sweden, words fail me. It beggars description. I'm the citizen of a government which is totally impotent. In fact it took me quite a considerable amount of aggravation, I mean punishment, in order to be able even to write to the Irish Government. I was informed by prison governors in four prisons that I could not write, and they contacted the Home Office. The Home Office wrote back and said that I could not possibly raise my treatment with a foreign government. I informed the Home Office that I was an Irish citizen and was told that I was not. I have only been visited twice by representatives of the Irish Government, on both occasions by a Third Secretary, and both within the last year, and only as a result of publicity given to my case — publicity which I hasten to add was given in January (1987) by English people, by the English media, which has a considerable amount of blame to carry. I view the British media as in 1974 generating the hysteria that made it possible for totally innocent people to be arrested and sentenced.

'I've been told that I shall never be released, except in the case of severe old age or severe infirmity. I try not to think about that because I don't think I could really cope with it. It's not so much the coping with that, it's the coping with my treatment, with the complete hopelessness of the situation now that it's purely a political football. I don't think in the long run that I could sustain the mental attitude to get through that. There will come a time sooner or later when I'll say to myself that I just can't have any more of that. I don't say that in any suicidal form because that's the last thing that I would ever do in my life, simply because that spells defeat, and I'm totally innocent. Defeat I can't contemplate.

'Since my imprisonment I've lost three members of my family — my sister who died in infancy from meningitis, and my grandparents on my mother's side whom I was particularly close to, having spent a large period of my childhood with them. When my grandfather died he was dying of cancer, and on the last visit with my grandfather the prison staff were well aware that he was dying of cancer. I was given forty minutes the last time I saw my grandfather alive. When my grandmother died I was in solitary confinement with nothing. I was sitting in the corner of the cell, the door opened, I was asked by a prison officer if I had a grandmother called Cushnahan, and I said I did. He said "she's dead" and closed the door, and that was it. I spent four or five days of anguish because I wouldn't go along to the prison staff and enquire about this. I thought this was — I was pretty paranoid — I thought that they were only possibly trying it on or trying to depress me. I also got a telegram sent at that time which I never received, and so it was a period of almost a week before I received a letter informing me that in fact my grandmother had died.

'It's patently obvious that the ordinary prison officer is told from higher up to generally harass the Irish prisoners. In particular, I've had the most severe harassment, aggravation, confrontation, for the smallest of matters. For example I'm moved every six weeks from cell to cell. There's no logical reason for it whatsoever. I'm told that this is done on security grounds. The vast bulk of my indiscipline record has been taken up by confrontation, by matters of generally being harassed, by my resistance to harassment.

'Basically the procedure in every punishment block I've been in is the same. Once I arrive I'm stripped and I'm told by ten or twelve prison officers that I'll get a bloody good kicking as it were. My prison record obviously follows me from segregation unit to segregation unit. That prison record contains pretty detailed reports on evidence that I gave against prison officers in the aftermath of assaults. In the aftermath of the Hull riot eight or ten prison officers were found guilty of assault on myself and several other inmates, assaults for which I was compensated in the paltry sum of £1500. I've been told by prison governors that my prison record was so diabolical that there was every possibility that I would be removed from the dispersal system — i.e. the long-term prison system — and lodged on the circuit in local prisons, which I would spend in solitary confinement. To use the words of one governor, I wouldn't see daylight for a very, very long period.

'This is in total contrast to an incident which occurred in a workshop in 1983, when an inmate, a black inmate who was serving a pretty minor sentence of four years, had an altercation with a civilian instructor during the course of which he assaulted the instructor. The riot bell was pressed. A heavy team of screws descended on the youth. The youth lifted a hammer and went to further assault the civilian instructor who was prone on the ground. I thought this was a pretty pointless exercise on behalf of the youth in view of the fact he was only serving four years, so I subdued the youth. I took him to the other side of the table and I said to him don't be crazy, you're serving four years and you'll get yourself life. I indicated to the prison staff that myself and other inmates would witness that the black prisoner wasn't marked, and that he would walk to the segregation unit with the staff, which he did. I was stopped several days later by an Assistant Governor who praised me for this action, and I told the AG several times that I didn't do it to be praised, and I said we did it in order to prevent the youth from getting a life sentence. This isn't entered in my prison record, and in fact it never was.

'Whilst in solitary confinement in one prison I was held with another inmate, a prisoner who was mentally bemused who was goaded by prison staff to attack us. He took a piece of glass from his window and on exercise he attacked us from the side with this piece of glass. The person was deranged and he ended up considerably damaged about the face, and we were totally unmarked. I view this as a simple example of prison officers geeing up inmates to attack Irish prisoners. This has happened to us on several occasions. On one occasion an Irish prisoner had his door marked by prison staff so that another inmate came into the cell when he was sleeping in bed in the morning and he was attacked by a battery in a sock and beaten about the head.

'It would also appear that harassment and aggravation intensifies around periods when we're receiving maximum publicity, and I can only equate that to the face of the reactionary British State.

'I was taken back to Hull prison last year, 1986, in spite of the fact I was told that I would never be taken back to Hull prison after being assaulted there in 1976. I was taken back there during a period when I was suffering from what I can only describe as pleurisy, and I had severe pain in my back. And I was told to take this matter up with the medical officers at Hull. I wasn't completely happy about this. Hull was completely unsuitable for visits, and it was creating considerable hardship with my mother and my young daughter. Their protests met with complete deaf ears. After a week's visits at Hull, when my mother had returned home, the day after their last visit I was then moved to London, and the sham I hope shows up the whole farce, the whole nonsense, of my being removed out of London two weeks before my visits even started.

'I'd like to thank every single person who has had the moral fibre to stand up and to speak out against this. I'm not a gunman. I'm not a bomber. I'm a totally innocent person. I've spent thirteen years in prison, thirteen pretty harsh, severe years. How I got here I don't really know, how I endured thirteen years of this, basically I can't tell you. I don't know. I suppose I owe a good deal to my family, and I've been lucky that I've had an aunt and an uncle and a mother who have given me basically all their time and turned their whole life over to the pursuit of justice. I appeal to every single person, for my sake and the sake of all my co-accused: "No, don't be silent. Speak up. Tell them like it is, that we're hostages. We can't continue to live like this. Sooner or later there will come a breaking point in us, and if this issue is not won then future generations of people, and in particular future generations of Irish people, will experience the same things which we are experiencing now."'

# EPILOGUE

INSIDE TIME is where I've been, just visiting. I was never in residence, and thank each one of the stars for that. Inside with the inside mob, over 54,384 as last counted, and half as many again of their custodians, in and out men, short-timers and long-haul jobbers, con-men, divs, piss artists, wind-up merchants, dog-end men and poets, among the allsorts, the innocent and the unconvincing and the simply guilty. It seemed to me like a zone suspended and separated in time from the rest of chronology, or beyond time as it measures them in the sentences they do, as if time were the real illusion. Everything seemed refracted in there, like sticks in water, bent out of shape, variously coded, mirror twisted. But for the one rule of compulsion, and the one rule of survival, all other rules were suspended.

In there, is where society punishes its miscreants, shuts them away from itself for its own safety and to teach them a lesson, and variously attempts to train them to behave themselves the next time. Mostly this training consists of being locked up for long periods of time away from whatever normality might be outside and regardless of whatever commitments they may have, being allowed to do routine work and to associate with other prisoners. Those who don't learn the lesson quickly, get trained a little harder by being sent to the block, by losing remission, by being fined or confined to their cells. When that fails, there's being messed about, shoved around the system, dumped or sectioned off, and the rabbit vanishes into the hat forever. The hope is they'll get the point eventually and come out decent citizens. Some do, but the system doesn't encourage it.

This attempt to teach the basic rules of social behaviour to those who have broken them might have more chance of success if prisoners didn't, from their upside-down view up the law's skirts, see the rules always being shifted or reinterpreted or by-passed or simply broken whenever it suits those who make them to do so. From time to time great pronouncements are made on these matters, as to how thoroughly disgusting our prison system is; and prisons like the Scrubs go on being disgusting. Here's the retiring Chief Inspector of Prisons, Sir James Hennessy, making his annual report on the state of British prisons in December 1987: 'The physical conditions in which many prisoners have to live continues . . . to border on the intolerable.' He says there's a great lack of constructive activity, that bored, inactive prisoners become discontented and a control risk. I like that careful 'border' to soothe the politicians and Civil Servants responsible for it all. But here it is: even from a control viewpoint it makes sense, as Sir James recommends, to use prison less, to use less prison, to build more open prisons; to have shorter sentences or alternative means of imprisonment.

Inside, no one believes any of it. They prefer governments with social consciences, but fear the do-gooders, and expect what usually happens: that attempts at change fizzle out and eventually get lost in the paperwork. We are proving again what we should already know: that repressive regimes create rebellion and defiance, that boredom makes people desperate, that reform does not follow from reaction and squalor.

They didn't believe Mr Hurd when he said he would end police remand custody by Christmas 1987, and he didn't. They do believe that the poor go to prison ahead of the rich, that it's harder for the unemployed to get bail and that they are more likely to be imprisoned, that social security cheats get jail and tax fiddlers don't, and they note that inside-traders and City fraudsters and bent politicians get a slap on the wrist and a fine they can afford. They know that prison is society's dustbin, and that many of the mentally unstable who have been discharged from one institution into non-existent community care end up here. Prison, often said to be the microcosm of society, is the mirror of its inequality, where the rules are inconsistent. Prison is at worst authoritarian, at best paternal. They note that the rule of segregating remands from convicted prisoners is often broken. They believe all kinds of things that may or may not be true and that no one inside can check: that in the event of war, all Cat. As will be taken by the Army and shot, that the razor wire is contrary to the European Convention but the British Government goes on using it and paying the fine. Whether any of these things are true or not, they become the apocrypha, the assumptions underlying thought and act. Inside, by and large, they don't believe anyone, not each other, nor the Chaplain, nor the Governor, nor the officers, who tell them nothing anyway. They don't believe the Government and they don't believe the press. Many of them know, from the media reporting on their cases, how reality gets short-handed and highlighted into news.

And, like them, I'm a doubter, blighted or blessed by disbelief, and think that anything is believable but not much of it is true: the only verifiable facts are the bars and bolts and keys, the wall and the utter separation from the world. And death. One evening in the summer of 1986, watching the news on TV, I heard a Government spokesman say there were no prisoners with aids in British prisons. One such had recently been discharged from the Scrubs to Hammersmith Hospital to die, and that same afternoon I'd talked with a man on B Wing doing a year for a motor offence who said he thought he'd only got a sentence to get him off the streets, and that when he'd come in, someone had chalked AIDS next to his name on the board opposite the movements desk. He was completely ostracized, and segregated from another man with the same diagnosis. Now there's a unit in Brixton for prisoners with aids, and it's admitted there are currently 100 prisoners found to be HIV-positive, and there's talk of issuing condoms, but in prison the fear is very sharp. Where the only choice is homosexuality or celibacy, and where men spill blood often enough, they point out: what do the experts know anyway? After Chernobyl the experts from the East and West wrung their hands in public admitting they didn't know what might happen or what they might do about it.

In prison, aids has now become part of the nightmare, woven into the apocrypha; tales go the rounds of the man, now deceased, who was said to have worked in the kitchens chopping vegetables for coleslaw. Whatever the truth, it seems the Home Office prefers to remain innocent of the problem; it recently decided against a major research project to be conducted confidentially in three prisons into drug use and homosexuality, figures for which are unknown, details unavailable. The project had been proposed by its own appointed Aids Advisory Committee, headed by the Scrubs' principal psychologist, in order to discover the scale of the problem and take avoiding action. The fact is that some men in prison turn homosexual for the duration, reverting to heterosexuality on release. As potential centres for the spread of aids, prisons concern us all, yet here the Home Office is caught in a hypocrisy. It cannot reconcile that drug taking and homosexual acts take place in prison, against the rules; a prison cell is not regarded as a private place. Therefore they can't investigate either act, for fear that doing so would sanction them. So what to do, now we can't look at the problem.

Questions without answers, and the questions go round and round in this poky corner of the State's dwindling enterprises. This has always been Cinderella's house, and no one, including its inhabitants, would expect it to be otherwise. There are moves now to privatise, starting with remand and open prisons, and surely something must be done about remand. Sir James hints at privatisation in his report, it is as if the report were written to support it. In America, he says, there are private enterprise prisons where the inmates aren't bored and unruly; maybe so, and maybe next we'll try the captive food outlet and cheap labour formula. Now there's news of a riot in a Corrections Corporation 'Facility' in Tennessee. Prisoners don't want it, being conservative in the sense they prefer the devil they know to the devil they don't, and they recall the hulks at Woolwich. Officers don't want it, for obvious reasons. Privatisation will cream off the well-behaved, and exploit them as cheap labour, but it is irrelevant to the crisis in our prisons. It will break the monopoly of the POA but it will ensure a vested interest in a high sentencing policy. Back in 1877, when the Prison Commission was set up, all contractors and privately-owned prisons and the last of the hulks were bought out; a long history of exploitation and abuse of their captive workforce had finally come to an end. There's no reason to suppose that in the last century human nature has much changed and greed gone out of style, for if that were the case many of these men wouldn't be here, and the crisis wouldn't exist. As to the electronic tag, most find the idea unbearable and say they'd prefer prison, and if tagged they'd break the rules, and go inside. As to shorter sentencing, all say Aye, though they point out that many magistrates allow for remission time, and bang another third onto the number they first thought of. Talk to the sentencers, is what they say. In 1986 when 3000 prisoners were released early to ease the pressure in the jails, the numbers were up again within a month.

That we need to make less use of prison and to explore forms of punishment and treatment within the community, if only to decrease the prison population and its consequent recycling effect, are aims held in common by the Howard League, NACRO, NAPO, the Prison Reform Trust and PROP and — now — by the Home Office itself. In November 1988 the Government allocated another £370m to the prison building programme, intended to provide another 3,000 prison places, and the Home Office announced measures to divert offenders from prison, and a new parole package. These moves to tackle overcrowding and to experiment with alternatives to prison are laudable; at the same time it was admitted in the prison service's annual report to March 1988 that prison overcrowding had reached 'nightmare' levels. The Home Secretary is now distinguishing between violent crimes against the person, for which the punishment must be prison, and non-violent and first offenders' crimes — minor offences for which prison is clearly not the answer. Indeed, it compounds the problem. Clearing out many of the short sentence and petty offenders would free resources within the prison service to explore less barbarous regimes and more effort at rehabilitation.

No conclusion. There is no objectivity, only competing viewpoints, and this viewpoint has been mine — that the truth is elusive and stranger than fiction, but that fiction is mostly what I found. What will probably happen is that people will go on committing crimes and getting arrested, that we'll go on building prisons and filling them and have to build more, in that perverse law of nature that abhors empty spaces; more prisoners will be caught up in the spiral, and crime will get worse and civil life less possible. No doubt experiment will follow experiment, failure follow failure, and things grow worse inside and out. We thought to build a prison, and isolate the danger of ourselves from ourselves, and found we can't.

Prison is an evil place. Don't go there. Or: don't go there again.

# GLOSSARY

| | |
|---|---|
| Accumulated visits | Convicted prisoners serving a year or more in prisons far from home can save from three to twelve visits. Cat. As and lifers must petition, others apply to the Governor for transfer to a local prison, usually for 28 days, where all the saved visits are taken. |
| Acker Bilk | Milk. |
| Active | Criminals who are planning or committing crime. |
| Adjudication | Governor's or VC's hearing to decide punishment for offences. |
| AG | Assistant Governor. |
| Ag | Aggravation. Hassle. |
| AKA | Also known as. |
| Almonds | Socks (rocks). |
| Ap | An application to the Governor. |
| Association | Free time, usually two hours in the evenings, when prisoners are allowed to associate with one another unless under punishment or restriction. |
| Baby burgler | Young thief. |
| Batter, On the | Soliciting. |
| Bent cozzer | Dishonest policeman. |
| Bird | Doing time. |
| Bit of work | A robbery. |
| Blade | Knife. |
| Blag, blagger, to blag | Armed robbery. |
| Blank, A | Ignoring someone. To blank. |
| Block, The | Punishment cells. The seg-unit. |
| Board | Committee of officers and others who periodically review prisoners' cases. |
| Boat | Face (boatrace). |
| Body, Bodies | Prisoners. |
| Bogging off | Being watched by a nosey person. |
| Boiled | Mix of boiling water and sugar thrown over someone. |
| Book, On the | Category A prisoner. |
| Bottle | Nerve, courage, cheek. Also rectum. |
| BOV | Board of Visitors — outside observers appointed to look into complaints and check on prison conditions. |
| Brass | Prostitute. |
| Brief | Barrister, solicitor, or QC. |
| Brown bread | Dead. |
| Bubble | Greek (bubble & squeak). |
| Bubbled | Informed on. Noted up. |
| Burglars | Screws who search cells. |

| | |
|---|---|
| Burn | Tobacco. |
| Buzzin | Stoned on whizz or cannabis. |
| Cabbage patch (abbrev. Cabbage) | Match. Also used of HMP Kingston (Portsmouth). |
| Cane | Jemmy for forcing doors. |
| Canister | Head, skull. |
| Career | Lifer's career plan — moves from prison to prison, recatting, out to open prison, etc. |
| Case Officer | Officer who writes progress reports. |
| Cat. A | 'A' Category prisoner classified as dangerous to the public, the police or the security of the State. |
| CC | Cellular confinement. Punishment awarded by Governor or VC, with only privileges closed visits and prison library books; no tobacco, no radio; mattress and bedding taking out of cell 8 am–8 pm; segregated exercise, etc. |
| Chasin | Smoking heroin off silver paper. (Chasing the dragon). |
| Chief | Chief Officer. |
| China | Mate (china plate). |
| Chiv | Knife, razor, or any other sharp weapon. |
| Chokey | Punishment block. |
| Civvies | Workshop instructors employed by HO. Civilian prison employees (i.e. not officers). Also tailor-made cigarettes. |
| Clothing Board | Between 5 and 8 weeks prior to release a prisoner tries on his own clothes; if they don't fit or he doesn't have respectable clothing he can then be supplied with clothing by the prison department. The rules state that a prisoner must be respectably dressed leaving prison. |
| Coat, To | Slag off, abuse verbally. |
| Cockle | £10 note (cock & hen). |
| Codgled (also Coshled) | Having plenty of something. |
| Control units | Special units (now closed) at Wakefield and the Scrubs for disruptive prisoners given 90 days in strict block conditions. Any infringement of regulations would mean sliding down the ladder to start again at day one. Order signed by BOV member. |
| Corned beef | Chief (Chief officer). |
| Corner | Share of the proceeds of a robbery. |
| Crank | Injection. |
| Creeper | Burglar who operates at night. |
| CRO'd | Checked with Criminal Record Office. |
| Currant bun | Sun. |
| Dairy, The | Suspicion, heat. |
| Death, In the | In the end. |
| Dep | Deputy Governor. |
| Derby, A | Fat stomach. |
| Diamond | Someone highly thought of. |
| Diesel | Nick tea. |
| Dipping | Picking pockets. |
| Dispersal prisons | Eight maximum security prisons set up in England after the Mountbatten Report that followed the escape of 22 prisoners in 1965, and that of George Blake, from the Scrubs, in 1966. They contain Cat. A and E–men, and disperse lifers and long-term prisoners through the prison system. |
| Div, Divvy | Mentally backward person. |
| Do a runner | Escape, get away. |
| Dog | Applied to certain screws. |

| | |
|---|---|
| Dog and bone | Phone. |
| DPP | Department of Public Prosecutions. |
| Draw, To | To get a sentence, as in drew a 5, an 8, a ten. |
| Drink, A | Payment for a favour. |
| Drums, Doing | Burgling houses. |
| Dry bath | Strip search. |
| E–man | Potential escaper. |
| Earwigging | Listening furtively. |
| EDR | Earliest date of release. |
| Egg and spoon | Black person (coon). |
| Face, A | A well-known villain. |
| Fireman's | Nose (fireman's hose). |
| Firm | A gang of criminals. |
| Fishbowls | Small glass-sided interview rooms on Scrubs' D Wing. |
| Fitted up | Victim of fabricated evidence. |
| Flop | Safe house or flat. |
| Flop on | Accost or impose on someone. |
| Form | Previous convictions. |
| Four handled mattress | Mattress used vertically to squash troublesome prisoner to wall. |
| Front wheel | A Jew. (Front wheel skid). |
| Gear | Cannabis. |
| Ghost, ghosted | To vanish. An inmate moved suddenly without warning. Also Shanghaid. |
| Ginger beet (Abbrev. Ginger) | Homosexual. |
| Go to Crown | Case heard in Magistrates' Court which goes on to Crown Court. |
| GOAD | Good order and discipline. Rule 43(B). |
| Going QE | Turning Queen's Evidence, informing on co-accused. |
| Gouchin | A dopey state induced by drugs. |
| Goofing out | Same as gouchin. |
| Grass, grassing | Informer, informing. |
| Gregory | Neck (Gregory Peck). |
| Grot, A | Dirty person. |
| Groyn | Ring, signet ring (Romany). |
| Hairy ape | Rape. |
| Hampsteads | Teeth (Hampstead Heath). |
| Heavy, At the | Armed robbing. |
| Hobbit | Nonce, moron, div, arse-licker. |
| Hoistin' | Shoplifting. |
| Home leave | Fixed-sentence prisoners are allowed a few days out 9 months and 4 months before EDR. |
| Hooch | Illicit home brew, usually made with potatoes, rice and/or fruit. |
| Hooky | Something snide. |
| Iron hoof (Abbrev. Iron) | Puff (homosexual). |
| Island, The | Isle of Wight. |
| Jackanories | Lies. Stories. |
| Jack & Jills | Pills. |
| Jack's | £5 note (Jack's alive). |
| Jam jar | Car. |
| Jam roll | Parole. |
| Jam sandwich | Police car (white with red stripe). |
| Jeckle | Snide (Jekyll & Hyde). |
| Jockey's whips | Chips. |
| Joe Blake | Steak. |

| | |
|---|---|
| JR | Judge's Rules, applied when a prisoner has been found guilty but is awaiting sentence. |
| Jug | Bank. |
| Jump, The | A counter jumped over during a robbery. |
| Kangaroos | Screws. Also Kangers. |
| Kettle | Wristwatch. |
| Knock-back | A refusal on something. Aka KB. |
| Kyting | Passing forged cheques. |
| Laggin' | A short sentence. |
| Lamp | Tramp (paraffin lamp). |
| Landings | In the barn-like interiors of the wings the landings are the tiers of cells beginning with the ground floor — the ones, the twos, threes, fours, etc. |
| Landing officer | Officer, i.e. of wing landing. |
| Licence | Life Licence, issued on release from life. |
| Lie-down | Spell on the block. |
| Lifer Induction Board | Lifer's initial interview board consisting of AG, Wing PO, Welfare, Dept Heads, etc. |
| Line | Snorting cocaine or amphetamine. |
| Line-up | Identification parade. |
| Liquid cosh | Drugs used to quieten a prisoner, most frequently Largactil. |
| Location | Where the prisoner lives in the prison: 'on location'. |
| Loid | Bit of celluloid for Yale locks. |
| Lollied | Grassed. |
| Long Term Training Board | Committee of prison officials who review inmate's conduct and progress. |
| Long 'un | £100. |
| LOP | Loss of privileges. Punishment in the block with no privileges, i.e. radio, newspapers, only half hour visit, etc. |
| Loss of association | Disciplinary punishment. Confined to cell. |
| LRC | Local Review Committee. Parole Board. |
| Lucozade/Lemonade | Black person (spade). |
| Lump, A | A big man. |
| Macca | Black person (coon/macaroon). Also shit. |
| Making one | Joining an escape attempt. |
| Mars bar | Scar. |
| Meat waggon | Police van. |
| Meet, A | A meeting to discuss a robbery. |
| Michael Miles | Piles. Also Farmers (Farmer Giles). |
| Mickey (adj.) | Fake; not as it seems (Mickey Mouse). |
| Mickey Mouse | Scouse. |
| Mincers | Eyes (mince pies). |
| Minder | A bodyguard. |
| MO | Medical Officer (doctor). |
| Monkey | £500. |
| Moody | Something not as it seems. |
| Muffin | Someone mentally disturbed. |
| Mufti, The | Minimum Use of Force, Tactical Intervention. The riot squad: officers in brown overalls, boots, crash helmets, carrying perspex shields and 3' riot batons. |
| Mutt | Deaf (Mutt & Jeff). |
| NACRO | National Association for the Care and Resettlement of Offenders. |
| NAL | Non-associated labour. Punishment in the block but with block privileges. |

| | |
|---|---|
| NAPO | National Association of Probation Officers. |
| National, The | National Coaches. Civvy coach hired to ferry inmates between prisons. |
| Nicked | Put on report for breaking prison rules. |
| Nifty | £50. |
| Nonce | Sex-offender. |
| North & South | Mouth. |
| Noted up | Informed on. |
| Nut and gut | Remanded for social and medical reports. |
| Obbo | Under observation. Also 'obs'. |
| On his toes | On the run from police or prison. |
| On report | Given Notice of Report for breaking prison rules. |
| On top | Caught doing something illegal — 'it's on top'. |
| O.U. | Open University. |
| P2 | Home Office Prison Dept dealing with lifers. |
| Padded cell | Cell in block with double doors, bare but for chamber-pot. Occupants usually required to wear a 'space-suit' or strait-jacket. Some are padded. All such cells are windowless, unlike strip cells. |
| Patches, In | Potential escaper wearing yellow stripes. Also known as E–men. |
| Pavement, On the | Armed robbery in the street. |
| Pen & ink | Stink. |
| Peter | Cell, safe. |
| Petition | Request to P2, HO, HS or MP. |
| Pikey | Gypsy. |
| Pipe | Home-made pipe for smoking cannabis. |
| Pixie | Large green-barred windowed bus used for taking prisoners to court/prison. |
| Plates | Feet (plates of meat). |
| Plot, The | Local streets area, formerly manor. |
| Plotted up | To hide something (usually weapon or money). Also someone waiting in ambush. |
| PO | Principal Officer. |
| POA | Prison Officers' Association. |
| Poacher's coat | Special coat with large inside pockets used for hoisting. |
| Poncing | Begging or pimping. |
| Pony | £25. Aka crap (pony & trap). |
| Porkies | Lies (pork pies). |
| Porridge | A jail sentence. |
| Prize, The | Bag of money. |
| Progress report | Filled out on all prisoners every six months by case officers detailing any changes of circumstance. |
| PROP | Preservation of Prisoners' Rights. |
| PTA | Prevention of Terrorism Act (1974). |
| Puff | Cannabis. Also homosexual. |
| Ready-eye | Police ambush at scene of crime, from information received. Also to inform on. |
| Rec, The | At the Scrubs a building containing association facilities — TV, snooker, table tennis, stage for drama and weekly film. |
| Receivers | Ears. |
| Reception | Section that receives and processes new intakes (also known as receptions), stores prisoners' property, discharges them at end of sentence. |
| Recess | Alcoves containing WCs, sinks, dustbins, etc. |
| Region PMO | Troubleshooter. Principal Medical Officer. A doctor. |
| Regional Director | Troubleshooter. Official who operates between regional office, HQ, |

| | |
|---|---|
| | and regional prisons. |
| Result, A | Good sentence (less than expected). Any positive outcome. |
| Richard | Shit. Turd (Richard the Third). |
| Ringer | Car with number plates changed. |
| Roasting | Confined within walls. |
| Rocks & boulders | Shoulders. |
| Robber's dog | A girlfriend used selfishly. |
| Rub down | Quick body search. |
| Ruby (Murray) | Curry. |
| Ruck | Fight or argument. |
| Rule 43 (A) | Prisoner segregated for his own protection. |
| Rule 43 (B) | Better known as GOAD. Inmate kept in block. After 24 hours and thereafter every 28 days a BOV member must check on circumstances and sign order. Not necessary to be on report — suspicion will do. |
| Rule 48 | Remanded in the block or on the wing for resumption of adjudication. Aka Governor's 48. |
| Safe | An inmate's cell. Aka peter. |
| Salmon | Tobacco (salmon and trout/snout). |
| Sardine tins | Skins (cigarette papers). |
| Scag | Heroin smoking. |
| Schvarza | Black person. |
| Score | £20. |
| Sectioned (off) | Declared insane and removed to criminal mental asylum. |
| Seg unit | Segregation unit; punishment block, the block. |
| Sent down | Sentenced. |
| Sherman tank | Yank. |
| Sky rocket | Pocket. |
| Slag | Derogatory male/female term. |
| Slaughter | Splitting stolen property. |
| Smack | Heroin injecting. |
| Smash | Cash. |
| Snide | Counterfeit. |
| Snow-dropping | Secretly sniffing underwear. |
| SO | Senior Officer. |
| SOE | Stoppage of earnings — fines. |
| Sort, A | Attractive woman. |
| Sovs | Pound notes. Or coins. |
| Space-suit | Untearable pyjamas worn in strip cell. |
| Special watch | High escape risks or attempted suicides checked every 15 minutes. |
| Spliff | Joint. Cannabis cigarette. |
| Spin | Cell search. |
| Squirter | Liquid soap container filled with ammonia used on robberies. |
| SSB | Special Security Block. |
| Sterile area | Area inside the wall but outside the 17′ security fence usually containing administration buildings. On reception inmates are first brought here. |
| Stiff | Smuggled letter. |
| Stitched, stitched up | The victim of fabricated evidence. |
| Straightener | Fist fight. |
| Strip | Body search. |
| Strip cell | Cell in punishment block bare but for chamber-pot. |
| Strong box | Cell in block with double doors, no windows, empty but for chamber-pot. |
| Sulph | Amphetamine sulphate. |

| | |
|---|---|
| Suss | Done for suss — arrestable offence — being a suspected person. |
| Sweat-box | Many-cubicled van used for taking prisoners to court/prison. |
| Sweaty sock | Jock. |
| Syrup | Wig (syrup of figs). |
| Targeted | Made a target criminal under 24 hour surveillance by police or agency employed by police. |
| TDA | Taking and driving away a motor vehicle without consent. |
| Telegram | Notice of report (usually delivered after bang-up or before unlock). |
| 10/74 | Form 10/74, from the date of its introduction in October 1974. Prisoner ghosted to the block in another prison for 28 or 56 days. |
| Tickle | Nice bit of stolen money. |
| Tin lid | Jew (as in Yid). |
| Tin tack | Sack. |
| Tom | Jewellery (tom foolery). |
| Tom & Dick | Sick. |
| Tom shop | Jewellers. Also Tommers. |
| Tool, tooled up | Flash car. Weapon. |
| Top-hatting | Gambling term. Slipping a high value chip on a low value stack. |
| Trading bodies | Informing to the police for a favour. |
| Trouble | Wife or girlfriend (trouble & strife). |
| Tucked up | Had over, ripped off, or made a fool of. |
| Turtles | Gloves (turtle doves). |
| Twirls | Keys. |
| Two and eight | State, physical or mental. |
| Valium sandwich | Two tablets of valium. |
| VC | Visiting Committee of magistrates who hear serious charges. |
| Verballed | Fitted up by fabricated oral evidence by police. |
| Ville, The | Pentonville. |
| VO | Visiting order issued to anyone visiting a sentenced prisoner. Not required for remands. |
| Vonga (or wonga) | Money (Romany). |
| Walked | Acquitted at court. |
| Wedge | Bundle of money. |
| Weighed off | Sentenced. |
| Welfare | Probation officer who works full time in the prison. |
| Whistle | Suit (whistle & flute). |
| Whizz | Amphetamine sulphate. |
| Wings | Prisoners' accommodation buildings. In some prisons they radiate like spokes from the central hub. At the Scrubs they lie laterally in line, with workshops, kitchens, etc in between. |
| Wonno | Wandsworth. |
| Works, A | Hypodermic needle. |
| Wrap up, A | Aggravated burglary where occupants are trussed up. |
| YPs | Young prisoners, 17–20. |
| Zero Zero | Good hash. Aka double zero. |
| Zoo, The | 43 Unit. Nonce wing. |